D1478373

Critical Issues in Educational Leadership Series
Joseph Murphy, Series Editor

TAKING ACCOUNT
OF
CHARTER SCHOOLS

What's Happened
and
What's Next?

KATRINA E. BULKLEY
PRISCILLA WOHLSTETTER

EDITORS

FOREWORD BY PAUL T. HILL

Teachers College, Columbia University
New York and London

Published by Teachers College Press, 1234 Amsterdam Avenue, New York, NY 10027

Library of Congress Cataloging-in-Publication Data

Taking account of charter schools : what's happened and what's next? / Katrina E. Bulkley, Priscilla Wohlstetter, editors ; foreword by Paul T. Hill.
    p. cm. — (Critical issues in educational leadership series)
    Includes bibliographical references (p.) and index.
    ISBN 0-8077-4394-1 (cloth) — ISBN 0-8077-4393-3 (paper)
    1. Charter schools—United States. I. Bulkley, Katrina E. II. Wohlstetter, Priscilla, 1953– III. Series.
LB2806.36.T35 2004
371.01—dc22   2003058023

ISBN 0-8077-4393-3 (paper)
ISBN 0-8077-4394-1 (cloth)

Printed on acid-free paper

Manufactured in the United States of America

11   10   09   08   07   06   05   04   8   7   6   5   4   3   2   1

Contents

Foreword

This book reflects the maturation of the charter school movement and the debate about it. Ten years ago only a handful of charter schools existed, and few of the states that had charter laws on the books had any charter schools up and operating. Today, 37 states have some form of charter law, and nearly 2,000 charter schools exist nationwide.

Ten years ago the debate about charter schools was entirely theoretical. Charter schools would unleash creativity, supporters said. Charter schools would look different, use different instructional methods, and attract new people into teaching and school leadership. They would also work far better than existing public schools, especially for poor and minority children as well as for those who needed unusual forms of instruction.

Charter schools would create privileged enclaves for families that wanted to escape the mainstream, opponents said. Charter schools would avoid the poor, harm public schools by drawing away the most talented children and taking away money, and harm the teaching profession by hiring poorly trained people and allowing entrepreneurs to exploit teachers. They might appear to work better than existing public schools, but only because they "creamed off" the easiest to educate.

As this book shows, the charter school debate is still alive, but it is now driven at least in part by facts. Supporters and opponents were right in some cases and wrong in others. But for the most part predictions missed the boat, because charter schools were different from what anyone expected and so diverse as to resist generalization.

Charter schools are diverse because state laws differ profoundly. Under some state laws (e.g., Arizona's), charter schools are independent entities that receive public funds but otherwise have no clear relationship with state or local oversight agencies. Under other state laws (e.g., Georgia's), charter schools are so closely tied to school districts that they have scarcely any more control over spending or teacher hiring than do regular district schools.

Charter schools also serve very different populations, depending on state law. In states that require charters to serve disadvantaged students, charter school populations are heavily poor and minority. In states that impose no requirements about who is to be served, charter schools serve a whiter and more advantaged population.

It also matters whether a charter school is a brand-new school, an existing private school that has sacrificed its independence to come under the charter umbrella, or a conventional district school that sought charter status in order to gain a little more freedom of action. Not surprisingly, former private schools are smaller and more sparsely staffed than former public schools. New charter schools are less stable and more prone to conflict among staff, and between staff and parents, than other kinds of charter school.

When it is possible to generalize, charter schools confound the hopes of supporters and the fears of critics. On average, charter schools are not more effective than regular public schools. This is due in part to the fact that many charters that have converted from private or regular public schools have not changed much. It also reflects the difficulties of starting new schools, a process that takes more time and leads to worse performance in the early years than anyone expected. Finally, as the Brookings Institution's Tom Loveless (2002) has recently reported, charter schools' indifferent performance might reflect the fact that some serve an extremely difficult population—children and parents who have never felt they "fit" in any school and have turned to charters as the latest best hope. It is safe to say this is not what either critics or proponents expected.

Whatever else can be said about it, the charter school movement is unlikely to go away. Too many legislators and parents are committed to it. Moreover, despite its problems, chartering provides needed options; for example, for parent groups that cannot get districts to improve schools in poor neighborhoods, for superintendents who cannot move their bureaucracies, and for cities that cannot build conventional school structures fast enough to house growing student populations. The new federal No Child Left Behind Act will probably force many heretofore unwilling districts to use chartering to create options for children entitled to leave consistently failing schools.

In bringing together the best evidence and argumentation about charter schools, this book founds an important tradition. Readers should expect new, similarly surprising, and contentious updates on the charter school experience every few years from now on.

—Paul T. Hill

Acknowledgments

This volume grew out of a national conference, Educational Issues in Charter Schools, held in Washington, D.C., in November 2001. The conference, funded by the U.S. Department of Education, was sponsored by the Consortium for Policy Research in Education and co-sponsored by the Center on Reinventing Public Education (University of Washington) and the Center on Educational Policy Analysis (Rutgers, the State University of New Jersey).[1]

This volume benefited from the contributions of many people. First, the participants at the Educational Issues in Charter Schools conference provided valuable insights and critiques during the original presentation of many of the ideas discussed in the following chapters. Among the discussants were Sue Bragato of the California Network of Educational Charters, Jane Hannaway of the Urban Institute, Rick Piercy of the Lewis Center for Educational Research, Sarah Tantillo of the New Jersey Charter Public School Association, and Todd Ziebarth of the Education Commission of the States.

Duc-Le To, Alex Medler, and Ram Singh of the U.S. Department of Education also offered advice throughout this project. Terrie Polovsky (with the able assistance of Jessica Teale) proved masterful at organizing the many small details for the conference. Jennifer Fisler, Jennifer Hicks, Courtney Malloy, and Melinda Mangin assisted with the conference, and Jennifer Hicks also provided valuable assistance in pulling together the manuscript for the book. Thanks also for support from William Firestone and Beth Rubin. Finally, the authors would like to thank their families for all their support during this project.

NOTE

1. Funding for the preparation of the chapters in this volume was provided by the U.S. Department of Education's Institute for Education Sciences (formerly the Office of Educational Research and Improvement) through a grant (#OERI-R308A960003) to the Consortium for Policy Research in Education (CPRE), and by Rutgers, the State University of New Jersey. The opinions expressed in these chapters are those of the authors and do not necessarily reflect the views of the Consortium for Policy Research in Education, the Institute for Education Sciences, the United States Department of Education, Rutgers, the State University of New Jersey, or the institutional partners of CPRE.

Taking Account of Charter Schools

What's Happened and What's Next?

Introduction
Katrina E. Bulkley
Priscilla Wohlstetter

Charter schools have become an important part of the landscape of public education over the last decade. Since Minnesota's first charter school opened in 1992, the charter school population has grown to more than 2,600 schools serving more than 575,000 students in 36 states and the District of Columbia. Pressure to create and expand charter schools in the coming years is likely because of the provisions in the federal No Child Left Behind Act that mandate public-choice options for students in low-performing schools.

While charter schools are now operating in all areas of the country, there are still many unanswered questions about the impact of this reform on the processes and outcomes of public education. Who are the teachers in charter schools? How are charter schools governed and managed? What educational practices are used in charter school classrooms? How are students in charter schools performing? This volume offers a set of new empirical studies that explore these potential impacts of charter schools.

Charter schools, by definition, are schools of choice that operate with more autonomy (and fewer regulations) under a charter or contract issued by a public entity, such as a local school board, public university, or state board of education. Charter school contracts, usually 3 to 5 years in length, provide school operators with more decision-making responsibility than district-run public schools. In exchange for this autonomy, charter schools have enhanced accountability: A charter school contract can be canceled if the school is not able to provide evidence of success by the end of the contract period (for overviews of the history of charter schools and research in this area, see Bulkley & Fisler, 2002b; Murphy & Shiffman, 2002; Nathan, 1996).

To date, much of the research on charter schools has focused on analyzing charter school laws, with the general conclusion that laws vary in important ways, in terms of both their specific components and the overall intentions that policymakers had when adopting them (Buechler, 1996; Lake

& Millot, 1998; Wohlstetter, Wenning, & Briggs, 1995). Termed respectively "strong" and "weak" laws, these analyses have shed light on the prevalence of charter schools in some states compared to others but have added little knowledge about the operations or impact of charter schools.

Despite variations in charter school laws, there are some common elements to the idea that, taken together, offer a theory of action for how charter schools can lead to improved student performance. With more autonomy and fewer regulations, charter school educators are expected to make better decisions tailored to the particular needs of their local school communities. As schools of choice, charter schools are expected to offer diverse educational programs that appeal to various groups of consumers—parents and students. Finally, the theory of action emphasizes enhanced accountability, which is expected to focus charter schools on student outcomes and improving student performance. In effect, the theory underlying charter schools rests on the idea that greater autonomy is traded for enhanced accountability to both government and consumers of the educational program (for a full discussion of the charter school concept and theory, see Murphy & Shiffman, 2002).

In the minds of reformers, the combination of reforms reflected in charter schools—autonomy, choice, and accountability—was expected to lead to schools that operated in different ways, including the teachers they hired and the experiences of those teachers in each school, their educational programs, the organization of the schools and their place in the broader educational system, and ultimately the outcomes for students. There was also an implicit expectation that increasing choice and improving school quality would lead to a more equitable public school system for individuals and society. At a minimum, charter schools were expected to increase the numbers of schools of choice in the public sector. At a maximum, charter schools were expected to serve as incubators for innovation and improved student performance.

Our focus in the chapters that follow is on the value-added by charter schools. We were most interested in how charter schools contribute to the landscape of public education and, especially, how they compare to district-run schools.

CHARTER SCHOOLS: MERGING AUTONOMY, CHOICE, AND ACCOUNTABILITY REFORMS

Autonomy

Decentralization, including providing additional autonomy to individual schools, has been an aspect of numerous reforms over the last 40 years, including alternative schools, magnet schools, and site-based management in addition to charter schools. In general, autonomy encompasses the ability of individual schools—within boundaries determined by government—to make budgeting, staffing, and educational decisions that affect both internal operations and external relationships (Wohlstetter et al., 1995). The strength of autonomy derives in part from the extent to which the school is independent from higher levels of government (deregulation, for instance) and in part from the ability of stakeholders in a particular organization to effect the direction and decisions of that organization. The basic logic behind school-level autonomy is that those people who work most closely with students are in the best position to determine what is educationally most effective for those students (Hannaway, 1993). Specifically, the argument for decentralization centers on the ideas that teaching is complex and dynamic and that teachers and other school-level personnel should have primary control—not the central bureaucracy, which is remote from the school.

Charter school advocates have generally considered more autonomy to be better (cf. Kolderie, 1990), but the research is not completely clear on this matter. One study found, for example, that schools with greater autonomy from their districts were better able to create and sustain a learning community and respond quickly to problems but were more consumed by managerial decisions (Wohlstetter & Griffin, 1998). Another study suggested that, despite their desire for autonomy, charter schools often turn to their district's bureaucracy when they need help (Wells et al., 1998). Some schools, particularly those with weak organizational structures, may have more difficulty capitalizing on their autonomy (Wohlstetter & Griffin, 1998). In this book, the authors grapple with the effects and challenges of charter school autonomy across a range of areas—from student achievement to special education, staffing patterns to classroom practices, and innovation to equity.

Choice

Embedded in the charter school theory of action is the idea that charter schools would develop a range of educational programs to appeal to the diverse needs of consumers—parents and students. As schools of choice, charter schools would operate like magnet schools, attracting consumers who were now free to use their sovereignty to select a school that best fit their needs. The charter school movement called into question the idea of the common school and in its stead offered diversification linked to the market. Several chapters in this book examine the issue of diversity—Do charter schools add diversity to the public school system?—and its ultimate effects, which some argue steer us away from equity.

Accountability

As noted earlier, charter schools are premised on the idea that one can trade autonomy for accountability—specifically, that if one provides greater autonomy to individual schools, through deregulation and/or school-site control over budgeting, staffing, and the educational program, then one can place greater demands on the educational performance produced by those schools (Kolderie, 1990; Nathan, 1996). Accountability for charter schools has two facets. The first facet involves accountability to government, both to the authorizers that grant charter contracts allowing individual schools to operate and to other governmental entities that set legal requirements involving charter schools. Authorizers all address the same basic issues: evaluating and approving applications, overseeing the school during the contract period, and determining whether or not to renew the charter when the contract period ends (Bulkley, 1999; Lake & Millot, 1998; Vergari, 2000).

The second facet, based on market theory and related to choice, involves accountability for satisfying the consumers of charter schools—parents and students. The assumption here is that consumers will demand, among other things, high-quality education and that charter schools, as schools of choice, will have the authority to respond. Accountability to the market essentially means that those who participate in the different charter school markets— for students and staff—are either satisfied with the "available products" or exit schools with which they are dissatisfied. The idea behind these two facets of accountability is that they will be mutually reinforcing. In general, Finn, Manno, and Vanourek (2000) argue that "the chief aim of accountability is to find and sustain good schools while weeding out or repairing bad ones" (p. 127).

OVERVIEW OF THIS VOLUME

The charter school theory of action argues that if schools are given autonomy and enhanced accountability, then charter schools, as schools of choice, will operate in creative ways to design programs that effectively increase student performance, thus attracting parents and students. While researchers to date have explored the *extent* to which charter schools are, in practice, autonomous organizations, few studies have focused on *how* charter schools operate in better, different, or more innovative ways. The impact of charter schools is closely tied to how autonomy, accountability, and choice provide opportunities for charter schools to impact their immediate stakeholders and, more broadly, public education.

Impact on Teachers

Teachers and their knowledge and skills are among the most important aspects of an educational program. Chapters in Part I explore two central issues—the characteristics and quality of teachers hired in charter schools and the professional opportunities available to those teachers. In Chapters 1 and 2, cross-state quantitative data are used to provide evidence that goes beyond a particular set of schools or an individual state.

In Chapter 1, Marisa Burian-Fitzgerald, Michael Luekens, and Gregory Strizek of the American Institutes for Research explore one aspect of organizational autonomy touted by charter school advocates—that such schools, if released from state requirements around teacher certification, would hire different and "higher-quality" teachers. They present a detailed portrait of teachers in charter schools, examining their characteristics, qualifications, and work experience, using data from the 1999–2000 Schools and Staffing Survey (SASS) produced by the National Center for Educational Statistics.

In Chapter 2, Christopher Nelson and Gary Miron of the Evaluation Center at Western Michigan University look beyond who has been hired in charter schools to examine the professional opportunities offered to charter school teachers. Drawing on original survey data in four states, the authors assess the extent to which teachers in charter schools experience enhanced professional opportunities and offer some explanation for why such opportunities vary across states. The chapter concludes by identifying policy levers that are likely to enhance professional opportunities for teachers—in both charter and traditional public schools.

Impact on Educational Practices

The increased autonomy of the schools (especially from states and school districts), the fact that they are schools of choice, and the use of contracts that allow a variety of parties to operate public schools all distinguish charter schools from district-run public schools in important ways. As cited in most authorizing legislation, a key policy objective for many charter school reformers is to promote innovations in instructional strategies. As Ted Kolderie (personal communication, October 24, 2001), one of the creators of the charter school idea, notes, "the chartered school is not a kind of school; not a learning program or method. The opportunity the law provides is an empty institutional structure, as a building is an empty physical structure. Students learn from what the organizers put into it" (see also Kolderie, 1998). The chapters in Part II offer new research on the extent to which charter schools' enhanced autonomy and accountability have led to altered educational practices.

In Chapter 3, Priscilla Wohlstetter and Derrick Chau of the University of Southern California examine the extent to which school-site autonomy in nine schools has influenced classroom practices around literacy. They build on research involving autonomy that suggests that educational policies—school-based management plans and charter school laws—offer different levels of school-site autonomy that may cause variations in school performance. The study finds that, in their sample, the presence of research-based literacy strategies was higher in schools with more autonomy.

In Chapter 4, Christopher Lubienski of the University of Iowa analyses the forces influencing innovation in charter schools. Using research from four states, he argues that, although charter schools are diversifying options for parents and implementing organizational innovations at the administrative level, autonomy is not necessarily leading to innovations in curriculum and instruction. Indeed, he suggests that charter schools with less institutional autonomy may be more successful in experimenting with new and different approaches in the classroom, while schools with greater autonomy are often more likely to embrace traditionalist approaches to instruction.

Impact on School Governance and Organization

Arsen, Plank, and Sykes (1999) argue that "the most important charter school innovations are not about teaching and learning, but rather about control over school operations" (p. 52). In the context of an institutional innovation, it is not surprising that governance structures are where the most change has been noted (Kolderie, 1998). The first chapter in Part III, which explores charter schools as a governance mechanism, examines the opportunities charter schools do—or do not—offer to the students and communities most in need of improved education. The other two chapters in this section report on new empirical studies of two important aspects of governance and organization for charter schools—the burgeoning role of for-profit management companies and the critical issue of special education.

In Chapter 5, Bruce Fuller, Marytza Gawlik, Emlei Kuboyama Gonzales, and Sandra Park of the University of California at Berkeley examine the issue of equity in charter schools from an organizational perspective. They argue that the state's move away from the ideals of common schooling—manifest in highly decentralized and particular forms of schooling—is legitimating new conceptions of fairness. The idea of equity gauged by comparable, universal benchmarks is being replaced by localized and particularistic conceptions of *opportunity* and organized options. The authors explore inequities and unfair opportunities observed among charter schools nationwide, illustrating how universal and particular forms of fairness play out within the movement itself.

In Chapter 6, Katrina Bulkley of Rutgers University examines the growing phenomenon of for-profit educational management organizations (EMOs) as service providers for charter schools. Based on interviews with the leaders of for-profit EMOs, she identifies different approaches to decision making for education used by EMOs. In doing so, she highlights how the increasing role of EMOs alters our understanding of organization and governance in charter schools.

In Chapter 7, Lauren Morando Rhim and Margaret McLaughlin of University of Maryland, Eileen Ahearn of the National Association of State Directors of Special Education, and Cheryl Lange of Lange & Associates draw on a large federal study of special education in charter schools to explore how these deregulated schools address federal requirements that state laws cannot waive. Specifically, they examine how charter schools are amassing the fiscal and human capacity and organizational structures necessary to educate children with a wide range of cognitive and physical disabilities. Their study reveals inherent policy tensions between special education and charter schools as well as a fundamental knowledge gap on the part of charter school authorizers and operators in terms of what they need to know about special education.

Impact on Student Outcomes

The impact of charter schools—the subject of Part IV—includes changes in educational practices, the characteristics of the teachers and the opportunities they have to develop and contribute to a broader school vision, and organizational structures. However, the focus for policymakers has often been on the outcomes for students that might result from these other changes. Of particular concern has been the issue of student achievement. What is the value-added by charter schools in terms of improved student performance?

In Chapter 8, Gary Miron and Christopher Nelson tackle the challenging issue of student achievement in charter schools. While advocates argue that there is strong evidence of charter school success in this area, a closer examination of the research reveals a more complicated picture. The authors point out that charter schools are granted enhanced autonomy on the assumption that they will use it to select and implement educational practices that will raise student achievement. Drawing on 17 studies in 11 states and the District of Columbia, this chapter provides a systematic cross-state comparison of student achievement in charter schools. Combining characteristics of the quality of the studies and their findings, the authors offer an overall "impact rating" of charter schools on student achievement across this body of research. Miron and Nelson's work demonstrates the critical importance of learning more about the effects of charter schools on student achievement as well as the complexity of explaining why schools in some states are having a more positive impact an achievement than schools in others.

In the Conclusion, David Plank and Gary Sykes of Michigan State University draw on the broad themes raised throughout the book, with a particular focus on the impact of charter schools, to identify key findings and contributions. They build on the empirical studies included in this volume to offer policy implications and an agenda for future research in this area. In particular, they stress the critical ways in which charter school research can inform practice and policy both within the charter school world and in broader efforts at school reform.

PART I

The Impact of Charter Schools on Teachers

CHAPTER 1

Less Red Tape or More Green Teachers: Charter School Autonomy and Teacher Qualifications

Marisa Burian-Fitzgerald
Michael T. Luekens
Gregory A. Strizek

"Sarah" recently accepted a job as a French teacher in a large, urban charter school. She is 32 years old, a fluent French speaker, and holds bachelor's and master's degrees from highly competitive universities. Sarah began her teaching career in 1993 at a private boarding high school in Massachusetts, before moving on to a private day school in the same state. In total, Sarah has 9 years of experience teaching French.

While seemingly qualified, Sarah would be unable to teach French in a traditional public school because she lacks appropriate certification. She is drawn to this charter school because of the charismatic principal and energetic teachers who share her vision of education. Although she would have to take additional courses to teach in a traditional public school, Sarah and her impressive résumé were welcomed by the school and its principal with open arms.

The case of Sarah and similar teachers provides one of the leading arguments in favor of the decade-old charter school movement. Granted autonomy from cumbersome regulations, charter school leaders are free to recruit and hire uncertified, but otherwise qualified, teachers who would be turned away from traditional public schools. In exchange for this autonomy, charter schools are held accountable to produce satisfactory results. A charter school that does not use its flexibility effectively risks losing its charter and, more importantly, its clientele, the parents and students.

This chapter seeks to shed light on one of the most important contributors to the success or failure of the thousands of students enrolled in charter schools across the United States: their teachers. It explores how charter schools are using their flexibility in teacher hiring. In particular, are charter schools taking advantage of their autonomy from traditional teacher-hiring restrictions to attract experienced and educated teachers like Sarah? By comparing the charter school teaching force to their colleagues in traditional public and private schools, this research provides information on the characteristics of the charter school workforce and tests the hypothesis that charter school flexibility in teacher hiring has implications for the types of teachers hired by charter schools.

The first section reviews the literature about charter school autonomy and teacher quality. The following section discusses measures of teacher qualifications along with hypotheses about their prevalence in charter schools. The study methods are then described. Next, findings are presented and discussed. Finally, the chapter concludes by placing this study in the larger context of research on charter schools and provides recommendations for future research.

CHARTER SCHOOL AUTONOMY AND TEACHER QUALITY

Charter school advocates claim that the increased autonomy provided to charter schools in hiring teachers will lead to more effective schools. Charter school supporters call for autonomy from higher levels of government (Wohlstetter, Wenning, & Briggs, 1995). Constraints imposed on traditional public schools and staff by districts, states, the federal government, and unions, scholars argue, limit the effectiveness of educational policies aimed at improving schools (Ballou & Podgursky, 1997). For example, bureaucratic constraints such as lengthy district screening processes may impede public schools' ability to hire the most effective teachers (Ballou & Podgursky, 1997). Many state and local policies reduce the efficacy of teacher recruitment practices in traditional public schools (Wise, Darling-Hammond, & Berry, 1987). Ballou (1996) also found that public schools may hire teachers from local schools or colleges rather than the most qualified applicants.

Waiving Teacher Certification

Like private schools, charter schools, through state charter laws and the terms of individual charters, may be exempt from many of the regulations with which traditional public schools must still contend and, therefore, may be more effective in hiring teachers. Private schools utilize these exemptions to hire teachers from a broader pool of candidates, regardless of their certification status, than do traditional public schools. Some argue that this has led to a higher-quality teaching force in private schools (Ballou & Podgursky, 1997). Charter school proponents claim that this freedom from traditional public schools' restrictive teacher certification requirements will produce similar results. With certification restrictions lifted, these researchers contend, charter schools will have the ability to recruit otherwise qualified individuals who did not, for various reasons, obtain a teaching certificate.

Others, however, argue that providing charter schools with such autonomy will result in charter school faculties that are less qualified than their certified colleagues in traditional public schools (American Federation of Teachers, 1999; National Education Association, 2002). Certification requirements, they claim, help to "weed out" unqualified teachers and ensure that teachers receive training in areas such as pedagogy and classroom management.

As Table 1.1 demonstrates, state laws differ considerably in terms of the freedom they provide charter schools to hire teachers and staff. Laws regarding teacher-hiring policies are especially salient to this chapter's discussion of the relationship between charter school autonomy and teacher quality. Some states, such as Arizona, place few if any regulations on charter schools' hiring practices, granting charter school leaders a great deal of autonomy in selecting the schools' faculty. Other states, including California and Rhode Island, place severe restrictions on charter schools in selecting teachers. However, many of the state charter laws requiring teacher certification include provisions allowing schools to waive this requirement or allowing charter schools to hire applicants who possess emergency or alternative forms of certification. Thus, it has been reported that certification is generally not a required element of charter legislation (Bomotti, Ginsburg, & Cobb, 1999).

Local Control of Teacher Hiring

A second theme in the research involving teacher-hiring policies in charter schools involves the second aspect of autonomy articulated by Wohlstetter and colleagues (1995): local or organizational autonomy. Wohlstetter and colleagues describe how schools operating with this autonomy feature principals with control over personnel, curriculum, instructional methods, and disciplinary policies. This autonomy provides principals with the freedom to hire teachers with a shared vision, thus creating a sustained learning community that will be more effective in attaining common goals (Wohlstetter & Griffin, 1998). Johnson and Landman (2000) also claim that increased autonomy will empower school leaders to recruit and retain teachers with a shared educational vision. There is evidence that a shared vision does lead

Table 1.1. State teacher certification requirements for charter schools: 1999–2000

Teacher certification required	Teacher certification waived	Teacher certification required for specified percentage of teachers	Teacher certification requirements specified in charter application*
Alaska	Arizona	Connecticut (50%)	Colorado
California	District of	Delaware (65%)	Georgia
Hawaii	Columbia	Louisiana (75%)	Kansas
Idaho	Florida	Mississippi (90%)	
Massachusetts (or pass MA Educator Test)	Illinois	Missouri (80%)	
	Texas	Nevada (70%)	
Michigan (except charter schools sponsored by a university may have faculty teach)		North Carolina (75% in elementary schools, 50% in secondary schools)	
Minnesota		Pennsylvania (75%)	
New Jersey		South Carolina (75% in new schools, 90% in converted schools)	
New Mexico			
Ohio			
Rhode Island			
Wisconsin (but special license available if no candidate found)			

* Includes states whose charter school laws specify that the certification status of teachers be negotiated in charter applications and states whose laws state that certification is required but may be waived.

Note: The states above include all states that had charter schools in operation in 1999–2000. It does not include states that had charter legislation in 1999–2000 but no charter schools in operation.

Source: American Federation of Teachers, 1999; Center for Education Reform, 2001a.

to a more effective learning community in the noncharter setting (Marks & Louis, 1997).

An extension of this is the power of teachers within an organization to make decisions with respect to how they will achieve their school goals. Educators will have the opportunity to own and run these schools, implementing their visions of education that the conventional public school structure stymies (Kolderie, 1990; Manno, Finn, Bierlien, & Vanourek, 1998a). For all of these reasons, the ability of schools to control the hiring process, free from state regulations and district control, should lead to more effective schools.

MEASURES OF TEACHER QUALITY

Past research argues that high-quality teachers can positively and significantly raise student achievement (Sanders & Horn, 1998; Wright, Horn, & Sanders, 1997). Furthermore, the effect of teachers on student achievement can accumulate over several years (Ferguson & Brown, 2000; Sanders & Rivers, 1996). Researchers have tried to isolate the impact of various measures of teacher quality on student learning, with varying degrees of success. This chapter focuses on four measures of teacher quality: teacher certification, subject-matter knowledge, teaching experience, and college selectivity. This section reviews the literature on each of these measures by examining their link to student achievement and reviewing previous studies comparing charter school teachers to public and private school teachers.

Teacher Certification

Teacher certification is one measure of teacher quality, around which much debate exists regarding its link to student achievement. There is evidence that teacher certification is related to higher student achievement (Darling-Hammond, 2000; Darling-Hammond, Berry, & Thoreson, 2001; Sanders, Skonie-Hardin, Phelps, & Minnis, 1994). Although many researchers agree that certified teachers produce higher student achievement than noncertified teachers, some research indicates that full or regular certification is most strongly related to achievement (Darling-Hammond, 2000; Ferguson & Womack, 1993), while other research indicates that alternative forms of certification have positive effects on student achievement similar to those associated with full certification (Goldhaber & Brewer, 2000; Goebel, Ronacher, & Sanchez, 1989). This inconsistency may be explained by the large variance in type and quality of alternative certification programs (Darling-Hammond et al., 2001). Furthermore, research has shown relationships between subject-specific certification and student achievement in the particular subject. Goldhaber and Brewer (1997), for example, found that teachers certified in math produced higher student scores on standardized math exams. Hawk, Coble, and Swanson (1985) reached a similar conclusion regarding the effects of certification on student achievement in math and also found evidence that teachers with certification in math were more likely to use effective teaching practices in their classes.

In addition to certification itself, many researchers have examined the effects of the processes teachers undergo to gain certification. In a review of existing research, Ashton and Crocker (1987) conclude that the number of education courses a teacher has taken is a strong predictor of student performance. Coursework in education and pedagogy lead to improved performance (Everston, Hawley, & Zlotnik, 1985; Ferguson & Womack, 1993; Monk, 1994), as does spending school resources on more educated teachers (Greenwald, Hedges, & Laine, 1996). The influence on student learning of teacher education coursework, often obtained while pursuing certification, supports the argument that teacher certification leads to higher student performance.

Some researchers, however, argue that evidence regarding a positive effect of teacher certification on student learning is not convincing. Ballou and Podgursky (2000) write that the research on teacher certification is not rigorous and is often misrepresented in research reviews. Some researchers contend that studies advocating teacher certification frequently overlook other studies that do not support certification, do not properly control for student background variables, use old or unavailable research, and are often not subject to peer review (Abell Foundation, 2001). Although the debate over the impact of certification has not been resolved, there is some evidence that certification is linked to student achievement and thus remains an important indicator of teacher quality.

This chapter explores whether charter school teachers are more or less likely to be certified than their public and private school counterparts. Initial research indicates that charter school teachers are less likely to be certified than traditional public school teachers (Gill, Timpane, Ross, & Brewer, 2001). For example, using the 1993–1994 Schools and Staffing Survey data for public and private schools and an independent sample of charter schools, Podgursky and Ballou (2001) found that charter school teachers, like private school teachers, were less likely to be certified. Hoxby (2000) also concluded that traditional public schools had a higher demand for certified teachers. The difference between charter and traditional public schools should be related to the flexibility in statutes, with charter school teachers in states that do not provide waivers from state certification standards more closely resembling teachers in traditional public schools. Likewise, charter schools in states that provide broad waivers from state certification requirements should have a percentage of certified teachers that is comparable to that of private schools.

Subject-Matter Knowledge

In-depth knowledge of one's teaching field is increasingly recognized as an important indicator of teaching quality. The No Child Left Behind Act, passed in 2001, requires teachers to demonstrate that they have sufficient content knowledge of the subject they teach—by having a major in or passing a subject-matter test in that subject—to be considered a highly qualified teacher (U.S. Department of Education, 2002). Further, the importance of in-depth knowledge of the subject matter is cited by many researchers. The large number of teachers who are teaching a subject in which they do not have a college major or minor is often used as a measure of the lack of qualified teachers in schools (Ingersoll, 1999). Students whose teachers have a college degree in the field they are teaching perform better on standardized tests (Darling-Hammond, 2000). Teachers who demonstrate content mastery through high subject-specific GPAs and scores on the National Teacher Exam have been shown to be more effective (Ferguson & Womack, 1993). Goldhaber and Brewer (1997, 2000) found that students of teachers with a master's degree in math scored higher on standardized math achievement exams than students of teachers with a master's degree in any other subject. Weglinsky (2000, 2002) also concluded that teachers with a major in the field they are teaching contributed to increased student learning.

However, the evidence for subject-matter knowledge in relation to teacher education knowledge remains mixed. Monk (1994) found that both undergraduate courses in pedagogy and courses in the subject matter contributed to increased student performance. Additional evidence supports the argument that coursework in education consistently leads to higher student achievement, while the impact of coursework on subject-matter content is less clear (Ashton & Crocker, 1987; Everston et al., 1985). The evidence seems to indicate that while content knowledge is necessary for effective teaching, it may not be sufficient without appropriate pedagogical training (Ferguson & Womack, 1993).

This chapter compares the percentage of math and science teachers with a major in the subjects they teach in charter, public, and private schools. Very few studies of charter school teachers examine their subject-matter knowledge or the presence of out-of-field teaching in charter schools. Hoxby (2000) found that public schools and charter schools demanded math and science teachers with majors in their teaching fields equally. Advocates of charter schools argue that traditional certification prevents people with college degrees in particular fields, but no certification, from becoming teachers. Charter schools, like private schools, should be able to attract individuals working in other professions who have relevant subject-matter expertise. If this is so, more individuals with relevant college coursework might be expected to teach in charter schools.

Teaching Experience

Evidence indicates that teachers gain competency as they gain experience. Teachers with higher levels of experience are more successful than less experienced teachers in facilitating student learning (Fetler, 1999; Greenwald et al., 1996; Klitgaard & Hall, 1974). Although there is some evidence that teaching experience does not lead to greater student achievement (Ferguson & Ladd, 1996; Hawk et al., 1985; Weglinsky, 2000), the bulk of the evidence indicates that there is at least some benefit to having a teacher with more experience. For example, Summers and Wolfe (1977) found that teaching experience led to higher student achievement for students already identified as high achievers but that this relationship did not hold for lower achievers. Furthermore, the influence of years of teaching experience on student performance is confounded by characteristics of individuals who begin teaching in a certain year (Murnane & Phillips, 1981). Teachers who began teaching at a certain point in time may be more or less prepared than other teachers, thus reducing the effect of teaching experience. Murnane and Phillips (1981) found that teaching experience does have a positive impact on student achievement after controlling for the average quality of new teachers in a given cohort. This conclusion is supported by research that claims the effect of teaching experience is greater for new teachers and may level off after 5 years (Ballou & Podgursky, 1997; Darling-Hammond, 2000).

This chapter compares the teaching experience of charter, public, and private school teachers. Previous research indicates that charter schools have more new teachers than public schools (Bulkley & Fisler, 2002b; Texas Education Agency, 2001). Furthermore, teachers in charter schools have fewer years of experience than both public and private school teachers (Podgursky & Ballou, 2001). Moreover, the fact that charter schools may be newly created schools decreases the likelihood that teachers will have many years of experience. Similarly, charter schools that are newly created should have more inexperienced teachers than charter schools that were converted from a previously existing public or private school.

College Selectivity

Teacher verbal ability may be the most consistent indicator of teacher quality (Hanushek, 1989). Ferguson and Ladd (1996) found that higher teacher ACT scores, a test of general education development used for college admissions, led to increased student achievement in reading and math in the fourth grade. Another study found that teachers' scores on a basic skills test required for certification helped predict student test scores (Ferguson & Brown, 2000). Meta-analyses have shown that teacher verbal ability is consistently related to student performance (Abell Foundation, 2001; Greenwald et al., 1996). Hanushek (1971) found that teacher verbal ability was associated with higher student achievement. Teacher aptitude is also related to student failure rates on competency examinations (Strauss & Sawyer, 1986).

The selectivity of the college from which a teacher graduated is often used as a measure of teacher aptitude in research on teacher qualifications and supply and demand (Ballou, 1996; Ballou & Podgursky, 1997; Hoxby, 2000). Colleges use measures of verbal ability and general aptitude in selecting students, such as SAT and ACT scores. Thus, a degree from a more selective college may indicate that an individual has greater verbal ability. Summers and Wolfe (1977) found that teachers who attended more selective colleges had higher-achieving students. Furthermore, they found that students from low-income backgrounds benefited most from teachers who had attended selective colleges.

Do charter schools hire teachers from more selective colleges than do public and private schools? Few studies of charter schools examine college selectivity, verbal ability, or other measures of the general knowledge of charter school teachers. Hoxby (2000) found that public schools and charter schools demanded teachers from more competitive colleges equally. Additional evidence suggests that individuals from more selective colleges do not enroll in teacher education courses or apply for teaching positions (Ballou, 1996). The increased autonomy given to charter and private schools, and the flexibility to hire teachers lacking traditional teaching credentials, may increase their potential pool of teaching applicants and allow them to attract individuals not previously disposed to teaching.

STUDY METHODS

This chapter utilizes the charter, public, and private school teacher components of the 1999–2000 Schools and Staffing Survey (SASS). Administered by the National Center for Education Statistics (NCES), SASS sampled teachers from a stratified probability sample of public and private schools as well as from the universe of charter schools open in the 1998–1999 school year that were still operating in 1999–2000. The sample includes approximately 3,000 charter school teachers, 42,000 public school teachers, and 7,000 private school teachers (Gruber, Wiley, Broughman, Strizek, & Burian-Fitzgerald, 2002). Only public and private school teachers in states that have charter schools are included in this analysis. Due to the wide variability within the charter school sector as well as the possibility that national estimates may mask trends stemming from different school populations, the data are disaggregated by school community type, school level, and the status of the state charter school law pertaining to teacher certification. In a separate comparison, we included only charter schools that have been open for at least 3 years in order to control for the possible impact starting a new school may have on staff qualifications. The teacher questionnaires collected data on teachers' education, training, experience, teaching assignment, and certification, among other topics. SASS includes questions that allow the construction of indicators for the four teacher quality measures discussed above.

SASS asked teachers to provide information on all teaching certificates held. In this chapter, "certified teachers" include teachers with regular or standard certificates, probationary certificates, provisional certificates or those obtained through an alternative certification program, or temporary certificates in their main or other teaching assignment field. The term does not include teachers with an emergency certificate or waiver who have insufficient teacher preparation.

SASS contains a series of questions regarding teachers' college training as well as their teaching assignments. This information was used to create measures of out-of-field teaching. Out-of-field teaching refers to teachers who are teaching courses in which they are not certified or in which they did not have a college major or minor (Seastrom, Gruber, Henke, McGrath, & Cohen, 2002). This chapter compares the percentage of public, private, and charter teachers who are "in-field" in math and science—that is, the percentage of teachers teaching math and science who had a college major or minor, at the undergraduate or graduate level, in that subject.

SASS also collected information on previous teaching experience. This chapter measures the total years of teaching experience that teachers had through 1999–2000 in public, private, and charter schools, including both full-time and part-time teaching. Teachers with 5 or fewer years of experience are considered new or inexperienced teachers.

Teachers reported the name of their undergraduate college or university on SASS. A measure of college selectivity was computed using the 2001 *Barron's Guide to Colleges*. Barron's ranks colleges in seven categories based on the selectivity of their admissions process, as measured by, among other things, SAT scores and acceptance rates (Ballou & Podgursky, 1997; Hoxby, 2000). This chapter excludes colleges that were categorized as "special" or having specialized admission criteria, such as performing arts colleges. The measure reported below represents the percentage of teachers who obtained a bachelor's degree from the most selective or highly selective colleges.

FINDINGS

Teacher Certification

Charter school teachers are less likely to be certified than public school teachers but more likely to be certified than private school teachers (see Table

1.2). About 93% of public school teachers are certified, compared with only 72% of charter school teachers. In contrast, only 57% of private school teachers are certified. This finding holds across all school community types and instructional levels. For example, in central-city schools, 65% of charter school teachers are certified, compared with 92% of public school teachers and 58% of private school teachers.

Although there is very little variation in the public school sector according to state policies regarding teacher certification, there is substantial variation among charter schools. Not surprisingly, charter school teachers in states that grant waivers to charter schools for teacher certification are less likely

Table 1.2. Percent of teachers with certification, by school characteristics

	Charter school teachers	Public school teachers	Private school teachers
All teachers	72.2	93.4*	57.3*
Community type			
Central city	65.4	92.6*	58.6*
Urban fringe/large town	78.4	93.6*	56.6*
Rural/small town	77.6	93.7*	54.8*
School level			
Elementary	76.0	93.4*	64.1*
Secondary	65.9	93.5*	57.4*
Combined	66.6	89.4*	47.0*
State certification status			
Teacher certification required	76.8	93.8*	56.9*
Teacher certification waived	61.5	93.0*	58.5
Teacher certification required for specified percentage of teachers	64.8	92.7*	59.0
Teacher certification requirements specified in charter application	84.8	94.3*	51.5*

* Statistically different from charter school teachers at the .001 level.

Source: National Center for Education Statistics, Schools and Staffing Survey, 1999–2000.

to be certified than public school teachers in those states. More surprising is that charter school teachers in states in which teacher certification waivers are granted on a charter-by-charter basis are the most likely charter school teachers to be certified. However, charter schools in these states still have fewer certified teachers than public schools.

Teacher certification does not seem to be related to the year the charter school began operating. The pattern of teacher certification, compared with public and private schools, holds for those charter schools that have been in operation for 3 or more years. Indeed, the percentage of teachers in charter schools who are certified is not statistically different between charter schools that were not open for at least 3 years in 1999–2000 and those that were open for 3 years or more. In only 2 of our 11 comparisons were older charter schools statistically more likely to have a higher number of certified teachers than charter schools still getting off the ground. However, these differences are small compared to the differential certification rate between charter and public school teachers. About 67% of teachers in central-city charter schools that have been open for 3 years are certified, compared with 63% of teachers in new charter schools. Likewise, 78% of teachers in elementary charter schools that have been open for at least 3 years are certified, compared with 75% of teachers in newer charter schools. Both central-city and elementary charter schools that are more established have fewer certified teachers than public schools.

The lower rate of teacher certification is not surprising considering that waiving certification requirements is a key component of the charter school movement.

Subject-Matter Knowledge

The findings about whether charter school teachers are more or less likely to have a major or minor in math and science are more contradictory. Charter school math teachers are less likely to have a major or minor in math than public school teachers (see Table 1.3) and are about as likely as private school teachers to have a major or minor in math. Approximately 38% of charter school math teachers majored or minored in math, compared with 51% of public school math teachers. Although secondary school math teachers in charter schools are most likely to have a major or minor in math within the charter school population (55%), they are still less likely to have a major or minor in math than public secondary school math teachers (70%). They are also less likely than private secondary school math teachers to have advanced knowledge in their field (68%). Charter school math teachers are more likely to be teaching out-of-field than public school math teachers in urban, suburban, and rural schools.

Table 1.3. Percent of math teachers with a college major or minor in mathematics, by school characteristics

	Charter school teachers	Public school teachers	Private school teachers
All teachers	38.5	51.0***	42.5
Community type			
Central city	42.2	50.7*	48.6
Urban fringe/large town	33.6	51.8***	39.5
Rural/small town	37.6	49.4***	33.8
School level			
Elementary	28.2	27.3	23.4
Secondary	55.5	70.0***	68.6***
Combined	32.6	44.0**	45.0**
State certification status			
Teacher certification required	42.4	54.5***	44.5
Teacher certification waived	37.2	46.7*	40.5
Teacher certification required for specified percentage of teachers	39.2	54.1	37.7
Teacher certification requirements specified in charter application	29.0	43.0**	49.9*

* Statistically different from charter school teachers at the .05 level.

** Statistically different from charter school teachers at the .01 level.

*** Statistically different from charter school teachers at the .001 level.

Source: National Center for Education Statistics, Schools and Staffing Survey, 1999–2000.

Charter school math teachers in states that do not waive certification requirements, in states that grant broad waivers to charter schools, and in states that grant certification waivers on a charter-by-charter basis are all less likely to have sufficient subject-matter preparation than corresponding public school teachers. Those charter school math teachers in states in which teacher certification requirements are specified in the charter are also less likely to have a major or minor in math than private school teachers.

The pattern is somewhat different for science teachers. Nationally, about 60% of charter, public, and private school science teachers have a major or minor in science (see Table 1.4). This is true regardless of the school's locale. However, in secondary schools, charter school science teachers are less likely than both public and private school teachers to have a major or minor in science. About 66% of charter secondary school science teachers have advanced knowledge in the field they are teaching, compared with 78% of public secondary school science teachers and 84% of private secondary school science teachers. Elementary school science teachers in charter schools are more likely to have a degree in science (52%) than public elementary school science teachers (34%).

Charter school science teachers in states that grant broad waivers for teacher certification requirements are more likely to have sufficient subject-

Table 1.4. Percent of science teachers with a college major or minor in science, by school characteristics

	Charter school teachers	Public school teachers	Private school teachers
All teachers	60.6	60.4	60.0
Community type			
Central city	63.7	58.4	61.5
Urban fringe/large town	55.7	62.6	61.0
Rural/small town	67.7	57.5	50.2
School level			
Elementary	52.0	34.4***	34.9***
Secondary	66.8	78.1***	84.4***
Combined	63.4	53.7	65.3
State certification status			
Teacher certification required	56.6	68.5**	59.3
Teacher certification waived	62.3	50.6**	47.7**
Teacher certification required for specified percentage of teachers	54.8	59.4	67.5
Teacher certification requirements specified in charter application	73	55.2*	65.4

* Statistically different from charter school teachers at the .05 level

** Statistically different from charter school teachers at the .01 level.

*** Statistically different from charter school teachers at the .001 level.

Source: National Center for Education Statistics, Schools and Staffing Survey, 1999–2000.

matter preparation than their public and private school counterparts. Charter school science teachers in states that specify teacher certification requirements in individual charters are also more likely to have a major or minor in science than public school science teachers. In states that do not grant waivers to charter schools for certification, science teachers in charter schools are less likely to have advanced content knowledge in science than their traditional public school counterparts.

There does seem to be a start-up effect for charter schools regarding the percentage of science teachers who studied science in college. Science teachers in charter schools that have been in operation for at least 3 years are more likely to have a major or minor in science (66%) than science teachers in charter schools that opened more recently (54%). Furthermore, science teachers in more established charter schools in central cities and urban fringe/large towns are more likely to have a degree in science (68% and 66%, respectively) than those in newer charter schools (54% and 53%, respectively). Science teachers in central-city or urban fringe/large town charter schools that have been open for at least 3 years are not statistically different in terms of having a major or minor in science than teachers in public schools. Also, secondary charter schools that are more established are not statistically different from secondary public schools in terms of the percentage of science teachers that have a major or minor in science.

These findings suggest that charter schools are not taking advantage of their increased autonomy to hire more qualified math teachers. In secondary schools, where subject-matter preparation should be most important, charter school science teachers are less likely to have adequate subject-matter knowledge than both public and private school teachers. However, in states that grant broad teacher certification waivers to charter schools, in states that grant waivers on a per-charter basis, and in elementary schools, charter school science teachers are more likely to have sufficient content knowledge than public school teachers.

Teaching Experience

Charter schools appear to have more inexperienced teachers than public and private schools. More than twice as many charter school teachers (62%) than public school teachers (26%) have 5 or fewer years of teaching experience (see Table 1.5). Charter school teachers are also almost twice as likely as private school teachers (33%) to be new to the profession. This is true across school levels, locales, and differences in state charter school laws.

Charter school teachers in all state policy environments analyzed here are more likely to be new teachers than their public and private school counterparts. States that specify teacher certification requirements in individual

Table 1.5. Percent of teachers with 5 or fewer years of experience, by
school characteristics

	Charter school teachers	Public school teachers	Private school teachers
All teachers	61.5	25.5*	32.6*
Community type			
Central city	65.9	25.1*	32.3*
Urban fringe/large town	59.9	26.7*	32.5*
Rural/small town	47.2	22.9*	33.8*
School level			
Elementary	62.0	25.9*	31.0*
Secondary	57.7	24.8*	29.2*
Combined	64.1	26.7*	36.7*
State certification status			
Teacher certification required	60.1	26.2*	29.8*
Teacher certification waived	67.5	25.4*	38.0*
Teacher certification required for specified percentage of teachers	65.5	24.2*	31.3*
Teacher certification requirements specified in charter application	50.7	26.1*	35.1*

* Statistically different from charter school teachers at the .001 level.

Source: National Center for Education Statistics, Schools and Staffing Survey, 1999–2000.

charter applications are least likely to have new teachers in the charter school population.

Although charter schools that have been in operation for at least 3 years have fewer new teachers, they still have twice the percentage of new teachers than that found in traditional public schools. More established charter schools have 56% of teachers with 5 or fewer years of experience, compared with 64% of newer charter schools. The pattern across different school and state environments is similar for newer and more established charter schools. Even charter schools that were preexisting public schools have almost twice as many inexperienced teachers (47%) as public schools (26%).

Over half, and in some cases almost two-thirds, of teachers in charter schools have 5 or fewer years of experience. Not only is this double the percentage of inexperienced teachers found in public and private schools, but it is an alarming finding on its own. Research indicates the benefits of veteran teachers mentoring new teachers (Spuhler & Zetler, 1994; Thomsen & Gustafson, 1997), but the opportunities for mentoring of new charter school teachers seem slim when new teachers outnumber veteran teachers. Furthermore, the burden on teachers in charter schools is often higher than in traditional public schools, since these teachers may be called on to help develop curriculum and discipline policies (Corwin & Flaherty, 1995). Thus, teachers in charter schools often must perform a wider range of tasks than public and private school educators despite having less experience. Although some improvement is visible as charter schools exit their start-up period, a striking difference remains. The prospect of improvement in terms of teacher experience is even more grim considering that teacher attrition is highest in the early years of teaching (Southern Regional Education Board, 2001; Theobald, 1990). It is expected that charter schools will experience higher teacher attrition rates than public schools due to their higher number of new teachers, which will cause charter schools to hire even more new teachers. Additional study of the experience of charter school teachers is necessary as the charter school movement continues to mature.

College Selectivity

Finally, evidence suggests charter school teachers are more likely to come from more selective colleges than public school teachers. While 14% of charter school teachers graduated from a more competitive college, only 10% of public school teachers did (see Table 1.6). A similar number of charter school and private school teachers graduated from more selective colleges. This pattern is evident in both central-city and urban fringe/large town school settings. Charter school teachers are about as likely as public and private school teachers in rural/small town settings to have graduated from a more selective college. Charter school teachers in elementary schools are more likely than both public and private school teachers to have graduated from a more selective college. About 18% of both charter school and private school secondary teachers attended a more selective college, compared to 11% of public school teachers. Charter school teachers in combined-grade schools were more likely to have graduated from a more competitive college (14%) than public school teachers (11%) but less likely than private school teachers (20%).

Charter school teachers in states that required teachers to be fully certified, and that required a certain percentage of teachers in each school to be certified, come from more selective colleges than public school teachers in those states. Charter school teachers in states that grant broad teacher certification waivers to charter schools were not statistically different from pub-

Table 1.6. Percent of teachers in most or highly selective colleges, by school characteristics

	Charter school teachers	Public school teachers	Private school teachers
All teachers	14.0	9.6***	14.3
Community type			
Central city	14.5	9.4***	13.8
Urban fringe/large town	14.9	10.7***	15.3
Rural/small town	8.0	6.8	11.5
School level			
Elementary	12.7	8.8***	9.8*
Secondary	18.1	11.2***	17.9
Combined	14.0	11.0*	19.6***
State certification status			
Teacher certification required	15.8	9.6***	14.6
Teacher certification waived	12.9	11.8	14.5
Teacher certification required for specified percentage of teachers	11.3	6.3**	10.9
Teacher certification requirements specified in charter application	12.7	10.1	21.1**

* Statistically different from charter school teachers at the .05 level.

** Statistically different from charter school teachers at the .01 level.

*** Statistically different from charter school teachers at the .001 level.

Source: National Center for Education Statistics, Schools and Staffing Survey, 1999–2000.

lic or private school teachers in the likelihood of having graduated from a more selective college (13%, 12%, and 15%, respectively).

There are mixed results in terms of the effects of any start-up period for charter schools and the academic background of their teachers. Overall, there is no difference between charter schools that have been open for at least 3 years and newer charter schools in terms of the percentage of teachers that graduated from a more selective college. This is true for elementary, secondary, and combined-grade schools. More established charter schools in central cities are more likely to have teachers from more selective colleges (17%)

than new charter schools (13%). However, the situation is reversed in large town/urban fringe charter schools, with more established charter schools less likely to have teachers from more selective colleges (13%) than charter schools that have opened more recently (17%). Further, states that do not waive teacher certification for charter schools and those that waive them on a charter-by-charter basis have not seen any change in the percentage of charter school teachers that come from more selective colleges, while charter schools in states that grant broad certification waivers are about twice as likely to have teachers from more competitive colleges if they opened within the last 3 years (16%) than if they have been open for at least 3 years (8%).

Charter schools do seem to be tapping into a pool of highly able individuals interested in teaching more frequently than traditional public schools. However, this analysis could not determine whether the increased prevalence of graduates from more selective colleges in charter schools is due to the ability of charter schools to hire noncertified teachers or to the fact that graduates from these colleges prefer to teach in charter schools.

CONCLUSION

The findings presented in this chapter suggest that charter schools are using their autonomy in staffing policies to recruit a teaching force that is different from the teaching force hired by traditional public schools. Overall, charter school teachers are less likely to be certified, have adequate training in math, and have 5 or more years of experience. They are more likely to have attended more selective colleges than public school teachers. Further, charter school teachers in secondary schools are less likely to have sufficient preparation in science than public school science teachers in secondary schools. They are also more likely to be certified but more likely to be inexperienced than private school teachers. These differences suggest that despite some flexibility in staffing, the charter school workforce remains different from the private school workforce. This difference may be due to remaining regulations or bureaucratic structures that constrain teacher hiring, or to the different types of teachers attracted to private and charter schools.

The increased number of uncertified teachers in charter schools is not surprising given that waivers of certification requirements are a common element of charter school laws. However, the argument for waiving certification requirements is that there is a pool of uncertified, but otherwise highly qualified, potential teachers into which charter schools could tap. Despite autonomy from certification regulations, charter schools are hiring significantly fewer math teachers with adequate knowledge of math, twice as many inexperienced teachers, and somewhat more teachers from more selective colleges.

An examination of the two extremes of state charter school policy environments may help shed light on how charter schools are using autonomy to hire a different teaching force. Charter schools in states that are most restrictive in terms of charter school hiring policies (those that do not allow charter schools to waive teacher certification requirements) have fewer certified teachers, fewer math and science teachers with adequate subject-matter knowledge, twice as many new teachers, and more teachers from more selective colleges than public schools. These states do not seem to be trading increased autonomy for more highly qualified teachers, except with regard to teachers from more selective colleges. However, it could be that charter schools in these states are still constrained by regulations that curtail their ability to hire the teachers they would like. States that are least restrictive in terms of charter school hiring policies (those that grant broad teacher certification waivers to all charter schools) have fewer certified teachers, fewer math teachers with a major in math, more science teachers with a major in science, more new teachers, and a similar percentage of teachers from more selective colleges than public schools. These states also do not seem to be trading increased autonomy for more highly qualified teachers, except with regard to teachers with a science degree.

According to some of the measures explored here, charter school teachers seem to be less qualified than teachers in public schools, except for the increased percentage graduating from more selective colleges. This calls into question the assumption that charter schools are successful in creating more effective schools. However, we should note that this does not mean that charter schools have a lower-quality teaching force than traditional public schools. Although evidence suggests that certification, subject-matter preparation, and years of experience are indicators of qualified teachers, quality teaching is a complex phenomenon. In addition, the relative impact these measures have on teaching quality, along with college selectivity, are not addressed here. Charter school teachers may be more qualified by measures not discussed in this chapter and not measured by the Schools and Staffing Survey.

For example, this chapter does not address whether charter schools are successful in hiring teachers who share a common vision or purpose for schools and education. Charter schools may hire teachers who have fewer qualifications but are more committed to implementing the shared mission of the school. Many teachers are attracted to charter schools precisely because of the educational philosophy of the school (Malloy & Wohlstetter, 2003). Although research suggests that a common school mission is important for student learning, it does not discuss its relative importance to a highly qualified teaching force.

This chapter provides a first attempt at addressing some of the issues related to charter school autonomy, teacher-hiring practices, and teacher quality. The available measures tap a number of aspects of teacher quality and objective qualifications that add to our understanding of this process. However, this chapter does not capture all dimensions of teachers that are relevant to charter schools. The finding that charter school teachers appear to be less qualified than their public school counterparts does not suggest that charter schools are failing; rather, it may point us in other directions as we explore the characteristics of charter school teachers and evaluate the role teachers play in the charter school movement.

CHAPTER 2

Professional Opportunities for Teachers: A View from Inside Charter Schools

Christopher Nelson
Gary Miron

One of the many uses to which proponents hope charter schools will put their autonomy is the development of enhanced professional opportunities for teachers. One charter school statute phrases the goal as follows: "to create new professional opportunities for teachers, including the opportunity to be responsible for the learning program at the school site." Behind this formulation lies the assumption that teachers currently possess useful knowledge that, if freed up from bureaucratic constraints, might be better directed toward the pursuit of academic achievement and other educational goals.

The purpose of this chapter is to describe professional opportunities in charter schools as perceived by charter school teachers themselves. Evidence for the chapter comes from surveys of charter schools and site visits to approximately 120 charter schools in four states.

The chapter is divided into three main parts. First, we describe how we conceptualize professional opportunities for teachers and how such opportunities might be related to charter school laws and to improved educational outcomes. Second, the chapter summarizes findings from four states that represent wide variation in legal provisions related to charter school teacher autonomy and professionalism. Finally, we explore the extent to which perceived professional opportunities vary across states and provide a preliminary exploration (based on examination of particular cases) of why some schools appear to provide more professional opportunities for teachers than others and how policymakers, school leaders, and others might leverage improvements in professional opportunities.

Overall, we found that most charter school teachers appear to be quite satisfied with the professional opportunities available to them. However, it is less apparent that the teachers regard these opportunities as new and different. Analysis of variations in perceived professional opportunities indicates, in turn, that most of the variation is at the school level rather than the state level, suggesting that policymakers might best focus efforts to enhance professional opportunities at the building level.

PROFESSIONAL OPPORTUNITIES AND CHARTER SCHOOL AUTONOMY: EVIDENCE FROM THE LITERATURE

Before proceeding to the analysis, it is necessary to address three conceptual questions: (1) What are professional opportunities and how would we know them if we saw them? (2) By what mechanisms do charter school laws and policies seek to create enhanced professional opportunities for teachers? (3) How should we expect enhanced professional opportunities to be linked to student achievement and other school outcomes?

Defining Professional Opportunities

The concept of professional opportunity is difficult to define with precision. Nor do charter school laws provide much conceptual clarity. Of the four states included in this analysis, the statutes of two of them simply assert that enhanced professional opportunities are an important goal of the reform without providing any definition whatsoever. The two remaining statutes provide, in addition, that professional opportunity includes "the opportunity to be responsible for the learning program at the school site." For the purposes of this analysis, professional opportunity involves three core components:

- Classroom autonomy
- Influence in schoolwide decisions (schoolwide influence)
- Professional culture[1]

The remainder of this section briefly discusses each component.

One important aspect of professional opportunities is autonomy, which in general terms involves freedom from obtrusive rules and other constraints. *Classroom autonomy* for teachers involves the latitude to use individual professional judgment to assess and address specific student needs. As such, it is most closely related to the charter concept's emphases on deregulation and decentralization. The literature on public school teaching suggests that classroom autonomy is quite common and flows from the view of public schools as loosely coupled "organized anarchies" (Weick, 1976).

Yet autonomy might be a hollow victory for charter school teachers if they lack the ability to influence the operation of the school beyond the classroom—in short, to help influence the larger environment in which their classrooms exist. Thus, whereas autonomy involves "freedom from" bureaucratic and other constraints, *schoolwide influence* involves the "freedom to" participate in the construction of the school organization, climate, and culture. Influence might include teacher participation in decisions about academic grouping and tracking, the allocation of resources, and the overall direction of the school. The literature on teaching suggests that teacher influence in these areas is less common than teacher autonomy in the classroom (see, e.g., Ingersoll, 1996).

Other authors argue, in addition, that an important component of teacher professional opportunity involves the creation and nurturing of a *professional culture*. Louis, Marks, and Kruse (1996), for instance, note the following key components of professional culture: (1) shared norms and values, (2) a collective focus on student learning and collaboration among teachers, (3) deprivatized practice (which involves discussion of professional practice among teachers), and (4) reflective dialogue among teachers.

How Do Charter School Laws Seek to Enhance Professional Opportunities?

Just as charter school laws are vague on the definition of professional opportunities, they are also rather vague on the link between the structure of charter school laws and the expansion of opportunities for teachers in charter schools. First, waivers of teacher certification requirements might allow talented people without traditional teaching credentials to bring their talents to charter school teaching. Second, the relaxing of collective bargaining requirements might foster more teacher collaboration by allowing school leaders to recruit a team of like-minded teachers and to manage that team in ways that maximize performance in light of the school's unique blend of student needs. Relaxed collective bargaining might also make it easier for school leaders to dismiss teachers whose styles and preferences turn out to be at odds with the school and its mission. Similarly, provisions in some states' laws that allow tenured teachers in noncharter public schools to work in charter schools without losing their tenure or seniority might encourage innovative and experienced teachers from traditional public schools to bring their talents to charter schools. Finally, the notion of school-based autonomy embedded in most charter school laws frees charter school teachers from the direction of central office administrators.

Do Professional Opportunities Matter?

In most discussions of the charter concept, enhanced professional opportunities are justified in terms of their ability to bring about improved student achievement. The literature on schools and school reform—along with the broader literatures on organizational behavior and industrial organization—suggests a number of distinct (though related) mechanisms through which enhanced professional opportunities for teachers might bring about such improvements.

The first mechanism linking enhanced professional opportunities and student outcomes derives from an analysis of the nature of the educational task. According to contingency theory from the field of organizational behavior, organizational processes used to structure behavior should be matched to the nature of the task at hand. The fact that education is a nonroutine, nonrepetitive task that involves uncertainty and shifting requirements implies that teachers are best governed through "organic" forms of management that feature participatory decision making and collaboration among teachers (Rowan, Raudenbush, & Cheong, 1993). Quite simply, what works for one group of students might not work well for other groups of students. Organic management structures that empower teachers, therefore, will better allow them to assess individual student needs and develop customized educational interventions to address those needs. In this respect, the educational task is quite different from the production of machine parts and other repetitive, routinized, and regularized processes better managed through more mechanistic and hierarchical decision structures (Masten, 1984; Perrow, 1986; Wilson, 1989).

The second mechanism relates to the professional culture component of our definition of professional opportunity. Specifically, professional culture might facilitate improved student and school outcomes by encouraging (1) the sharing of knowledge among teachers (deprivatization of practice) and (2) the development of norms of shared responsibility for student outcomes (Marks & Louis, 1997). More generally, professional culture can help overcome the loose coupling endemic in public schools. As Lee, Dedrick, and Smith (1991) observe, "[g]roup consensus [around an organizational culture] . . . reduces the uncertainty and ambiguity of roles—factors that make general functioning difficult" (p. 194). Indeed, culture is a particularly important mechanism of coordination among actors in organizations that grant considerable autonomy to individuals and have open and flexible organizational structures (Miller, 1992).

The third causal argument linking enhanced professional opportunities and improved student and school outcomes is that by giving teachers a greater stake in the school, such opportunities engender more commitment and higher levels of effort (see, e.g., Weiss & Cambone, 1994). This is linked to the idea of property rights in the industrial organization literature (see, e.g., Miller, 1992) and the notion that workers are more likely to make substantial investments in their work if they expect to capture a greater share of the financial and psychological gains from their work.

Not all arguments for enhanced teacher professional opportunities are instrumental, however. One noninstrumental argument draws on notions of justice. Indeed, it is only fair to give greater autonomy to teachers and other school officials if educational policies are also going to hold them more accountable for outcomes than is the case in other schools. This follows from an old and venerable maxim of public administration that power (autonomy) must be commensurate with responsibility (accountability) (see, e.g., Wilson, 1887). Another noninstrumental argument derives from an understanding of political feasibility. Malen (1994), for instance, argues that decentralizing reforms in education can serve the political purposes of preserving legitimacy in the face of intense conflict over education and can help to diffuse such conflict by allowing people to choose their own educational strategies. This political argument is given some empirical backing by Ingersoll's (1996) finding that increases in teacher autonomy in schools are associated with decreases in intraschool conflict.

These theoretical arguments notwithstanding, empirical evidence for the connection between enhanced professional opportunities for teachers and student outcomes is limited. Taylor & Bogotch (1994), for instance, could find no links between the two. Marks and Louis (1997) find evidence of a linkage between teacher empowerment and student achievement, but only if the former is clearly focused on improving instructional practices, not on noninstructional issues. More generally, Wohlstetter, Smyer, and Mohrman (1994) caution that decentralizing reforms are unlikely to work unless policymakers provide mechanisms through which newly autonomous teachers and school staff can acquire the skills and capacity to use their autonomy in productive ways.

STUDY METHODS

Having a professional opportunity does not require that a teacher will *act* on it. Accordingly, instead of attempting to observe actual teacher professional activities, we simply asked charter school teachers to provide their perceptions about available opportunities, largely through closed- and open-ended survey responses. The survey data were supplemented by qualitative data collected during site visits at most of the charter schools in the sample.[2]

Data were collected in four states between the 1997–1998 and 1999–2000 academic years. The four states represent considerable variation in charter school statutes, with one state law receiving a rating of A (most permissive) from the Center for Education Reform (CER), one a B, and two Cs (see Table 2.1).

The four states' charter school laws also exhibit considerable variation in provisions specifically related to teachers. Beginning with teacher certification requirements, state I requires all charter school teachers to be certified (with limited exceptions), while state IV allows uncertified teachers to work in charter schools provided they have college degrees, relevant nonteaching experience, and other characteristics. The remaining states lie in the middle of the continuum, with state II requiring that 75% of charter school teachers hold traditional certification and state III requiring 50% to hold such certification. There is less variation in collective bargaining provisions across the four statutes; states I and II provide collective bargaining coverage for teachers in some schools, but not others, while states III and IV allow but do not require collective bargaining at the school level.[3] Three of the four states represented in this study allow teachers in noncharter public schools to take leaves of absence to teach in charter schools without loss of seniority or tenure. Finally, returning to the issue of autonomy vis-à-vis "central office" pressures, there is considerable variation among the states in the prevalence of schools managed by educational management organizations (EMOs), which might compromise teacher autonomy (see Bulkley, 2001; Miron & Nelson, 2002). In state I, some 53% of the schools were managed by EMOs at the time the surveys were administered. The proportion in the other states was considerably smaller.

We sought to include all charter schools in three of the states. In the fourth state the scope of the project was restricted to schools outside the largest metropolitan area. In the remaining three states we were able to gain access to nearly all schools, with the exception of state IV, where a small number of urban schools declined to participate. Within schools we sought a census of all staff involved with instruction as well as key administrators. However, only classroom teachers are reported on in this chapter. Intensive follow-up limited nonresponse bias and generated an overall response rate of 85%. Table 2.2 provides a breakdown of response rates by state.

THE CONTOURS OF PROFESSIONAL OPPORTUNITY IN CHARTER SCHOOLS

In light of the conceptual discussion above, this section explores survey evidence related to the three components of professional opportunity discussed above: (1) classroom autonomy, (2) opportunities for schoolwide influence, and (3) professional culture. The section also explores

Table 2.1. Attributes of state charter laws pertaining to teachers

	State I	State II	State III	State IV
CER Ranking in Terms of "Strength of Charter School Law"	3rd of 38 laws A	17th of 38 laws B	29th of 38 laws C	22nd of 38 laws C
Certification	Required, except that faculty at a university or community college may teach in a charter school sponsored by that institution	Up to 25% of teachers may be uncertified	Up to 50% of teachers in charter school may have alternative or temporary certification and be working toward standard certification; the other 50% must have regular certification	Charter schools may employ uncertified teachers if they have a bachelor's degree, 5 years experience in area of degree, passing score on state teacher tests, and evidence of professional growth; mentoring must be provided to uncertified teachers
Collective Bargaining/ District Work Rules	Teachers in charter schools authorized by local school boards are covered by district bargaining agreement; other charter school teachers are not; they may negotiate as a separate unit with the charter school governing body or work independently	The staff may bargain collectively, but not as part of the school district's bargaining unit	For locally sponsored charter schools, teachers are covered by district bargaining agreement, but the agreement may be modified by a majority of charter school teachers and governing council; for state charters, teachers may negotiate as a separate unit with the charter school governing council or work independently	Charter school teachers may remain covered by district bargaining agreement, negotiate as a separate unit with the charter school governing body, or work independently
Leave of Absence from District	No	Up to 5 years	Up to 4 years	Up to 5 years
Retirement Benefits	Employees hired by charter school board are eligible for state retirement benefits; employees hired by for-profit corporation contracting with a charter school are not	Yes	Yes	Yes

Data for this table are derived from state information presented by the Center for Education Reform (www.edreform.com) and the U.S. charter schools website (www.uscharterschools.org).

Table 2.2. Sample of charter school staff by state

State (year of sample)	Targeted Sample	Achieved Sample	Response Rate	Number of Classroom Teachers in Sample
State I (1997–1998)	812	728	89.7%	486
State II (1999–2000)	649	537	82.7%	281
State III (1999–2000)	270	257	95.2%	152
State IV (1999–2000)	192	126	65.6%	62
Total	1,923	1,648	85.7%	981

Note: In order to ensure comparability across states, we have restricted our analysis to surveys that were administered during the third or fourth year of each state's charter school reform.

whether teachers in charter schools regard their professional opportunities as new.

Evidence for the Components of Professional Opportunity

The first aspect of teacher professional opportunities we examine is *autonomy in the classroom*. On the whole, more than two-thirds (68%) of charter school teachers responding to the survey said that the statement "Teachers are autonomous in their classrooms" was true. However, this is considerably less than the 81% who had expected such autonomy when initially joining the charter school's faculty. Of the 30% of respondents reporting a gap between expected and actual experience, the overwhelming majority reported moving from "True" to "Partly True," indicating that the change was not very dramatic. Only 2% of respondents moved from "True" to "False." Overall, the difference between the distributions for the initial expectation and current experience was statistically discernible ($p < 0.01$, Wilcoxon signed rank test).

The second aspect of teacher professional opportunities examined was *influence in schoolwide decisions*. One survey item asked teachers to indicate their agreement with the statement "Teachers are involved in decision making at this school." The mean response to this item was 3.7 on a scale of 1 to 5, with 1 indicating "Strongly Disagree" and 5 indicating "Strongly

Agree." Put more concretely, 53% of respondents either agreed or strongly agreed with the statement.

A related item asked respondents to report the extent to which the statement "Teachers are able to influence the steering and direction of the school" was true. Just over half of the respondents said that the statement was true, another 37% that it was partly true, and 12% that it was false. Once again, we found that teachers expected more influence than they were currently experiencing, with 74% of respondents reporting that they had initially expected schoolwide influence. Not surprisingly, responses to the two schoolwide influence items were closely related (Spearman's rho = 0.70, $p < 0.01$).

Interestingly, the percentage of teachers agreeing that they had opportunities to influence schoolwide policy was considerably lower than the percentage who believed they were autonomous in their classrooms ($p < 0.01$, Wilcoxon signed rank test). This comports with findings from the literature on noncharter public schools. Ingersoll (1996), for instance, found that the average score on a survey index for perceived policy influence in instruction was considerably lower than for classroom autonomy in instruction. The findings are also similar to those reported by Bomotti, Ginsberg, and Cobb (1999) on charter school teachers in Colorado.

Of equal interest, there was considerably more *variation* in perceived levels of schoolwide influence than perceived levels of classroom autonomy. At the individual level, the amount of variation in the influence variables ($s = 0.69$) was higher than the amount of variation in the classroom autonomy variable ($s = 0.52$). Thus, perceived schoolwide influence is both less prevalent and more variable among charter school teachers than perceived classroom autonomy.

The third component of teacher professional opportunities discussed in the literature is the existence of a shared *professional culture*. One facet of professional and organizational culture often discussed in the literature on industrial organization is the mechanisms through which employees select themselves (and are selected) into the organization (see, e.g., Miller, 1992). In some sense, charter schools are schools of choice for teachers as well as parents and students; the assignment of teachers to schools is generally not governed by collective bargaining agreements (which often rely heavily on seniority rules). According to the theory of choice, teachers (as well as parents and students) will select schools on the basis of their agreement with its educational approach and philosophy. The end result of this process of quasi-market sorting (Tiebout, 1956) should be that charter school teachers will be more focused around a common set of educational goals than teachers in other schools (Lee, Bryk, & Holland, 1993; Lee et al., 1991; Newmann, Smith, Allensworth, & Bryk, 2001). We assessed the degree of preference sorting among charter school teachers both by examining the reasons they provided for choosing a charter school and by asking about their commitment to and satisfaction with their school's mission.

Beginning with reasons for choosing the charter school, the one rated most highly by teachers was the desire to work with like-minded educators, with an average response of 4.1 on a scale of 1 to 5 (with 1 indicating "Not Important" and 5 indicating "Very Important"). More concretely, 79% of responding teachers rated this reason as either "Important" or "Very Important." The two lowest-rated reasons for seeking employment at the schools were location and difficulty in finding other work, which received mean responses of 2.8 and 2.6, respectively (on the same 5-point scale). Thus, the survey evidence indicates that charter school teachers in the four states we studied are choosing to work in charter schools largely on the basis of their agreement with the schools' culture and philosophy.

Turning to mission commitment, 67% of responding teachers said that the statement "Teachers are committed to the mission of the school" was true. As with the items above, however, commitment to the schools' missions did not quite live up to the teachers' expectations, as 87% initially expected such mission commitment. This differences, as before, was statistically discernible ($p < 0.05$, Wilcoxon signed rank test). However, as before, most teachers (69%) reported no difference between their initial expectation and current experience, and most teachers who did report changes moved from "True" to "Partly True." Another item asked teachers to rate their *individual* level of satisfaction with their school's mission. Responses to this item confirm that teachers, overall, are satisfied with their school's mission. The average response to this item was 4.0 on a scale of 1 to 5, with 1 indicating "Very Dissatisfied" and 5 "Very Satisfied." More concretely, 75% of responding teachers said that they were either "Satisfied" or "Very Satisfied" with their school's mission.

The individual satisfaction item also provides an opportunity to observe more directly the degree of normative coherence in charter schools around school mission. Specifically, for each school we calculated the proportion of teachers who were either "Satisfied" or "Very Satisfied" with their school's mission. In 83% of the schools, the proportion of teachers satisfied with their school's mission exceeded 50%.[4] In only four of the schools sampled did the proportion satisfied fall below 20%.

Up to this point, we have examined teacher professional opportunities piece by piece, beginning with classroom autonomy and ending with organizational supports. It is possible, however, that some teachers and schools score highly on one component but lower on others. Thus, we created a *composite index* of the items discussed earlier in this chapter.[5] As with most of the items discussed above, examination of the index scores indicated that most charter school teachers are satisfied with available professional opportunities (the average value was 29 out of a maximum value of 37). (See Figure 2.1.)

Once again, we examined the data at the school level, since the operation of a school depends upon how individuals (each with their individual attitudes) are clustered together. Interestingly, we found that schools with lower values on the professional opportunity index also showed greater within-school variation (Pearson's $r = -0.63$). More concretely, teachers in schools with more perceived professional opportunities perceived them more consistently than teachers in other schools. It is perhaps fortunate that schools with lower average values on the index also have high standard deviations, since in these schools at least some teachers generally have more positive perceptions of professional opportunity.

Are Charter Schools Providing New Opportunities for Teachers?

Overall, we have found that most charter school teachers are reasonably satisfied with the professional opportunities afforded them. The charter school concept, however, promises not just satisfactory professional

Figure 2.1. Distribution of standardized index of perceived professional opportunities

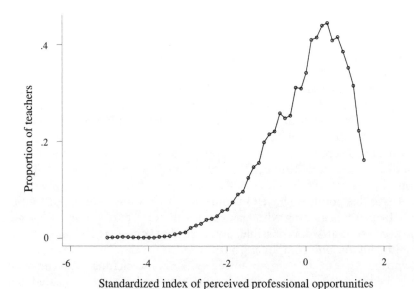

Standardized index of perceived professional opportunities

opportunities but also *new* opportunities. Has the charter concept delivered on this promise?

The charter school teacher survey included an item that asked teachers whether the professional opportunities afforded them were new, comparing their current experience with their initial expectations. Only 46% of responding teachers said that the statement "There are new professional opportunities" was true. Thus, while the previously discussed findings suggest that charter school teachers are generally satisfied with the level of available professional opportunities, many do not consider these opportunities to be new or innovative. The 46% of teachers agreeing that their professional opportunities were new is considerably lower than the 68% of teachers who said that they currently had autonomy in their classrooms and the 67% who said that teachers at their school were committed to their school's mission. It is, however, similar to the 51% of teachers who said that teachers currently had opportunities to influence the steering and direction of their school.

As with the other items, current experiences appear to fall short of initial expectations, with 67% of teachers saying they initially expected new professional opportunities, compared with 46% who said they currently did. As before, the difference between the initial expectation and current experience distributions is statistically discernible ($p > 0.01$, Wilcoxon signed rank test).

We considered the possibility that the larger variations in some schools were simply a proxy for lower sample sizes in those schools. However, a multivariate analysis (robust regression) confirmed that the negative relationship between the average index score and within-school variation persists even after we control for school size.

Also, it is commonly held that teachers in nonpublic schools have greater professional opportunities than those in public schools (see, e.g., Lee et al., 1991). Thus, teachers' assessments of the newness of professional opportunities in charter schools might be sensitive to the comparison group they used. To test this we examined the relationship between the perceived newness of professional opportunities and (1) the number of years teachers had previously taught in public schools and (2) the proportion of their total past teaching experience spent in public schools. In both instances there was virtually no relationship (Spearman's rho = 0.03 and 0.04, respectively).

Overall, then, most charter school teachers appear to be quite satisfied with the professional opportunities available to them. However, it is less apparent that the teachers regard these opportunities as new and different.

SOURCES OF VARIATION IN PERCEIVED
PROFESSIONAL OPPORTUNITIES:
A PRELIMINARY EXPLORATION

Describing the typical opportunities and variations among teachers' perceptions is itself a valuable exercise. However, the lack of good comparison data from noncharter public school teachers limits our ability to interpret and evaluate our findings. We can, however, examine variations across charter schools and charter school teachers. We begin by exploring variations across states and within schools on survey responses and then turn to qualitative evidence for some preliminary explanations for these variations.

Inspection of average scores on the overall professional opportunity index suggests that there are, indeed, differences across states, with teachers in state III having the highest overall score and teachers in state II the lowest (see Table 2.3). Because the scores in the table are standardized to have a mean of 0 and a standard deviation of 1, the score for state III shows that, overall, its perceived professional opportunity index score was approximately one-fifth of a standard deviation above the typical value for all sampled teachers. Similarly, the score for state II shows that teachers in that state scored on average approximately one-fifth of a standard deviation below the grand mean for all sampled teachers.

Returning to the discussion of the characteristics of the state laws, we found little relationship between the Center for Education Reform's ratings of the laws' permissiveness and states' scores on the professional opportunity index. Indeed, state III, which received the highest index score, received only a C from CER. Similarly, state II, to which CER gave a B, scored –0.20 on the professional opportunity index. Focusing on the provisions of the charter school laws that directly concern teachers, we find no apparent relationship between certification requirements, for instance, and scores on the professional opportunity index. While state II has rather permissive certifi-

Table 2.3. Variation in index of perceived professional development
opportunities by state

State	CER Grade for Law	*N*	Mean	Standard Deviation
I	A	486	0.07	1.00
II	B	280	-0.20	1.02
III	C	152	0.18	0.86
IV	C	62	-0.08	1.02

cation requirements (allowing up to 50% of teachers to hold alternative certification), state I, which scored next highest on the index, grants no teacher certification waivers at all.

This is not to say, however, that states' legal provisions have nothing to do with teacher professional opportunities. If they do, however, the mechanisms are not captured by the factors identified in this chapter. An analysis of variance suggests that school-level (between-school) factors do a better job of explaining variance in the professional opportunity index scores than state-level factors (see Table 2.4). Indeed, nearly one-seventh of the variation in index scores can be accounted for by school-level differences compared with one-hundredth for state-level differences. This suggests that policymakers should look more to school-level policy instruments than to changes in state statutes should they wish to nurture greater perceived professional opportunities among charter school teachers.

As noted above, the teacher surveys were accompanied by site visits to most of the schools included in the sample. Thus, we also examined schools that had particularly high and low scores on the index of professional opportunities in order to gain some preliminary insights on the reasons teachers in some schools perceive more professional opportunities than those in other schools. In this way, we follow the strategy employed by many researchers in school effects research of using quantitative indicators to identify outlier schools and qualitative methods to explore some of the likely reasons these schools score either high or low on the quantitative indicators (Stringfield, 1994; Teddlie & Stringfield, 1993). Six case studies were developed based on existing qualitative data collected during site visits.[6] The first three case schools scored nearly a full standard deviation *above* the grand mean on the index. The remaining three schools, by contrast, scored approximately one standard deviation *below* the grand mean. In total, we identified six factors that are likely to explain variance between charter schools.

Table 2.4. Analysis of variance of professional opportunity index scores

Source of Variance	Partial Sum of Squares	Degrees of Freedom	MS	F	P-value
Model	163	59	2.77	3.12	<0.01
State	10	3	3.36	3.79	0.01
School	145	56	2.58	2.91	<0.01
Residual	815	920	0.89		
Total	979	979	1.00		$R^2 = 0.16$

School-Based Decision Making. While it may seem self-evident, it is likely that there will be more teacher influence and greater perceived opportunities for professional development when decisions are made at the school as opposed to the headquarters of a management company. Likewise, teachers will exercise more influence when they are involved in planning.

Effective School Leadership. Schools that scored well on the index had administrators who struck a careful balance between providing a clear vision of the school's mission and methods versus micromanagement. The danger of an administrator with too clear a vision or too dominant a role was clearly illustrated in one of the case schools that had a very low index score.

Clearly Defined Mission and Goals for the Schools as Well as Clearly Formulated Professional Development Plans. The schools with high index scores appeared to have better accountability plans, and they often had specific plans for professional development (these plans often included setting aside at least half a day each week for collaborative work and professional development activities). Schools with low index scores often did not have staff development plans or other documents to steer the vision and development of the school. One lesson from the case schools was that professional development activities will have limited value if they are not keyed to the school's core mission.

Experienced Teachers among Staff. The evidence from the cases suggests that schools with high index scores had at least some experienced teachers on their staff. In two of the case schools these teachers also retained strong ties to the host district and its surplus of experienced teachers.

Job Security for Teachers and Staff. Many of the schools that had high index scores had arrangements such as collective bargaining agreements or had teachers who were granted leaves of absence from a district school. These arrangements helped ensure teachers that they had greater job security. Even with collective bargaining agreements, teachers were still considered at-will employees of the charter school. However, they could return to a district school if they lost their job at the charter school.

Low Levels of Teacher Attrition. Some of the lower-scoring schools were beset by high teacher turnover, which lends credence to the idea that the value of investments in professional culture and professional opportunities can be severely reduced if the teachers in whom the school invests leave too soon.

CONCLUSION

Our aim in this chapter was to describe and explain variations in perceived professional opportunities among charter school teachers. While professional opportunity is a murky concept, we identified professional culture, influence in schoolwide decisions, and classroom autonomy as key components.

Evidence from the surveys suggests that teachers in charter schools are, in fact, choosing schools in order to find communities of shared approaches and expectations. In most schools, considerable internal agreement on the school's mission existed and teachers reported being satisfied with those missions.

Given that they tend to be smaller and more cohesive, we might expect charter schools to be less disjointed than other public schools (Little, 1990; Weick, 1976), leading to greater perceptions of schoolwide influence and perhaps less classroom autonomy than in other public schools. Our findings suggest, however, that charter school teachers, like other teachers, perceive more classroom autonomy than schoolwide influence. This confirms an earlier finding by Bomotti and colleagues (1999) based on a study of Colorado charter school teachers. These results also comport with studies of traditional public schools, which find that teacher empowerment and influence vary by domain and that teachers generally have more influence in their classrooms than in the larger school setting (Ingersoll, 1996; Marks & Louis, 1997).

It is noteworthy, however, that the *magnitude* of the "influence deficit"—or the difference between perceived influence and autonomy—was smaller in our data than in the Colorado study.[7] Both differences, moreover, are considerably smaller than the difference reported by Ingersoll's (1996) study of noncharter public school teachers based on the 1987–1988 administration of the SASS.[8] Thus, it appears that charter schools are altering the balance between teacher empowerment in these two domains, even though teachers still perceive themselves as more influential in the classroom.[9] In spite of this, the survey responses cast at least some doubt on the claim that charter schools are providing *new* professional opportunities.

Our analysis also suggests that there are variations in perceived professional opportunities by state. However, while state differences were statistically significant in an analysis of variance, they were overwhelmed by school-level differences. This suggests that while state-level factors are not unimportant, policymakers would be advised to focus most of their efforts on school-level policy levers. Qualitative evidence from charter schools that scored particularly high and low on the professional opportunity index suggests a number of possible correlates of professional opportunity. These include (1) small school size, (2) school-based decision making, (3) administrators and leaders who provide a clear vision without micromanaging, (4) professional development activities that are keyed to the school's mission, (5) the existence of at least some experienced teachers in the school, (6) job security for teachers and staff, and (7) the absence of high teacher turnover.

Priorities for future research should include further studies that do more to identify the particular characteristics of charter schools and charter school laws that facilitate professional opportunities for teachers. Moreover, given the heavy burdens placed on teachers at many charter schools—especially those in the start-up phase—policymakers should be concerned about teacher burnout, which seems evident from the high rates of teacher attrition in many schools (see, e.g., Miron & Nelson, 2000; Miron, Nelson, & Risley, 2002). Indeed, high rates of teacher attrition can vitiate investments schools might make to develop teachers' capacity to use their autonomy effectively.

In the end, we believe that the most important questions concern whether charter school teachers and staff possess the knowledge, skills, and capacity to make good use of their autonomy and influence in the service of student achievement. Therefore, the most important research priority should be to assess whether the professionalism–achievement linkage found in the literature on noncharter public schools applies to charter schools.

NOTES

1. These components are adopted, with modifications, from Bomotti, Ginsberg, and Cobb (1999).

2. All surveys were sent to schools by mail, completed individually, and returned to the research team in sealed envelopes either through the mail or during site visits by the research team. Site visits to charter schools generally lasted from half a day to a full day and included interviews with school directors, teachers, and parents as well as unstructured observations. In a limited number of cases, the site visits also included separate focus groups with parents and teachers.

3. To our knowledge, no schools in states III and IV have collective bargaining agreements. However, it is possible that the mere opportunity to engage in collective bargaining has influenced the environment in the schools.

4. For the purposes of this analysis, we excluded schools with five or fewer teachers, since in smaller schools the chance occurrence of a single dissatisfied teacher might unduly boost the within-school variance.

5. The index was constructed using an exploratory principal components factor analysis (with promax rotation). The index is the weighted and standardized sum of the items identified in the analysis and had a marginally acceptable level of inter-item reliability (Cronbach's alpha = 0.69).

6. Readers may consult Nelson and Miron (2002) for more extensive discussions of the cases.

7. Using effect size coefficients to make the comparisons, we find that the difference between the mean response to the influence and autonomy questions in our data was –0.58 standard deviation, while the difference in the Colorado data was –1.73 standard deviations.

8. Using the same effect size methodology, the difference reported by Ingersoll is –2.6 standard deviations.

9. Interestingly, among the four states we studied there were notable variations in the gap between perceived schoolwide influence and classroom autonomy. Using the effect size coefficient, the difference was –0.62 standard deviation for state I, –0.47 for state II, –0.43 for state III, and –0.57 for state IV.

PART II

The Impact of Charter Schools on Educational Practices

CHAPTER 3

Does Autonomy Matter?
Implementing Research-Based
Practices in Charter and
Other Public Schools

Priscilla Wohlstetter
Derrick Chau

Reformers, particularly in urban school districts, have experimented with various models of school autonomy, from magnet and site-based managed schools to in-district and independent charter schools. Proponents of school autonomy argue that increased decision-making authority enhances local buy-in and commitment to reform among school staff and parents. Local stake-holders (rather than district and state administrators) who are closest to students and have the most knowledge about their educational needs are expected to make better decisions on how money should be spent, who should be hired, and how and what students should be taught. The argument is that better decisions in these areas will lead to more effective classroom instruction and, ultimately, increased student performance.

While some empirical research has supported the link between school autonomy and instructional improvement, little research has investigated which *types* of decisions—budget, personnel, educational—are the most significant for schools in generating instructional improvements. In this chapter, we investigate the extent to which autonomy facilitated the adoption of research-based practices in classrooms. We also examine whether some dimensions of autonomy were more important than others for improving instruction.

We studied a sample of nine elementary schools that varied in terms of school autonomy, from site-based managed (SBM) schools to charter schools, and assessed their use of research-based literacy practices. Literacy instruction was used as a measurement device for assessing instructional improvement. Since school autonomy policies are designed to improve instruction, we hypothesized that the use of strategies that have been shown to be linked with success in literacy would be greater in schools with more autonomy. Further, we expected that schools with more control over decision making specifically related to instruction would utilize more research-based literacy practices. We expected charter schools in our sample to exhibit the highest levels of autonomy and, as a result, the fullest implementation of research-based practices. SBM schools, on the other hand, were expected to have less autonomy across the dimensions of budget, personnel, and the educational program and, consequently, less implementation of practices linked to success in literacy.

The following section reviews existing literature on the relationship between school autonomy and instructional improvement. In the next section, we present the two frameworks we developed from the literature to investigate school autonomy and research-based literacy practices. Literacy was selected as the focus of instructional reform because school districts, in recent years, have intensified their attention on improving literacy, particularly in urban elementary schools. The remainder of the chapter is focused on data from our sample of nine autonomous schools. We conclude with a discussion of the implications of our findings for policy and practice.

SCHOOL AUTONOMY AND INSTRUCTIONAL IMPROVEMENT: EVIDENCE FROM THE LITERATURE

The majority of studies on school autonomy in decentralized schools have found only limited or indirect impacts of these policies on improving instruction (Malen et al., 1990; Smylie, 1994). In many cases, local self-governance resulted in increased participation in school decision making by teachers and parents (Malen, Ogawa, & Kranz, 1990). However, the decisions were often trivial and peripheral to the instructional practices of the schools (Clune & White, 1988; Lieberman, Darling-Hammond, & Zuckerman, 1991). Some studies even noted that self-governance might hinder instruction, since teachers could become preoccupied with administrative duties, supplanting student instruction (Hannaway, 1993; Smylie, 1994).

Other studies of decentralized schools have identified several indirect effects of autonomy on instruction in schools. Increased teacher participation in decision making often resulted in increased teacher satisfaction, morale, and commitment to improving instruction (Malen et al., 1990; Rowan, 1990). This is encouraging, since schools with higher teacher satisfaction are more effective organizations (Ostroff, 1992) and high levels of teacher morale and commitment have also been found to encourage collaboration to improve instruction (Little, 1990). However, school autonomy was found to have only an initial positive impact on these indirect effects on instruction (Malen et al., 1990). Factors such as large time commitments, stress, and frustration tended to limit the impact of these indirect effects.

A smaller number of studies suggest that school autonomy may have a more direct effect on instruction. A study of SBM schools found that these schools were able to generate curricular and instructional innovations (Robertson, Wohlstetter, & Mohrman, 1995). The ability of these schools to improve was due largely to the presence of conditions associated with high-involvement organization—specifically, decentralization of power, knowledge and skills, information, and rewards. Smylie, Lazarus, and Brownlee-Conyers (1996) found that school-based participative decision making was related positively to instructional improvement and student achievement. This relationship was, in part, the result of renewed teacher enthusiasm and a strong focus on instruction. Similarly, Heck, Brandon, and Wang (2001) found that positive teacher involvement through site-based decision making can result in the selection of organizational, curricular, and pedagogical methods to improve instruction. Some evidence in this study also suggested that decentralized decision making led to improved student achievement.

While studies have found some direct effects of school autonomy on instruction, research on autonomous schools has recognized that local control over certain dimensions of decision making may have more impact on instruction. In a series of studies, researchers have investigated the effects of teacher empowerment in decentralized schools on instruction and student achievement (Marks & Louis, 1997; Marks & Louis, 1999; Newmann, Marks, & Gamoran, 1996). Marks and Louis (1997) found that overall teacher empowerment was an important but insufficient condition for changing instruction. A significant contribution of these studies was the recognition that teacher empowerment can be divided into different dimensions, such as teacher influence over school operations and classroom instruction. Their findings indicated that the dimensions of teacher influence were distinguishable, suggesting that not all forms of empowerment will have the same effects on instruction.

Research has identified three dimensions of autonomy—school control over budget, personnel, and educational issues—that are necessary for improving instruction (Odden & Busch, 1998; Wohlstetter, Wenning, & Briggs, 1995). Studies of budget autonomy have found some positive effect on the implementation of instructional improvements: Autonomous schools have the flexibility to focus resources on student learning (Knight, 1993; Odden & Busch, 1998). Other studies examining schools with control over personnel, especially hiring and professional development, have found that such autonomy can foster strong teacher professionalism in support of instructional improvements (Louis, Kruse, & Associates, 1995). Finally, studies investigating the effects of local control over the educational program suggest that autonomous schools are able to select curricula and materials more appropriate to the specific needs of students (White, 1992).

While past research recognizes the importance of school autonomy over budget, personnel, and educational issues, few studies have disaggregated which types of decisions are the most significant for generating improvements in instruction. Over what items in the budget should schools have control in order to improve instruction? What types of school control over personnel most directly affect instruction? What decisions about the educational program should schools control in order to improve instruction most effectively?

FRAMEWORKS FOR THE STUDY

This section utilizes existing research to develop a more refined definition of school autonomy and to identify effective research-based literacy practices for schools. We developed two frameworks composed of indicators to guide our assessments of autonomy and educational practice in our sample of schools. These frameworks also facilitated the development of hypotheses about the relationship between school autonomy and instructional improvement.

Refining School Autonomy

Previous research has argued that school autonomy will affect student achievement only if it focuses on improving instruction (Marks & Louis, 1997). In this study we go beyond earlier studies of autonomous schools by breaking autonomy down into the elements of control within three areas of decision making. Table 3.1 shows the indicators that we developed for each dimension to classify the degree to which the sample schools in our study had been vested with control.

Budgetary control was expected to allow schools to allocate instructional resources more effectively. The literature suggests that when schools control curriculum and instruction-related expenditures, they can directly affect instruction by purchasing needed literacy materials such as texts and computers (Caldwell & Spinks, 1992; Odden & Picus, 2000). This control, moreover, can be viewed as distinct from the limited control that many schools have over only the discretionary portions of their budgets, which may or may not be applicable to curriculum and instruction. Additional research in decentralized schools concludes that schools with control over external resources

Table 3.1. Indicators of school control over budget, personnel, and educational program decisions

Control over Budget Decisions	Control over Personnel Decisions	Control over Educational Program Decisions
Extent of control over curriculum and instruction-related expenditures (limited, moderate, or extensive)	Extent of control over teacher socialization (limited, moderate, or extensive)	Extent of control over the literacy curriculum (limited, moderate, or extensive)
• How much control does the school have over expenditures for texts and other literacy materials?	• How much control does the school have over hiring teachers and the principal?	• How much control does the school have over selecting its literacy curriculum?
• Does the school require authorization from another authority to spend school funds?	• How much control does the school have over actively recruiting teachers?	• How much control does the school have over selecting supplemental literacy materials such as texts and periodicals?
Extent of control over external resources (limited, moderate, or extensive)	• How much control does the school have over the criteria for evaluating teacher performance?	Extent of control over instructional practices (limited, moderate, or extensive)
• How dependent is the school on the district for funding?	• How much control does the school have over rewards for teachers?	• How much control does the school have over literacy instruction in the classroom?
• To what extent is the school accessing external resources?	• How much control does the school have over the frequency, length, and content of teacher professional development?	• How much control does the school have over selecting interventions for low-performing students?
• Does the school have a formal procedure for accessing external resources?	Extent of control over personnel structure (limited, moderate, or extensive)	• How much control does the school have over scheduling instructional time for literacy?
	• Can the school implement team teaching or other forms of teacher collaboration in the classroom?	Extent of control over student assessment measures (limited, moderate, or extensive)
	• How much control does the school have over the use of aides for instruction?	• How much control does the school have over the selection of student assessment measures in addition to the required state assessment?
	• Can the school create specialist positions to assist with literacy instruction?	• Do teachers have access to timely student assessment data?
	Extent of control over parent involvement policies (limited, moderate, or extensive)	• Does the school determine how student assessment data will be used?
	• Can the school create requirements for parent involvement in the classroom?	
	• How much control does the school have over involving parents in school decision making?	

(e.g., grants, partnerships) have better access to supplementary resources and target those resources toward instructional goals (Odden & Picus, 2000).

For the dimension of personnel, school autonomy was expected to foster a professional school culture that included a focus on continuous improvement (Louis et al., 1995; Odden & Busch, 1998). Research in autonomous schools suggests that control over the socialization of teachers affects school instruction by facilitating a strong organizational culture. Teacher hiring, performance evaluations, rewards, and professional development all contribute to the consistency of implementing effective instruction in schools (Louis et al., 1995). Schools with control over personnel structure are able to determine the most effective distribution of personnel for instruction. Decisions about the use of teacher aides, parent volunteers, literacy specialists, and team teaching directly affect instruction in schools (Snow, Burns, & Griffin, 1998). Control over parent involvement policies allows schools to select and design such policies to support student instruction. Parent involvement policies that directly relate to instruction include parent contracts, requirements for parent involvement at home (reading nightly with students), and informational meetings about school literacy programs and assessments (Snow, Barnes, Chandler, Goodman, & Hemphill, 1991).

We developed indicators to assess schools' autonomy regarding the educational program in order to investigate whether schools were allowed to determine their own approaches to teaching literacy. Selection of literacy curricula by schools can lead to increased teacher commitment and satisfaction (Smylie, 1994). These positive teacher attitudes improve the quality of implementation and increase the effectiveness of the adopted programs (Dimmock, 1993; Snow et al., 1998). Further, when schools have control over instructional practice, they are better able to determine which practices are most effective for their student populations, since school personnel have the most knowledge about the educational needs of students. Schools with extensive control over instructional practice can select effective practices (Snow et al., 1998), such as intervention strategies, extended instructional time, or specialized teaching methods, in order to improve student achievement. Autonomy regarding the educational program was also defined to include control over student assessment. Selection of student assessment measures allows schools to focus on evaluating their students for the purpose of improving instruction rather than for external accountability (Calfee & Hiebert, 1991).

Defining Research-Based Literacy Practices

Significant public attention has been directed to improving literacy instruction in schools, particularly at the elementary (K–5) level (Manzo, 2001). Therefore, in studying classroom practices, we focused on literacy as a measurement device for assessing instructional improvement. We thought it reasonable to expect that improving literacy was core to the sample schools' reform agendas. For the purposes of this study, literacy was defined as the ability of students to read and write fluently. Literacy achievement is an important determining factor for student achievement in public schools. Students who are not at least modestly skilled readers by the end of third grade are unlikely to graduate from high school (Snow et al., 1998). In addition, students with fewer literacy skills will struggle to develop skills in other areas, such as content knowledge and verbal abilities (Cunningham & Stanovich, 1998).

Studies in education have noted an improvement in knowledge about "what works" in effectively instructing students (Hoffman, 1991; Louis, 1998). Effective research-based literacy practices have been identified by extensive studies on literacy (American Federation of Teachers, 1998; National Center to Improve the Tools of Educators, 1996; National Reading Panel, 2000). It is important to emphasize that our study focused on literacy practices rather than on literacy curricular content. In the past, debates have raged over the "correct" content of literacy programs, especially between phonics and whole-language curricula (Routman, 1996). We believe that the literacy practices employed in this study can support effective literacy instruction, regardless of the content of the curriculum.

Six research-based literacy practices emerged from our review of the literature and were used to assess instructional practices in the sample schools.

1. *Print-rich classroom*: Availability of supplemental literacy materials such as literature sets and student level periodicals encourages more reading and exposure to new vocabulary (Curriculum Development and Supplemental Materials Commission, 1999; Krashen, 1993; Snow et al., 1991).
2. *Use of technology*: Computers and other instructional technologies can help students produce text (Reinking & Bridwell-Bowles, 1991); technology frees students to concentrate on sentence structure and vocabulary rather than on handwriting skills.
3. *Instruction tailored to students' reading levels*: The selection of appropriate literacy materials for student reading levels optimizes opportunities for student learning and high performance (Curriculum Development and Supplemental Materials Commission, 1999; Hoffman, 1991; MacGillivaray & Rueda, 2001).
4. *Small-group instruction*: Small-group instruction allows teachers to customize instruction to meet student needs (Barr & Dreeben, 1991; Curriculum Development and Supplemental Materials Commission,

1999; Taylor, Pearson, Clark, & Walpole, 1999); this is most effective for classes with a range of student abilities.

5. *Assessment designed for instruction*: Frequent performance-based assessments designed to evaluate students' reading levels assist teachers in the planning of instruction (Calfee & Hiebert, 1991; Curriculum Development and Supplemental Materials Commission, 1999; Snow et al., 1998).

6. *Strong school–home connections*: Coordination of literacy instruction at school with parents reading nightly with students reinforces their learning (Snow et al., 1991).

Some types of decisions under school autonomy were hypothesized to have more impact on certain literacy practices than others. Budget autonomy was expected to have more impact on the availability of literacy materials and the use of technology because schools with extensive budget control were expected to direct dollars toward the purchase of supplementary literacy materials and technology. School autonomy over the educational program was expected to affect the ability of schools to tailor instruction to student reading levels, design assessments to support instruction, and use small-group instruction. High levels of autonomy over personnel were expected to allow schools to reduce student–teacher ratios in support of small-group instruction and to strengthen home support for instruction. While other relationships may certainly exist, these relationships were hypothesized to be the most important for autonomous schools to implement effective literacy practices.

To summarize, this study focused on the relationships between the various dimensions of school autonomy and the six research-based literacy practices, described in the frameworks. Data from sample schools with varying amounts of autonomy, from site-based managed to charter schools, were analyzed to assess the extent to which the various dimensions of autonomy correlated with the adoption of effective literacy practices. A description of the sample schools and the methods used to collect and analyze data are described next.

RESEARCH METHODS[1]

Sample Schools

The sample for this study consisted of nine elementary (K–5) schools from the Los Angeles area—three independent charter schools, three dependent charter schools, and three SBM schools. The three groups of schools were selected to capture schools with varying degrees of autonomy. From the

charter school population, we selected three schools that were fiscally dependent on their charter authorizers and three that were independent. California charter school law allows schools to negotiate, through their charter
petition, the extent to which they have fiscal autonomy (Powell, Blackorby,
Marsh, Finnegan, & Anderson, 1997; Wohlstetter, Griffin, & Chau, 2002).
The three charter schools with extensive control over their budgets—independent charter schools—were hypothesized to be the most autonomous of
the sample (school A, school B, and school C). The other three charter schools
selected for the study were dependent charter schools that still relied on their
charter authorizers for approval of their budgets (school D, school E, and
school F). Reflecting the state charter school population at the time, most
charter schools in the sample were conversions; only school A and school F
were new-start charter schools.

The three SBM schools in the sample (school G, school H, and school I)
operated under a district-sponsored SBM initiative and were hypothesized
to have the least amount of autonomy among the schools we studied. All
three SBM schools were located in the same Los Angeles area school district.
As described on the district's website, the SBM plan transferred "significant
decisions in instruction, budgeting, staffing and school operations" to schools.
However, the district revised its instructional policies in the fall of 2000 and
centralized decisions about reading instruction. As a result, all elementary
schools in the district were required to use the same published literacy program for the first through third grades during the 2000–2001 academic year.
SBM schools retained control over other decisions. Within the universe of district schools that had implemented SBM, schools were selected that had been
successful in improving student achievement in the area of reading; these schools
were expected to be more likely to use research-based literacy practices. To
identify SBM schools with improvements in scores, Stanford Achievement Test–
Version 9 (SAT-9) reading scores for third graders between the 1997–1998
and 1998–1999 school years were compared. For the three sample SBM
schools, the average scores for students at or above the 50th percentile increased
from 17% to 30% between the 2 years.

Across the three sample groups, schools were selected that had been
operating under their respective reforms for at least 3 years to ensure that
the schools' instructional programs were fully implemented. The only exception to this criterion was a newer dependent charter school, school F, operated by an educational management organization (EMO). We included the
school in the study because we felt it offered an interesting balance between
school-site autonomy and EMO authority.

To ensure the relevance of the study for urban settings, the ethnic diversity of student populations was another consideration in selecting sample
schools. For instance, within the universe of district SBM schools, schools

were selected for the sample only if their student populations included large percentages (over 85%) of non-White, particularly Latino and African American, students. Likewise, preference was given to charter schools with higher percentages of non-White students.

We recognize that the selected sample schools represent a unique set of high-capacity schools. The charter schools demonstrated initiative and strong community by voluntarily petitioning and creating their schools, while the SBM schools had successfully improved student achievement. The study was designed to investigate how school autonomy facilitated the adoption of literacy practices, so schools were selected with the highest likelihood that both conditions (autonomy and research-based literacy practices) would be present. Therefore, the study was intended to be exploratory in nature, offering new information that should not be generalized to all charter or SBM schools.

Data Collection and Analysis

Data for the study were collected from a variety of sources, including school-site interviews, teacher surveys of literacy practices, and a review of archival documents. Teams of two researchers conducted data collection during a 2-day site visit to each school. Site visits occurred during the 1999–2000 and 2000–2001 schoolyears.

One-on-one interviews at the school sites were conducted with individuals knowledgeable about school decision-making processes and about school literacy efforts, including principals, literacy coordinators, teachers, and parents. For interviews with teachers, we focused on the first and fifth grades to capture approaches used early and late in the schools' literacy programs. We also interviewed members of school governance councils and decision-making teams with responsibility for curriculum and instruction. At each school, 10 to 14 interviews were conducted. School documents such as budgets, annual reports, and charter petitions were also collected to supplement information from the interviews.

In order to assess the levels of autonomy in the sample schools, we compiled interview responses related to each indicator of autonomy (see Table 3.1) and analyzed them using cross-case analysis (Miles & Huberman, 1994). The extent of school control over each indicator was rated on an absolute scale (limited control = 1, moderate control = 2, extensive control = 3) to create summed indices for each sample school. For example, a dependent charter school that was able to decide how much money to spend on literacy materials but required district authorization to spend school funds was given a "moderate control" rating in the budget indicator of "control over curriculum and instructional expenditures." An SBM school that was not allowed to make any decisions related to the purchase of curricula was rated as having "limited control" over curriculum and instructional expenditures. In order to summarize these findings, ratings of school autonomy were summed for the areas of budget, personnel, and educational decisions and calculated as percentages of the total scale (budget = 6, personnel = 9, educational = 9).

As noted earlier, data collection also included a teacher survey to assess the extent to which research-based literacy practices were being used in classrooms. Survey items were developed based on the six research-based literacy practices identified earlier. The surveys were administered to all teachers in the sample schools, usually during a regularly scheduled faculty meeting. The average response rate across the nine sample schools was 76%. Survey responses were aggregated by school, and analysis of variance was used to confirm that school responses to survey items differed at statistically significant levels ($p < .001$). Since this study was exploratory in nature, we compared ratings of school autonomy to teachers' use of research-based practices from responses on survey items. The next section uses these data to explain the relationships observed between school autonomy and the use of research-based literacy practices.

RESULTS

Results from this study are presented in two sections. The first section profiles the nine sample schools, describing the levels of autonomy and the prevalence of research-based literacy practices in classrooms. The second section explores the relationship between autonomy and the use of research-based literacy practices to determine the extent to which autonomy facilitated the adoption of research-based practices in classrooms.

The ratings of autonomy in sample schools supported the expected distinctions across independent charter, dependent charter, and SBM schools, with independent charter schools exhibiting the highest levels of autonomy in all decision-making dimensions. A summary of the ratings of autonomy in sample schools is presented in Figure 3.1.

Overall, the difference in autonomy between charter and SBM schools was much more pronounced than the difference between independent and dependent charter schools. Although dependent charter schools have only moderate control over their budgets (charter authorizers must approve all financial decisions), they have few restrictions with respect to personnel and educational decisions. Not surprisingly, the autonomy ratings for the dependent charter schools on those two dimensions were quite similar to the ratings for independent charter schools in our sample. The three SBM schools

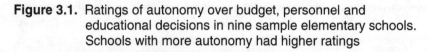

Figure 3.1. Ratings of autonomy over budget, personnel and educational decisions in nine sample elementary schools. Schools with more autonomy had higher ratings

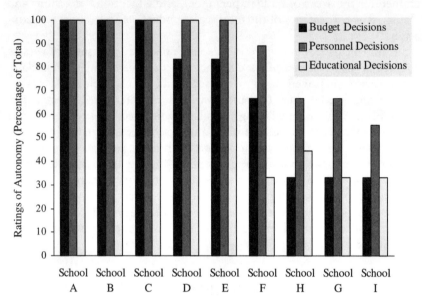

we studied had only limited control over most dimensions of autonomy. This finding is consistent with much of the previous research on SBM, which has found that SBM plans maintain district authority over decision making, especially in the dimensions of budget, personnel, and curriculum (Bimber, 1993; Malen et al., 1990).

The one exception to these trends in autonomy ratings among our sample schools was a dependent charter school that was managed by a national EMO. School F deviated markedly in autonomy ratings from other dependent charter schools in our sample. In the case of this particular EMO, many of the decisions related to the educational program were determined by the EMO. The EMO, similar to a district central office, retained control over several dimensions of autonomy, including the educational program. One teacher explained that "when it comes to curriculum and instruction we [school F] are limited in the decisions we can make."

Overall responses from teacher surveys indicated that research-based literacy practices were prevalent in the nine sample schools. Across the sample schools, teachers most often reported that they used assessments to assist in planning instruction. About 82% of teachers overall used this practice.

Moreover, in two schools 100% of teachers reported that they used this practice. Over 70% of teachers who responded also had print-rich classrooms, used small-group instruction, and had strong school–home connections. By contrast, tailoring instruction to students' reading levels had the lowest usage across teachers who responded. In five of the nine sample schools, 50% or fewer of the teachers used this practice. The widespread use of research-based practices by teachers in the sample schools confirmed both that literacy had been a reform focus in the schools and that the sample schools were indeed high capacity, that is, the collective power of the faculty was focused on strengthening student performance (Youngs & King, 2002).

Though the use of research-based practices was high in sample schools, responses from individual schools varied considerably. For instance, the use of technology across sample schools ranged from a high of 100% of teachers in one school to a low of only 17% of teachers in another school. There was also considerable variation among schools on teachers' reported use of print-rich classrooms, instruction tailored to students' reading levels, and the use of strong school–home connections. Such variation across the sample schools allowed us to tease out which types of autonomy influenced instruction.

In exploring the relationships between autonomy and the use of research-based practices, some indicators of autonomy were found to be more important than others. Specific indicators such as control over educational expenditures, external resources, curriculum, student assessment, and parent involvement policies had strong relationships with certain research-based literacy practices. The remainder of this section discusses these relationships in detail.

School Control over Educational Expenditures and External Resources

The strong trends between ratings of budget autonomy and the presence of print-rich classrooms suggest that schools with more budget authority allocated more funds to acquire literacy materials for classrooms. All six charter schools, which were rated with moderate or extensive control over educational expenditures, had higher percentages of teachers reporting print-rich classrooms than the three SBM schools, which were rated with limited control. The independent and dependent charter schools with significant control over external resources also had higher percentages of teachers reporting print-rich classrooms than the SBM schools.

Staff in schools with extensive budget autonomy—the three sample independent charter schools—were positive about their ability to acquire needed materials. A teacher at an independent charter school explained, "The power over our own finances that came with charter status really facilitates the ability of the school to make decisions and implement changes." On the other hand, school-site administrators and teachers at the three dependent charter and three SBM schools mentioned during interviews that school district requirements hindered their ability to make purchasing decisions. The principal in a dependent charter school described these financial restrictions by saying, "The fact that we're still tied fiscally to the district keeps us from going in different directions we'd like to pursue—we get lots of 'no's' from the district." Likewise, the principal at a SBM school remarked, "There are district requirements with strings attached to funding, so this limits the use of funds."

The results also demonstrated a pronounced difference between the presence of print-rich classrooms in the six charter schools (with moderate to extensive control over budget) and the three SBM schools (with limited control over budget). This difference also surfaced in the interview data. For instance, a first-grade teacher in an independent charter school explained, "The school's charter status has helped because I have all of the materials and anything else I need. They are all available to me." On the other hand, a teacher in an SBM school bemoaned, "Good instruction at our school is inhibited by a lack of materials. Some teachers are trying to teach without workbooks for the literacy program."

Schools with high levels of control over external resources were better able to focus resources directly on improving instruction, rather than on peripheral issues. The principal of an independent charter school explained, "The school gets funding for instructional assistants to help classrooms for 4 hours per week each. Private funding comes for books, supplies, and technology such as computers." Indeed, most of the charter schools in our sample had higher percentages of teachers using technology than the three SBM schools.

Schools with more external resources appeared to use them to purchase technology for instructional purposes. For instance, the principal of a dependent charter school explained that her school not only received a grant for computers but also obtained other grants over time to upgrade the computers. Among the autonomous schools studied, many schools directed efforts to acquire external resources, which included the purchase of computers. Additionally, schools with high ratings of control over external resources used their decision-making power to seek out new avenues to obtain needed educational resources. The use of external resources in SBM schools was less focused on instruction, often limited to occasional grants for small numbers of books or minor renovations of facilities.

School Control over the Curriculum and Student Assessment

Schools with greater control over their literacy curricula also had a higher presence of print-rich classrooms. Nearly all the charter schools had extensive control over the selection of their literacy curricula, and all these schools also had higher percentages of teachers with print-rich classrooms compared to the other schools, which were all rated with limited control. Only the dependent charter, operated by an EMO, was rated with limited control over its literacy curriculum, similar to the three SBM schools. In the case of this EMO, the company selected the literacy curriculum for its entire network of schools.

By being able to determine their own literacy curricula, schools with extensive control were able to decide on the instructional materials needed in classrooms. A first-grade teacher in an independent charter school explained this relationship by saying, "Every student has the necessary materials: books, workbooks, tests, all the supplements, and the classroom library from the literacy program. We chose our literacy program and we can make sure we have the materials to make it work."

As noted earlier, the three SBM schools and the dependent charter operated by an EMO had limited control over literacy curriculum decisions. In the SBM schools, personnel experienced more difficulty in acquiring instructional materials for the literacy program required by the district. The instructional coordinator at an SBM school complained:

> Some pieces of the literacy program are not available due to a lack of funds. For example, I like the idea of the literacy program picture files, but I have never seen a picture file. I myself did not do the ordering, so I could not control what materials would be used.

Though the EMO-run dependent charter was unable to select its own literacy curriculum, the company used its considerable resources to select and purchase a published literacy program. As a result, a high percentage, or about 81%, of teachers in this school responded that they had print-rich classrooms. The EMO's resources help to explain the high presence of print-rich classrooms in this dependent charter school, in spite of the fact that the school itself had only limited control over curriculum decisions.

In addition to selecting materials for their literacy programs, schools with control over the curriculum were better able to address weaknesses in their literacy programs. When weaknesses were identified, these schools often pilot-tested supplemental programs in order to determine whether those programs would be complementary to the existing curriculum. For instance, a teacher at an independent charter school described the adoption of a program for remedial reading instruction by saying, "The program was piloted first and then a written evaluation was prepared for the Curriculum Council. The Curriculum Council voted to adopt the program and then sent it to the Budget/Operations Council for final approval." Schools with limited control over their literacy curricula were subject to the decisions made by the district or EMO.

Schools with greater control over student assessment tended to have higher teacher use of assessments designed for student instruction in classrooms. In schools with extensive control over student assessment—all the charter schools except the EMO-run dependent charter—about 90% of teachers reported that they used assessment results to help plan instruction. The remainder of the sample schools, mostly SBM schools, were rated with only limited control over assessment, and only about 76% of teachers in these schools used assessments in planning for instruction. According to interview data, schools with extensive control over student assessment were better able to select assessments that aligned with curricular and instructional goals and informed instruction. Describing an example of this kind of school autonomy, the instructional coordinator in an independent charter school explained, "The school was not happy with using the district literacy test and wanted to align the writing diagnostics, so the school got all of its grade-level chairs together and compared the rubrics and decided on the new diagnostic."

Since schools with extensive autonomy were administering their own assessments, these schools also had greater control over the analysis of student performance data. The instructional coordinator at a dependent charter school discussed the use of the school's self-implemented assessments by saying:

> All of the grades are doing entry-level assessments and follow-up assessments during the year. Both of these impact instruction. The entry-level assessments help determine the instructional grouping that the student will be placed in. The follow-up assessments are used by the teachers to monitor both student progress and how effective the instructional programs are.

Personnel in other schools with extensive control over assessments also mentioned the development of on-site databases that included student performance data in order to improve access by teachers and administrators.

Personnel in schools with limited control over student assessment measures were unable to align assessments with their instructional programs. Even though all SBM schools were required to adopt a published literacy program that included assessments, these schools rarely used assessments to inform decisions on instruction. A first-grade teacher at an SBM school explained, "Individually, teachers conduct ongoing assessments as part of the published literacy program, but I do not know if this information will be collected and monitored schoolwide to evaluate the program." These schools relied heavily on the state-mandated assessment, administered by the district only once at the end of the schoolyear, for information on student performance. As a result, these schools had limited ability to analyze student performance data on their own and were only able to assess the overall impact of their literacy programs, rather than analyzing the progress of programs and students during the school year. In part this finding is likely due to the nature of assessments in the particular literacy program adopted by the district.

School Control over Parent Involvement Policies

In analyzing the influence of control over personnel on literacy practices, we expected autonomous schools to create parent involvement policies to support classroom instruction. The results do indeed indicate a strong relationship between control over parent involvement policies and the involvement of parents in home instruction. All of the charter schools in our sample were rated as having extensive control over parent involvement policies; they also had higher percentages of teachers who reported that parents were involved with reading nightly to students. By contrast, the three SBM schools that were rated as having only moderate control over parent involvement policies had lower percentages of teachers with strong school–home connections.

These findings complement earlier research and also suggest that charter schools may opt to adopt stronger and more specific parent involvement policies than less autonomous schools. Research on charter schools (Becker, Nakagawa, & Corwin, 1997; Finn, Manno, & Vanourek, 2000) suggests that parent involvement is significantly higher in charter schools than in district-run schools, in part because charter schools are schools of choice. Across the sample of six charter schools, nearly 90% of teachers responded that parents read nightly with their children. By contrast, only about 55% of teachers in the three SBM schools reported that parents read nightly with their children. Four of the charter schools in the sample—both dependent and independent—instituted schoolwide parent contracts that in part required parents to read nightly with their children.

Another interesting finding related to parent involvement in the sample schools concerned work to bolster the skills of parents so that they would be effective "teachers" with their children at home. Many sample schools with high numbers of parents who were English-language learners offered courses for parents in English as a second language (ESL) and held parent meetings to explain school literacy programs and student assessments. In some SBM schools, the district had even implemented English-language-learner programs for parents. The principal at an independent charter school described her school's program by saying:

Many of the parents at the school are not able to speak English, and the school has helped them in improving their English skills. The parent center on campus provides ESL classes for parents. The family literacy trainer works with 15 families at home to improve English literacy.

Schools with greater control over parent involvement policies tailored their methods to address the characteristics of their specific communities.

CONCLUSION

The intent of this study was to explore the relationship between school autonomy and the use of research-based practices in classrooms. Findings from the nine elementary schools confirmed our hypothesized distinctions between the levels of autonomy in charter and site-based managed schools. The charter schools in our sample had more autonomy than the site-based managed schools; furthermore, the independent charter schools had more autonomy than the dependent charter schools. As hypothesized, we found that teachers in schools with higher levels of autonomy also tended to use more strategies that have been linked with student success in literacy. On the other hand, we found that the SBM schools, which had less autonomy across the dimensions of budget, personnel, and the educational program, implemented fewer practices linked to success in literacy. Finally, as expected, specific types of autonomy seemed to have stronger relationships with the use of certain research-based practices.

While it was hypothesized that schools with more control over decision making specifically related to the educational program would utilize more research-based practices, the findings with regard to which types of autonomy were most important were broader, including school control over educational expenditures and external resources as well as control over curriculum, student assessment, and parent involvement policies. Data from teacher surveys as well as interviews with school personnel supported these relationships and indicated that schools utilized their autonomy to influence classroom practices. In particular, school control over educational expenditures and external resources was found to have a strong relationship with the presence of print-rich classrooms and the use of technology. The increased ability of schools to determine their curricula was also found to influence the presence of print-rich classrooms. Similarly, some relationship was found between school control over student assessment and the use of assessments designed for student instruction in classrooms. In addition, school control over parent involvement policies had a strong relationship with support for reading instruction at home. In effect, when autonomous schools were vested with autonomy, they directed decision making, particularly in areas related to the budget and the educational program, toward improving instruction in ways that were consistent with research-based literacy practices.

The design of this exploratory study suggests some avenues for future research. The selection of sample schools in this study was designed to provide some evidence of the use of research-based practices in classrooms. These schools could be described as high-capacity schools; faculties were willing to assume greater decision-making responsibilities and to mobilize efforts to address their own problems. Also, sample schools in this study possessed unique characteristics and operated under specific autonomy policies that limit comparisons with other schools. While the characteristics of the sample schools in this study served the purpose of this exploratory study, additional research is necessary to provide more generalizable results. The framework employed here for analyzing various dimensions of autonomy refines the concept of autonomy by delineating measurable indicators for assessing gradation. Future studies of schools that represent a broader range of school characteristics and autonomy policies would add to our understanding of the relationship between school autonomy and instructional improvement. With this expanded knowledge, educational policymakers and practitioners will be better able to put in place strategies leading to more effective classroom instruction and, ultimately, to increased student performance.

NOTE

1. For more detailed information about research methods, please contact the authors.

CHAPTER 4

Charter School Innovation in Theory and Practice: Autonomy, R&D, and Curricular Conformity

Christopher Lubienski

The idea of innovation undergirds the charter school concept. While charter schools represent a significant innovation in governance, even more importantly, many reformers and policymakers believe that such structural changes will foster new approaches in curriculum and instruction that will improve student achievement—an expectation that motivated much of the charter movement at its origins and is still very much in evidence today. In contrast to the uniformity associated with bureaucratic administration, charter advocates argued that reforms would create autonomy for individual schools, freeing them from burdensome top-down regulations and allowing educators to use resources as they saw fit. This autonomy would make them more flexible and responsive to local needs, thereby providing the opportunity to be innovative in responding to parents, raising academic achievement, and engaging students marginalized by standard practices. In view of these new opportunities afforded by structural innovations in governance, the question emerges as to how charter schools are using their autonomy to innovate around curriculum and instruction. Ironically, this analysis indicates that many schools may find themselves forced to exercise that autonomy in ways that undermine their innovative potential.

The chapter considers the theory and expectation that autonomy positions charter schools to serve as "laboratories" or "R&D" (research and development) centers for innovative educational practices. Theorists and policymakers advocate the reform of governance under the assumption that changes in school administrative structures lead to "different and innovative" classroom practices. Under that logic, charter enthusiasts anticipated not only that structural changes would *diversify* options for parents in local communities but also, as demonstrated below, that greater school autonomy from higher levels of government would precipitate classroom innovations—that is, new or substantially altered practices *not available in the broader public school system.* A review of research on charter school practices in four key states suggests that this is not happening in the ways theorists and reformers predicted. Diversification is evident in all the states studied. Yet, the "innovative" part of the different *and* innovative mandate appears to be more elusive than reformers had anticipated. While administrative activities in many charter schools are innovative, states where charter schools enjoy greater autonomy demonstrate no particular propensity for innovation in the classroom—where reformers anticipated change. Instead, this analysis suggests that the theoretical assumptions regarding autonomy are not only unsubstantiated but possibly wrong. Development of innovations often depends on greater autonomy not only from higher levels of governance but also from the immediate demands of seemingly capricious marketlike forces.

The first section of the chapter outlines the theoretical foundations and perceived potential of charter schools. Specifically, I look at policy goals associated with charter schools in light of public-choice theory—the rational-economic understanding of public-sector endeavors—particularly as this theory offers a cogent critique of public administration. As the predominant analytical perspective prescribing decentralization and deregulation, public choice endorses institutional autonomy as the key to innovation and improvement in the provision of public services. While there are a number of arguments (such as efficiency and equity) that motivate school-choice reformers, charter schools in particular incorporate the essential elements of public-choice theorists' advocacy of alternative institutional arrangements. Because they are premised on public-choice prescriptions for autonomy, charter schools can inform our understanding of the theoretical expectations of innovation and the types of changes we might expect from other forms of school deregulation that are consistent with public choice.

In the second part, I apply a framework for exploring the question of innovation in charter schools—consistent with the tenets of public-choice theory—in reviewing research on charter school practices in four states in order to understand the nature of change occurring in and through these institutions. I look for innovations that represent new or substantially altered practices in light of the R&D expectations of theoreticians, policymakers, and reformers for "different" *and* "innovative" educational methods. The final section considers patterns evident in charter school practices, focusing on the logic of autonomous schools as R&D centers in decentralized environments—indicating that the narrow and ideological focus on autonomy from higher levels of government may in effect undermine the innovative potential intended in charter schools.

THE THEORY OF CHARTER SCHOOL INNOVATION

Frustration with the state of public schooling over the last two decades mirrors the widespread dissatisfaction with "big government" in general and state administration and regulation in particular—a view popular with many policymakers (see, e.g., Bennett et al., 1998; Finn, 1997; Finn, Manno, & Bierlein, 1996; Osborne & Gaebler, 1992). Indeed, these concerns represent a compelling critique of current approaches to public administration and a coherent theory offering alternative models of public service provision. As the predominant perspective for public policy analysis in recent years, public-choice theory has been influential in policymakers' arguments for decentralizing, deregulating, or otherwise reforming the delivery of many public services through autonomous agencies. Much of the thinking behind charter schools embodies both the public-choice critique of public administration of education and its preferred remedy for the problems inherent in state-run schooling (Garn, 1998). For example, theorists and reformers note that the public school monopoly on state funding for education deprives bureaucratically administered schools of the incentives to serve their clients effectively; therefore, removing the "exclusive franchise" forces schools to respond to consumers or risk losing their funding (see, e.g., Kolderie, 1990; Nathan, 1996; see also Chubb & Moe, 1990). Advocates argue that these aspects of their design position charter schools as laboratories for innovative educational practices that are expected to benefit the school system as a whole.

Public-Choice Theory and Educational Innovation

Although there are several variants of public choice, theorists generally draw their fundamental assumptions and approaches from neoclassical economic principles in analyzing law, political science, and public administration. This perspective has been widely influential in the last three decades, as evident in the critique and reform of public services—endeavors that have traditionally relied on nonmarket mechanisms outside the scope of economic discipline (Mueller, 1979). Public-choice theorists assume that people, motivated by self-interest, most effectively express their individual preferences in the public sphere much as they do when dissatisfied with services in the private business sector—by exercising the "exit" option and finding a more suitable provider. Moreover, government officials also look after their own individual self-interest. Rather than serving the illusory public interest, public institutions often direct their benefits toward their bureaucrats, or—since they are shielded from market discipline—the special-interest groups to which they are susceptible and whose interests may conflict with those of the general public (Buchanan, Tollison, & Tullock, 1980; Kalt & Zupan, 1984; Romer & Rosenthal, 1979).

Public-choice theorists elevate the sovereignty of individual consumer preferences over other social or institutional goals, a priority often evident in, for instance, concern for user satisfaction indicators. Public institutions are thought to be most effectively organized if they are responsive to their immediate users rather than to messy and ineffective political and bureaucratic processes. Furthermore, people consuming public services are best arranged in small-scale groups of like-minded individuals—preference "bundles" or "clusters"—in order for their wishes to be most effectively heard and honored. These economic-style principles form the basis of public-choice analysis in its diagnosis of the problems of public administration and its prescription of market-style autonomy for providers.

Pathologies of Public Administration. A central tenet in public-choice theory is that there are certain institutional ills inherent in state provision of public services. Public-choice theory holds that self-interested officials will seek to enhance their own power by creating "empires" (a.k.a. fiefdoms, dictatorships) within and over bureaucracies and public resources (Niskanen, 1971; Romer & Rosenthal, 1979). Rather than promoting local autonomy in order to find new or more effective ways of serving local consumers, government administrators hope only to maintain the status quo or expand their budgets for their own sake; operating outside the incentives and discipline of a market environment, they are inherently incapable of considering true costs and benefits to the public, leading to inefficiencies and inflexibility (Greene, 1996; see also, e.g., Niskanen, 1971).

Similarly, public-choice scholars perceive regulations largely as a means by which entrenched interests insulate, enrich, and protect themselves, since these interest groups are better positioned to organize effectively in advancing their interests through regulatory institutions (Kalt & Zupan, 1984; Stigler, 1998). This line of reasoning presumes that public provision or regulation is fraught with anti-innovative constraints. As individuals, groups, or firms seek to control public resources, regulatory regimes are reoriented toward the needs of bureaucrats or the interests that control them (Borcherding, 1977; Buchanan et al., 1980; Rowley, Tollison, & Tullock, 1988). In the case of education, this notion is applied to the "education establishment"—teachers unions, school boards, administrators, and so on—as the entrenched interests that stand in the way of innovation and substantive reform (Levin, 1997). Thus, according to this view, the "over-regulation of traditional schools has stultified educational innovation and responsiveness" (Levin, 2000, p. 3; see also Chubb & Moe, 1990; Doyle, 1994; Peterson, 1990). The implicit solution is deregulation and enhanced autonomy for local providers.

As a consumer-oriented perspective, public choice emphasizes the diverse individual preferences of consumers and a perceived contradiction between those consumer preferences and the centralized monopolies that engender disincentives for developing different approaches. Indeed, particularly in the case of state schooling, public-choice theorists point to the uniformity associated with public provision (e.g., Peterson, 1990). Self-interested administrators employ top-down authority, which gives them control over inputs and processes, if not outcomes. Therefore, bureaucrats use such authority to impose standardized practices that maintain their power, rather than practices that may effectively educate diverse children. Minority ethnic groups, or marginal "affinity groups," or "preference clusters" of like-minded individuals are effectively disenfranchised by the bureaucratic and majoritarian political systems that support the status quo—hence the popularity of choice in polls of minority groups (Chubb & Moe, 1990; Gee, 2001; Maranto, 1999; Walberg & Bast, 2001). Broader forms of input that directly influence institutions—referenda, legislated mandates, and so on—are more likely to lead to conflict between groups, produce more bureaucracy to manage those conflicts, and result in less responsiveness to consumer preferences. The result, according to this popular line of reasoning, is that public administration leads to a deadening uniformity whereby each school is "essentially identical to every other" (Finn & Gau, 1998, p. 79; see also Fitzgerald, 1995; Little Hoover Commission, 1996). Furthermore, in view of the widespread sentiment that children learn in different ways, there is a growing backlash in policymaking circles against the "one-size-fits-all" approach associated with common schooling and the administrative-progressive "one best system" reforms (e.g., Finn & Gau, 1998). Thus, in this theoretical perspective, the primary goal of public education is the satisfaction of individual consumer preferences; indeed, public choice does not recognize lofty, value-laden, and seemingly unattainable goals such as civic coherence, the public interest, or the common good—purposes that only invite conflict (Bobrow & Dryzek, 1987). Essentially, choice advocates argue against the old common school as an antiquated approach in a society now characterized by pluralism and diverse parental perspectives on education (e.g., Coleman, 1990; Doyle, 1994).

Public-Choice Prescriptions and Charter Schools. In order to be responsive to individual preferences—rather than to the interests of bureaucrats or politicians—public-choice theorists advocate an approach that has been very popular in recent years: limited government through small, local, autonomous institutions that respond to their consumers in the delivery of public services. The antibureaucracy sentiment of public-choice theory is apparent in school reformers' concerns regarding uniformity in state-monopolized education (Garn, 1998; see also, e.g., Kolderie, 1990). In essence, the charter is a grant of autonomy from regulation with the expectation that the school will improve academic results; the particular processes by which it will enhance learning are not specified but are delegated to the school. In theory, decentralization and autonomy encourage experimentation and diverse options in many consumer markets. Therefore, theorists suggest that similar dynamics would be useful in forcing schools away from rigid, top-heavy administrative models and encouraging new approaches for educating students (e.g., Coleman, 1990; Hoxby, 1994).

Charter schools are premised on individual (or family) choices where such choices are thought to best reflect the diverse preferences of the choosers. Since communities are shaped around common interests and values, charter schools give form to such communities around educational issues (Clayton Foundation, 1999; Viteritti, 1999)—what public-choice theorists would see as homogeneous preference clusters that reduce conflict over school issues in the wider context (e.g., Chubb & Moe, 1990). Theorists argue that, in a deregulated and decentralized system, schools will have to strive to attract these groups, resulting in innovations in both the *types* of education available and the *processes* by which more efficient and effective education is provided. And if a school fails to meet the diverse needs of consumers, parents have the right or responsibility to seek satisfaction of education preferences elsewhere—thereby holding publicly funded providers accountable to users through the threat or exercise of an exit option not available in pupil assignment systems (Manno, Finn, Bierlein, & Vanourek, 1998b; Vanourek, Manno, Finn, & Bierlein, 1997).

Therefore, although there are other motivations and justifications (such as parental involvement, teacher empowerment, etc.) that serve as catalysts for school choice, charter reforms bear the unmistakable imprint of public-choice theory in the diagnosis of the pathologies of state provision and the adoption of alternative institutional arrangements. In bypassing bureaucratic regulatory authority, charter schools are expected to unleash the innovative potential of educators as autonomous schools compete to meet diverse needs within their local area.

Innovation as a Policy Objective for Charter Schools

Innovation is a frequently cited goal in charter school advocacy for three related reasons, which, together, demonstrate the perceived need for new approaches in the education system. First, in keeping with the values of public-choice theorists, a system of school choice presupposes a range of options from which parents may choose. Quite often, innovation is cast as the means of developing and diversifying options that meet the preferences of users, and charter schools are specifically designed to manifest the theoretical potential for innovation. Second, innovation may lead to improvements in educational practices, and, presumably, increased achievement. As laboratories or R&D centers for curricular and instructional strategies, charter schools have the autonomy to experiment with different approaches for finding more effective practices for educating children—"with the perceived assumption that such innovations will produce identifiable improvements in student achievement" (Wohlstetter & Griffin, 1998, p. 3; see also, e.g., Clayton Foundation, 1997, 1998; Lane, 1999). Finally, charter schools can innovate to meet the preferences of people traditionally marginalized by standard practices in the state system. Individuals and groups whose pedagogical or content preferences are not represented in the standard curriculum can choose a school geared to their needs.

Thus, by changing the governing structures in which schools operate, charter school reforms change the environment—the institutional autonomy of schools from centralized bureaucratic regulations, the opportunities to try new approaches, and the incentive to attract and maintain interest. These changes are intended to secure the ultimate goals of increased achievement and parent satisfaction. The logic can be outlined as shown in Figure 4.1.

While many school reform strategies specify particular processes, this approach reconfigures the institutional environment in which schools operate (Hentschke, 1997; Lubienski, 2001c). Such structural reforms are designed to create incentives and opportunity space for educators to use their autonomy and flexibility to develop processes for enhancing student achievement and meeting parental preferences. Many reformers frame choice, deregulation, and innovation as the intermediate goals necessary for increasing achievement. Moreover, innovation and diversification are primary goals for those reformers seeking to find ways of engaging children and communities traditionally marginalized by the one-size-fits-all uniformity associated with the status quo (e.g., Flaherty, 1995; Fulford, Raack, & Sunderman, 1997; Lane, 1999).

While not to be overstated, the significance of encouraging innovations in schooling should not be slighted, since it is often central to arguments for, and expectations of, school choice. Certainly, innovation should be seen as the means to other goals rather than as an end in itself (although its frequent and close association with charter schooling in the policy literature often suggests otherwise). Still, the notion that autonomous schools, motivated by competition, will develop innovative practices is an assumption widely embraced by many groups—theorists, legislators, teachers, and charter founders.

Such assumptions are explicit in the laws authorizing charter schools. The legislation varies across states, with laws allowing more autonomy and greater ease of entry generally regarded as "stronger" laws (Center for Edu-

Figure 4.1. Charter school logic model

INPUTS (Structural Reforms)		TRANSFORMED ENVIRONMENT (Opportunity Space/ Policy Objectives)		OUTCOMES (Final Goals)
• Decentralized autonomy		• Entrepreneurial management / administration		• Student achievement
• Consumer choice (open enrollment, mobile per-pupil funding)		• Teacher autonomy and professionalism		• Customer satisfaction
• Provider competition		• Curricular and pedagogical innovations		
• Deregulation		• Equity / access to new educational opportunities		
• Accountability to authorizer (public) for results		• Privatization		
• Accountability to parental (private) preferences		• Parental / community involvement		
		• Incentives for responsiveness to consumers		

Note: Adapted from Miron & Nelson, 2002.

cation Reform, 2001a; Viteritti, 1999). According to charter enthusiasts, stronger laws "shape the scope, adequacy, quality, innovative-ness, and educational value of charter schools" by providing more opportunities and incentives for educators to exercise autonomy (Vanourek et al., 1997, p. 3). Under the assumption that "public schools must be provided with an option for more autonomy over their administration, operations, and expenditures," the law in Washington, D.C., authorizes charter schools in order to "stimulate the use and development of different and innovative teaching methods" (D.C. Law 11-135, § 103, 43 DCR 1699). California's charter school law also seeks to "encourage the use of different and innovative teaching methods" (California Education Code 47600). In fact, innovation is specified as a policy goal in over 75% of the charter school laws, with virtually all of those explicitly seeking innovations in instructional practices such as teaching methods. No other goal—including academic achievement and the diversification of programmatic options—is mentioned more frequently.[1] Indeed, the rate at which this purpose is cited in legislation has increased substantially; it is cited in all laws passed since 1998. Hence, policymakers appear to assume a causal connection between structural reforms (e.g., school autonomy, competition, choice) and innovations in classroom practice. This is significant: *Legislators, consistent with assumptions of public choice theory, expect that changes in school administrative structures will lead to "different and innovative" practices in the classroom.*

Charter school authorizers display similar assumptions. For instance, the schools authorized by Central Michigan University—the most active chartering agency in Michigan—must "be pillars of innovation in instruction" (cited in Khouri, Kleine, White, & Cummings, 1999, p. 25). In Colorado, over 42% of individual charter schools identified innovations in teaching and learning as a goal in their mission statements (Clayton Foundation, 1997). Indeed, teachers often seek employment at charter schools anticipating more freedom to try "innovative methods" in pursuing their educational philosophy (Clayton Foundation, 1998, 1999; Vanourek, Manno, Finn, & Bierlein, 1998). Parents and charter school founders express similar assumptions (Clayton Foundation, 1998, 1999; RPP International, 1998; RPP International, 1999; SRI International, 1997; Vanourek et al., 1997). Medler (1996), for example, reports from his survey of 110 charter schools that innovation was one of the top three reasons for founding a school, well ahead of other objectives such as increased autonomy (see Education Commission of the States & Nathan, 1995). Reform advocates, policymakers, and analysts endorse the expectation for educational innovations with remarkable frequency.

Thus, a substantial, bipartisan, and consistent consensus presumes that structural changes—the decentralization and deregulation manifested in charter school reform—have the potential to induce innovation in educational practices. Many people from a wide variety of backgrounds and perspectives concur in the presumption that the likelihood of achieving innovation and uniformity is a result of institutional design. Indeed, many reformers cast charter schools as R&D centers or laboratories to break the mold of standard classroom practices (Wohlstetter & Griffin, 1997; see also, e.g., Halpern & Culbertson, 1994). In fact, prominent charter advocates agree that the *"R&D potential is an important part of any policy-oriented appraisal of the charter phenomenon"* (Manno et al., 1998b, p. 490; emphasis added).

ANALYZING INNOVATION IN CHARTER SCHOOLS

Relatively clear expectations for innovation have become more problematic when observers try to appraise the charter school movement. Semantic debates over what we mean by "innovation" slight the important goal of understanding the *potential* of structural reforms to bring about substantive changes in the core practices of schooling. Some argue that innovation should be defined "as conventionally understood (e.g., something new)" (Good &

Braden, 2000, p. 145; see also Stout & Garn, 1999). Others believe diversification of options for local residents is sufficient (Hassel, 1999b; Manno et al., 1998b). However, the question here is not so much *whether* charter schools are innovative in their own *individual* contexts. Instead, in view of the public-choice concerns with the pathologies of public provision, the question is whether charter schools—as R&D centers—can develop practices that are new within the publicly funded school system.

To examine the expectation that autonomy would encourage innovation, I reviewed 39 research and/or evaluation reports on charter school practices in Arizona, California, Colorado, and Michigan. Together, these four states are home to over 45% of all charter schools in the United States. According to charter advocates, they are among the most dynamic sites for this reform in terms of the strength of their authorizing legislation and extent of charter activity (e.g., Center for Education Reform, 2001b). Furthermore, they have been the subject of numerous evaluations and studies, providing a broad and often longitudinal basis for this analysis. The reports used here are studies that dealt with the issue of innovation in charter schools as either a central or ancillary yet significant consideration, and presented primary evidence on charter school practices from one or more of these states.[2] These reports are based on a range of methods and data, including examinations of curricular materials, classroom observations, interviews with employees and parents, and innovations self-reported by charter school operators; they were produced by researchers with a range of perspectives on charter schools.

This chapter employs two considerations for analyzing and understanding the significance of charter school practices reported as innovations.

At what level within institutions does the practice represent change? I distinguished between administrative changes (organization-level practices and structural designs that do not directly impact classroom techniques or content) and educational changes (practices regarding curricular content and instructional strategies with immediate impact at the classroom level) (following Daft & Becker, 1978, ch. 5; regarding juxtaposing innovations in form and content, see also Meyer, 1992). Of course, there is room for interpretation in classifying specific practices as such; thus, some practices are listed in both categories.

To what extent does the practice represent change across educational sectors? If, as public-choice theorists have argued, the problems with public schools are symptomatic of a top-down bureaucratic culture, and if those problems appear in the classroom as stagnant and uncreative teaching and learning, then modifying that governance structure by increasing autonomy would induce innovations in classroom practices. Under this logic, innovative practices developed in charter schools would not be developed otherwise in schools administered directly by district bureaucracies. Thus, the unit of comparative analysis is the school sector, as characterized by governance—that is, noncharter public schools (hereafter referred to as district schools) and charter schools. Therefore, I examined the unique and distinctive characteristics of charter school practices within the broader context of education.

According to the evidence reported in these studies, charter schools are engaging in a wide array of practices at many levels. Table 4.1 lists practices cited as innovations by charter schools and/or researchers in these states.

A survey of these practices suggests several discernible themes. First, charter schools are engaging in a number of activities at the administrative level that appear to be new and distinctive in the broader public sector. For instance, charter schools are experimenting with merit-pay plans, marketing, parental involvement contracts, and financial arrangements that give them access to private capital—most of which are substantially new to the publicly funded education sector. This notable list of innovations would seem to lend support to the public-choice thesis. However, under the charter school logic model (see Figure 4.1), these administrative innovations are an immediate result of the structural changes fashioned as policy *inputs* for charter schools, not an end in themselves. It is worth remembering that such changes in institutional conditions are intended to induce innovations in teaching methods, according to the expectations of policymakers, teachers, and others—as charter advocate and Education Leaders Council CEO (and former Arizona state superintendent) Lisa Graham Keegan (1999) notes in her critique of district schools, "You have to go beyond advertising and outreach and get down to the classroom level" (p. 193).

Second, by their nature, charter schools are increasing options for parents in specific localities. Whereas a district may have embraced new math, a charter school may now be offering Saxon math (a traditionalist curriculum emphasizing review and practice). In Colorado, charter schools were among the first to employ Hirsch's "core knowledge" curriculum. Thus, by diversifying the range of programmatic options available for some parents, charter schools are embracing practices that can be seen as innovations from the perspective of parents in a local education market.

However, the R&D argument from public-choice theory posits that the autonomy afforded to charter schools will encourage practices that are innovative not simply at the local level but also within the broader publicly funded sector—that is, practices not already evident in district-administered schools. Most of the studies reviewed here described a number of educational practices as innovative. Yet, on closer inspection, virtually all these activities are already in use in bureaucratically administered districts. While a Montessori approach, block scheduling, or integrated themes may appear innovative in a local context, they have not been developed by the charter

Table 4.1. Charter school practices reported as innovations in four states

STATE	ADMINISTRATIVE INNOVATIONS	EDUCATIONAL INNOVATIONS
\multicolumn{3}{l}{States granting *high* degrees of autonomy to charter schools[1]}		
Arizona[2]	• employment practices • block scheduling • nongraded classes • smaller class size • use of advertising • computer-based	• arts focus/integrated arts • back-to-basics • computer-based • core knowledge • great books focus • Montessori • multiple intelligences emphasis • Saxon math • Waldorf • thematic curriculum • business focus • portfolios • child-centered • active learning • block scheduling • nongraded classes • smaller class size
Michigan[3]	• management and operations • corporate governance • smaller school/class size • employment practices • parent involvement • contracting-out services • advertising • all-day kindergarten • finance arrangements • student uniforms	• ethnic-based curricula • technology theme • school-to-work focus • whole-school programs • theme-based • basics/core knowledge focus • character/citizenship focus • multicultural emphasis • parent involvement • smaller school/class size • all-day kindergarten • student uniforms

school sector but previously existed in district schools. Inasmuch as these practices are innovative, their prior existence in district schools challenges the R&D function for charter schools and undermines the public-choice diagnosis of bureaucratic administration from which it emerges.

Third, despite differences in the degree of autonomy afforded to charter schools in Arizona and Michigan, as opposed to California and Colorado,

Table 4.1. (*continued*)

States granting *moderate* degrees of autonomy to charter schools[4]

California[5]	• employment practices • finance arrangements • parental involvement requirements • home-based instruction • technology-based instruction • site-based decision making (SBDM) • focus on specific populations • individual education plans (IEPs) • block scheduling • multi-age classes	• parental involvement requirements • home-based instruction • project-based instruction • technology-based instruction • focus on specific populations • individual education plans (IEPs) • field trips • hands-on learning • arts focus • college prep • child-centered approach • leadership emphasis • basic math • block scheduling • service learning • Waldorf • Montessori • integrated curriculum • multi-age classes
Colorado[6]	• employment practices • merit pay • multi-age grouping • focus on at-risk/gifted students • extended schedule • block/nontraditional scheduling • SBDM • support for homeschooling	• thematic/ interdisciplinary instruction • technology focus • core knowledge curriculum • community-as-classroom • IEPs • multi-age grouping • focus on specific subjects • character education • hands-on/active learning • focus on at-risk/gifted students • extended schedule • block/nontraditional scheduling • foreign language requirements • student-centered • support for homeschooling

1. Center for Education Reform (2001a).
2. Gifford, Phillips, & Ogle (2000); Glassman (1998); Stout & Garn (1999).
3. Arsen, Plank, & Sykes (1999); Dykgraaf & Lewis (1998); Horn & Miron (1999, 2000); Khouri et al. (1999); Mintrom (2000); Miron & Nelson (2002); Plank & Sykes (1999); Reynolds (2000).
4. Center for Education Reform (2001).
5. Anderson & Marsh (1998); Becker, Nakagawa, & Corwin (1997); Corwin & Flaherty (1995); Flaherty (1995); Link, Gordon, & Khanna (1999); Little Hoover Commission (1996); SRI International (1997); Wells et al. (1998).
6. Clayton Foundation (1997, 1998, 1999); Colorado Department of Education (2001); Fitzgerald (1995, 2000).

there do not appear to be substantial differences in the types of activities reported as innovative in these states. This is a significant point: Whereas public-choice theorists argue that autonomy from centralized bureaucratic mandates is an essential element in inducing innovations, the very real differences in autonomy (the degrees of deregulation, institutional sovereignty, legal and operational integrity, fiscal independence from the district, etc.) in these states do not appear to generate substantial differences in the types, nature, or extent of charter schools innovations. In Arizona, for instance, local districts sponsor 23% of the charter schools, and the figure is about 16% in Michigan. While these states are often noted for the dynamic nature of their education markets, practices reported as charter school innovations are quite comparable to those in California and Colorado, where charters are typically sponsored by local districts.

Theoretically, charters do offer educators the opportunity to sustain alternative practices apart from shifts in district policy. For example, many of the practices in charter schools reflect child-centered progressive ideas that have fallen in and out of favor in various public schools. On the other hand, *the largest discernible proportion of charter schools by far are using their autonomy to provide "basics" or traditional curricula* (see Center for Education Reform, 1997, as cited in Price, 1998; Center for Education Reform, 2000; Hassel, 1998). Likewise, some charters may have an impact through ethnic-oriented themes, since many are effectively (if controversially) exempted from ideological commitments to common schooling (Lubienski, 2001a). Another area where charters may outpace district schools over the long run is in online learning, since for-profits are looking at new ways of delivering distance education, particularly to homeschooling consumers. Nevertheless, despite the potential for charters to develop innovations in these specific areas, the public-choice predictions regarding an educational laboratory function for charter schools appear to be misguided.

UNDERSTANDING PATTERNS IN CHARTER SCHOOL PRACTICES

Explaining the Lack of Innovation in Charter Schools

There are two readily apparent but unsubstantiated explanations for the paucity of new educational innovations emerging from charter schools. The most obvious may be the relative newness of the reform, which has existed for only slightly more than a decade. However, one might expect innovations to occur *more rapidly* at the advent of these reforms, particularly with new or start-up schools where high proportions of new teachers are not yet set in their instructional strategies. In fact, the patterns evident in U.S. charter schools are quite consistent with the outcomes of school reforms in other nations with a longer and more comprehensive track record of leveraging autonomy, deregulation, and decentralization. Research on comparable reforms in Chile, England/Wales, and New Zealand, for instance, indicates that anticipated innovations never really materialized in ways theorists and reformers predicted. Indeed, independent schools often used their administrative autonomy to *avoid* new and innovative educational practices, frequently embracing *traditionalist* approaches over time, while the bureaucratic sector often produced more innovations (Gauri, 1998; Lauder & Hughes, 1999; Lubienski, 2001b; Whitty, Power, & Halpin, 1998; Woods, Bagley, & Glatter, 1998).

The other obvious but unfounded explanation is that although policymakers may have wanted to promote innovation, in designating parents as choosers, they selected an inherently cautious group of consumers who are not particularly interested in innovation so much as a solid, basic academic education for their children (e.g., Arsen, Plank, & Sykes, 1999; Hassel, 1999b; Lane, 1999; Plank & Sykes, 1999). Apart from essentializing the motivations of parents, there may be some truth to this view. But it misses the point. The thinking behind charter schools is not simply that they will offer innovative "products" if parents want them. Instead, charter schools are granted autonomy with the expectation that they will use it to develop innovative *processes* for better satisfying consumers' demands. That is, consumers may not be looking for innovations, but consumer demand is supposed to *cause* innovation, even if the demand is not for innovation itself (see Hill & Jones, 1989).

Rethinking the R&D Objective

Policy analysts seem to be at a loss for explaining the patterns of practice apparent in charter schools. Yet, inasmuch as ideals such as innovation and diversity are worthy goals, understanding these patterns is crucial as policymakers increasingly embrace autonomy, decentralization, and deregulation through this and other school-choice reforms. Most frequently, policy recommendations focus on either expanding deregulation to free up marketlike mechanisms or adding support structures so that charter schools can use their autonomy more effectively in developing innovations. In this view, if authority were more decentralized, and autonomous schools were put in more marketlike environments, they would likely fulfill their presumed potential in inducing substantive change in core practices. Their uneven record to this point, in this line of thinking, indicates only isolated incidents of market failure—in view of start-up effects, peculiar consumer preferences, or continued state regulation, for example. Consequently, while reformers did not necessarily anticipate these problems, they believe they can address them through simple policy correctives (e.g., parent information centers, communication networks to diffuse innovations, etc.). Here I suggest another possibility: that the paucity of innovation in classroom practice evident in these states is not simply *in spite of* structural reforms. Instead, the very forces that were unleashed in the drive for autonomy may *encourage* curricular conformity and standardization.

Organizational Theory and Innovation. There is, in fact, an established perspective from organizational theory that considers the internal logic of marketlike environments—the conditions sought by structural reforms of school governance (DiMaggio & Powell, 1983). This descriptive theory suggests outcomes that are rather counterintuitive to public-choice prescriptions, but help explain the apparent disconnect between the seemingly tight logic of public-choice theory and the actual record of charter school innovation. While reformers have tried to make more schools autonomous within such environments, according to organizational ecologists, the uncertainties of these environments can have the unintended consequence of constraining innovation. Independent schools seeking to survive such conditions may more easily emulate successful models than engage in costly and risky innovations themselves.

For instance, DiMaggio and Powell (1983) observe that "in fields characterized by a high degree of uncertainty, new entrants, which could serve as sources of innovation and variation, will seek to overcome the liability of newness by imitating established practices within the field," focusing their activity on "appearances" (p. 156; see also Hannan & Freeman, 1977). Furthermore, such trends are typical with *established* organizations in environments where multiple providers offer services in a recognizable "product field" such as schooling—conditions referred to as "monopolistic competition" by economists. While providers may differentiate their services, the distinctions are often symbolic matters of image and advertising rather than the result of substantive innovation (Mansfield, 1970). Thus, it is conceivable that similar forces may be promoting administrative, image-oriented innovations while constraining educational change, even for those schools specifically designed to develop innovations in classroom practices.

Indeed, many educators are attracted to the charter concept because of the perceived opportunities for professional independence, autonomy from bureaucratic control, and the chance to pursue a specific vision (Clayton Foundation, 1998, 1999; Fuller, 2000; Vanourek et al., 1998). Yet many teachers change their initially optimistic views after working in the schools. For example, in a study of Michigan charter schools, the percentage of teachers agreeing with the statement "The school will support/is supporting innovative practices" declined significantly—down 25% from when they were surveyed on first joining a charter school (Khouri et al., 1999). Whereas teachers are often attracted by professional opportunities to develop new and exciting curricula in line with their educational philosophy, in some cases they simply implement curricular decisions made by bureaucrats in private organizations, such as educational management organizations, that are better positioned to survive in a capricious climate (Dykgraaf & Lewis, 1998; Horn & Miron, 2000; Triant, 2001). Innovation is often a costly undertaking, and larger organizations with the resources to withstand setbacks are often better equipped to shoulder the risks and expenses of innovation. The idealized small, independent, mom-and-pop charter school has less access to private capital, and thus its susceptibility to the immediate vagaries of the market may undermine its ability to pursue a distinct vision when attracting consumers is the critical consideration for start-ups.

Sources of Innovation and Conformity. Contrary to the logic apparent in public-choice theory, innovation can emerge from different sources. For instance, many professions have been successful in cultivating innovations without relying on market models. Indeed, the previous existence of many charter school innovations in the public-school sector suggests that extramarket factors are also at work. In more marketlike fields—such as technology in recent years—individuals often advance innovations through start-up firms, which attract venture capital, and are frequently then incorporated into larger corporate conglomerates. However, this pattern is the exception, since larger firms have typically been more successful at R&D (see Hill & Jones, 1989).

But the idea of charters as educational laboratories or R&D centers may itself be a misconception. It is true that charter schools are granted a substantial degree of autonomy as an *opportunity* to innovate, with market-style forces intended to drive innovation. Yet charters are often positioned in some of the *most* competitive environments, where they are expected to sink or swim. In other sectors that invest in experimentation and innovation, the R&D component of a firm is often relatively immune from the immediate effects of competition. That is, R&D units are usually shielded from immediate competitive imperatives to attract and retain customers, to prove the direct value of every idea, or even to stay out of the red (Hill & Jones, 1989). Instead, such components are typically granted additional resources and expected to try different approaches—many of which will fail—that may cultivate improvements over time. Therefore, while we often assume that innovation will emerge when schools have a degree of autonomy from bureaucratic administration, it may very well be that charter schools will be better able to develop educational innovations if they enjoy autonomy from the effects of marketlike conditions.

CONCLUSION

The issue of innovations in charter schools is complex and much more problematic than is presumed in the prescriptions of public-choice theory. Whereas theorists and policymakers expect decentralization, autonomy, and deregulation to encourage innovations, it appears that these forces may be more successful in inducing innovations in administrative behavior than in the classroom. In fact, many schools placed in uncertain conditions use their autonomy to pursue rather familiar conceptions of schooling. Thus, these structural reforms may generate incentive structures that have the unanticipated consequence of undermining the intended potential of charter schools to develop innovation in the classroom, where policymakers and reformers want to effect change. If charter schools are expected to serve as R&D centers, they may require autonomy not only from bureaucratic mandates but also from market-style imperatives.

Indeed, in some cases it appears that schools chartered by districts as the local lab or alternative school are often more successful in developing and sustaining a vision or approach outside the norm. In Arizona, for example, 77% of charters are granted by agencies other than local districts. Yet districts are disproportionately active in chartering schools that employ multi-age grouping, cultural themes, and extended calendars, for instance (Arizona Department of Education, n.d.). Inasmuch as these schools are established not to challenge but to accompany and complement district programs, many such charter schools may operate without immediate pressures impinging on their pursuit of unique or innovative practices. In that respect, further research is needed on how innovations emerge in charters in light of the nature of their relationship with local districts. The next step in this particular line of inquiry is to compare distinctive organizational and educational practices in schools enjoying greater degrees of autonomy from bureaucratic mandates to those practices in charter schools nurtured by their sponsoring district.

Charter schools often operate under uncertain conditions as a result of their position in an emerging quasi-market environment. However, the degree to which this new environment undermines the innovation it was intended to induce is an important factor in considering the potential of other market-oriented school reforms to develop new practices in teaching and learning. Theorists and reformers have given charter schools the Herculean task of changing core activities, in a system where classroom practices have been remarkably resilient in the face of structural reforms of governance and administration. Still, as a policy innovation, they represent for many what Tyack (1974) aptly terms "the lure of the structural panacea" for policymakers seeking to reform the entrenched practices of schooling (p. 169).

NOTES

1. The pervasiveness of public-choice perspectives on publicly administered schools explains—at least in part—the popularity of the view that district schools are plagued by a lack of classroom innovation while market forces engender innovation and diversification. We might also consider the degree to which state legislators adopt legislative language from advocacy organizations that offer templates of model school reform legislation. But regardless of how the wording of state laws came to be so similar in so many instances, it is important to note that lawmakers accepted the assumed link between market forces and classroom innovation.

2. In addition to the single-state reports, I drew on evidence from multistate and national reports that encompass one or more of these four states (e.g., Good & Braden, 2000; Hassel, 1999a; Manno et al., 1998a; Podgursky & Ballou, 2001; Rebarber, 1997; RPP International, 1998, 1999, 2000, 2001; RPP International & University of Minnesota, 1997; U.S. General Accounting Office, 1995; Vanourek et al., 1997, 1998). To manage the scope of this analysis, this chapter focuses on innovation in charter schools themselves rather than the intended "ripple effect" whereby innovative practices are expected to be adopted by other schools due to competition or other means of diffusion (e.g., Rofes, 1998; Vanourek et al., 1997; Wells et al., 1998). Furthermore, I did not analyze innovations in special education or assessment practices for this chapter. Otherwise, all studies known and available to the researcher as of 2001 were considered—regardless of how they defined "innovation"—so long as they presented evidence on the issue.

PART III

The Impact of Charter Schools on Governance

CHAPTER 5

Localized Ideas of Fairness:
Inequality Among Charter Schools
Bruce Fuller
Marytza Gawlik
Emlei Kuboyama Gonzales
Sandra Park

The ideals of common schooling still express the quite modern hope that institutions—through shared experiences for all children—will strengthen and integrate an otherwise disparate civil society.[1] Americans have long held faith in, and have invested heavily in, the public school and its alleged capacity to advance *universal* forms of learning that affirm the public facets of human life: a shared language, a commitment to democratic values and obligations, and fungible skills that allow individuals and groups to succeed in the economy.

All this has happened since the West's 18th-century rejection of an old regime that ensured dominance by particular groups, exclusive forms of culture and power, castelike boundaries defining class membership and who could accumulate capital. The modern state came to be seen as the public agent that could advance the individual's odds of moving up in a premodern class structure, reproduced by ascribed characteristics of the person, not his or her merit or achieved virtues. Premodern Europe had defined children's education as a private endeavor, advanced with the aid of tutors or local churches. This worked fine for some classes, some local "tribes." But for those of the lower classes and the fledgling middle class, the modern state was to build and advance the quality of public education.

RETHINKING WHAT'S FAIR

What is fascinating about charter enthusiasts, especially their spirited eagerness to be cut loose from the modern state, is their nonmodern return to local cultural forms and particular ways of raising children. The widening rejection of common schooling—or perhaps it's the impersonal, bureaucratic rendition of the one best system—is energized by strange bedfellows, from Latino and African American activists fed up with unresponsive city schools to affluent parents who seek a pristine school behind their gated community.

At both ends of this political spectrum, parents and educators within local enclaves believe that the present system is unfair, since it does not advance their *particular* cultural agenda, way of raising children, or local identity. But if the modern state no longer has the credibility to define what's fair and hold schools or educators accountable to meet common benchmarks, how should we think about fairness in such a radically decentered society?

THE END OF COMPARABLE FORMS OF EQUITY?

In this chapter, we review how grassroots activists and national advocates talk about fairness. These two groups are engaging in distinct discourses that are recasting how we think about equity and what is fair among public schools. We also briefly examine how researchers are giving little credence to these *localized conceptions of fairness*, instead evaluating charters according to the old indicators of *comparative equity*. Stemming from these alternative conceptions of fairness, we then devise operational measures to assess how charter schools themselves vary along the two sets of gauges. Third, we discuss the implications of our empirical findings, asking whether the state still holds the political authority for or interest in redressing disparities among charter schools.

The foundational assumptions of the common school are no longer credible in the charter movement. What is defined as fair is no longer attached to modern conceptions of equity in the eyes of many charter school proponents, as measured by comparable and universally valued benchmarks: providing equal access to any school by diverse children, making school resources more equal, and tracking comparable gauges of what children are learning.

Instead, charter advocates rightfully define as unfair the fact that so many schools are ineffective in boosting achievement and fail in socializing youngsters to follow the cultural tenets of their local communities (or the wider civil society's values). But the decentralist's critique also attacks the state's authority and the bureaucratic organization of schooling that government and urban educators have been so adept in creating. While modernists have viewed public agencies as pro-equity in character, many charter advocates see them as failing miserably at promoting fairness.

For charter advocates, it is *particular opportunities*—situated in a particular milieu and defined by ethnicity, language, or child-rearing beliefs—and the ability to *choose schools* with these attributes that have become the icons of what's really fair. This casting of fairness enables parents and teachers to create or select schools that fit their beliefs or preferred way of raising children. Charter advocates believe that public rules cannot, through bureaucratic means, assure such localized forms of like community. Instead, public authorities should charter particular opportunities for particular collectivities among which parents may choose. Some would say that public dollars are now allocated to an archipelago of charter schools, each of which pursues privately defined interests. This is seen by many charter activists as more fair.

The origins and unrelenting forces that are driving this shift toward localized conceptions of fairness are intriguing. Scholars are debating whether this return to particular forms of community and insulated forms of schooling might stem from *postmodern* identity politics: the rejection of central institutions that advance a homogenized conception of learning and teaching; human-scale democracy enacted by parents, after being alienated by huge and unresponsive downtown administrations; or the revival of ethnicity and local ties that lend meaning to and direct control over children's daily settings (Wells, Lopez, Scott, & Holme, 1999).

Alternatively, the move away from universals and comparable gauges of what's fair may be *premodern* in character: parents with more wealth or chutzpah seek out better schools, or display more wherewithal in creating new schools that reproduce their own cultural or moral values (Fuller, 2000). This interpretation assumes a wider presence of publicly sanctioned market rules and intense local cooperation as preconditions for creating effective charter schools. It's reminiscent of how better-off parishes hired tutors or built village schools prior to the modern era (Fuller & Rubinson, 1992). Yet recurring community-control movements, from New York in the 1960s to contemporary Chicago, have also discounted the technical expertise or the centralized logic of accountability advanced by the modern state.

CHARTER ADVOCATES AS CULTURAL RELATIVISTS

We focus not on these antecedent forces but instead on how these localized conceptions of fairness differ from classically modern definitions of comparable equity. In short, charter schools have come to be defined as fair when they provide a range of organizational opportunities that map against segmented communities. Many grassroots enthusiasts and movement leaders also define state controls over curriculum, standards, and testing as controlling and counter to local forms of communal participation. Thus, it is defined as more fair to break away from this oppressive state structure or to create alternatives to the homogenized, secular form of schooling that has come to be equated with *public* education in the minds of many.

In important ways, charter advocates have become the new cultural relativists—including those on the political right, who typically press for cultural convergence, and those on the left, who press for comparable forms of equity in other domains of public life. The "effectiveness" of each charter option is judged by some advocates only in terms of parental satisfaction and localized benchmarks for how children are to be raised. Whether my school with a Black nationalist curriculum in Lansing is more open, is more resourceful, or boosts test scores better than your school serving Mormon children outside Phoenix is no longer a relevant question when it comes to establishing their relative fairness. The two schools are just *different*, and this rise of institutional relativity is defined as being in the public interest, more fair than comparing schools along comparable gauges of equity.

TANDEM DISCOURSES OVER FAIRNESS: CHARTER ENTHUSIASTS AND CRITICAL SCHOLARS

Grassroots activists and national charter advocates, while talking in differing terms, are indeed concerned about fairness. After reviewing qualitative studies and media reports that contain the voices of charter adherents, we identified four features of their parallel conversations. These four dimensions counter historical and classically modern ideas about fairness, as summarized in Table 5.1. We cannot generalize to all advocates at national and local levels. Our aim in this section is simply to illustrate the localized conceptions of fairness that have arisen within the charter movement.

Talk of Fairness Inside Charter Schools

Selective Inclusion to Advance Community Cohesion. The common school ideal of bringing diverse children under one roof has come to be viewed as hollow and unfilled, or simply less important, by many charter activists. After spending several days inside the all-Black El-Hajj Malik El-Shabazz Academy in Lansing, researcher Patty Yancey asked Mr. Hollingsworth, the "at-risk specialist," whether such charter schools in Michigan were resegregating students along racial lines. He vehemently objected. The family feel of El-Shabazz bred trust between parents and teachers, and this sense of com-

Table 5.1. Conceptions of Fairness—Common Schooling Versus Charter
Schooling

Charter School Model— Modern Tenets	Charter School Model— Nonmodern Tenets
Equal access and affirmative policies for inclusion	Community cohesion, purposeful exclusion to reinforce (local) social unity
Professional management, hierarchical division of labor	School-level democratic participation, communal division of labor locally
Integrating diverse children, school as melting pot	Legitimating separate groups, schools that reproduce local cultures, classes, norms
A uniform school institution, accountable to public authority, managed choice among alternative schools	Diverse forms of school organizations directly accountable to neighborhood parents

munity was linked to being African American. Mr. Hollingsworth had earlier written an opinion piece in the *Lansing State Journal*:

> Racial segregation means to be excluded, to bar or prevent someone from a right or privilege. Therefore, to conclude that the highly Black populated charter schools . . . were developed with the evils of racial segregation is highly inaccurate. These schools are not practicing exclusion, but simply offering choices. We are catering to our clientele. This is the school we never had, a school for the community. This is why many Blacks have flocked to these schools, because children who seem to have no place have now found a place. (quoted in Yancey, 2000, p. 92)

Similarly, parents at the Yoder Charter School in Kansas—more than half of whom are Amish—sounded ecstatic about receiving public funds to pursue what many would consider private virtues. The school won a waiver to avoid having to cover sex education in their instructional program, and it explicitly advances "the values taught at home, including responsibility, compassion, honesty, and a strong work ethic" (Finn, Manno, & Vanourek, 2000, p. 232).

Some advocates inside the Washington beltway, such as Chester Finn (2000), argue that such community building is a primary policy goal. "Charter schools are not only education institutions. They also are examples—and wellsprings—of community rebirth. They are instruments of civil society as well as places of teaching and learning . . . imparting a sense of control to people, giving them status, and making them members of a community that embodies their values and transmits their norms" (pp. 221–222). Thus we hear a broader public strategy that is built on a collection of private interests. Whereas modernists view the state as provider of public goods when the market fails, charter advocates suggest that market dynamics can yield public virtues.

Democratic Management and Grassroots Participation. Few Americans believe that unresponsive, bureaucratic management is fair; it violates the individualistic tenets of our political culture. By breaking away from downtown school offices and voluminous state rules, charter enthusiasts hope to pursue a fairer, more invigorating form of participation.

This represents an ideological bridge from the 19th-century New England ideal of schools run by townships, a quaint model later situated within Horace Mann's argument that only the state could equalize school access and quality. Some charter advocates are reinvigorating a radically decentralized variant. Take, for example, the words of Nina Lewin, founding parent at the Chelmsford (Massachusetts) Public Charter:

> We were involved . . . in everything from serving on the planning committee, to finding a company to help with the management of the school, to cleaning up the building and painting the walls. It's been an intense experience. It takes an extremely dedicated group. (quoted in Finn et al., 2000, p. 229)

After studying charter schools in 12 California school districts, Amy Stuart Wells and colleagues (1999) were struck by school-level activists' desire to open-up "identity-building spaces," using the charter structure to express and operationalize their own local conception of how their children should be raised and how teachers' work should be crafted for particular communities. Rather than the school springing from culturally homogeneous New England villages, charters have become organizational devices for bounding and invigorating a pluralistic range of ethnic, linguistic, or religious collectives.

Legitimating the (Publicly Funded) Reproduction of Particular Social Groups. The images of a coherent and supportive community were vividly portrayed by teachers and students alike at Amigos Charter Academy in Oakland, California. Two former students from this small middle school told researchers:

> It was just really like a community setting . . . like we were learning at home . . . with a bunch of our friends. They had really nice teachers who were, you know, mostly Chicano and Chicana. . . . We could relate to them. . . . They know

your culture, your background. . . . [T]hey talk to your parents. . . . And your parents trust them, and it's like a family. (quoted in Wexler & Huerta, p. 100)

Other students reported feeling more comfortable because they could speak Spanish in class and on the playground.

Another intriguing example is the Valley Home School Charter, created by an enterprising school board that enticed more than 600 parents from their church-based networks to enroll in the public option, generating millions of dollars in new revenue for this small rural district. Many of the parents, a range of Christian fundamentalists, were delighted to now receive free curricular materials and send their youngsters to learning centers, dance classes, computer labs, and even the homeschool marching band. But the district superintendent candidly said that this approach "is not for everyone. . . . These parents prefer familial, church, and intergenerational educational experiences made possible through home schooling" (quoted in Huerta, 2000, pp. 187–189).

One parent said that "the main reason [for joining the charter school] was for religious reasons . . . different Christians take it from different viewpoints." Another parent said, "I'm raising my kids the way I want to raise them, not the way government-run schools think I should. I believe it's my right to pass on the values that I believe" (quoted in Huerta, 2000, p. 187). The school board also believes that public monies are appropriate in supporting this constructed "civil right" to a particular form of schooling.

Stimulating Growth in Alternative Forms of Schooling. The voices of charter advocates often celebrate the importance of having diverse forms of schools that are tightly linked to their immediate communities. Chicano activist Marcos Aguilar helped to found the *Academia Semillas del Pueblo* (Seeds of the Town) in East Los Angeles. At the school's opening, Aguilar promised an "alternative, community-based and culturally sensitive" pedagogical approach. "We are not following something we bought and paid for two months ago with a grant. What we are developing is a living, breathing way of teaching as a community." Veteran teacher Maria Isabel Rodriguez said that the new charter school "will give us a sense of unity . . . it helps us come in touch with our inner selves, a fine balance between mind and body" (quoted in Cardenas, 2002, p. B1). Surveys of local charter activists also reveal this legitimated commitment to "serving special populations," a major impetus among one-fourth of all charter directors in one survey (RPP International, 2000, p. 42).

Reminiscent of earlier research in the "effective schools" tradition (e.g., Rutter, 1979), charter founder Rosanne Wood in Tallahassee argued that "more choices allow schools to have a theme or focus instead of an all-purpose curriculum. We'll have more students with schools that fit" (quoted in Nathan, 1996, p. 5). This emphasis on a particular school mission is often coupled with the claim that direct accountability to local parents, and to charter teachers who will enjoy more democratic participation, will advance fairness. For example, one co-founder of another ethnocentric charter school said, "Speaker after speaker said [to the school board] that maybe we needed to have our own schools. We need to decide our own curriculum. We can decide how our children are going to learn, what they are going to learn" (quoted in Wells et al., 1999, p. 193).

Fairness Talk of Charter Wonks

Our earlier fieldwork revealed that many charter parents and teachers do not identify with a broader movement per se; they are too busy trying to stay afloat and strengthen their own school (Fuller, 2000). Nor do they necessarily compare their school to others on equity grounds; relative gauges of fairness are rarely cited.

But most professional charter advocates, working in state associations and national think tanks, must blend old and new conceptions of fairness. They do invoke the new discourse, emphasizing particular opportunities, crisp school missions and norms, and a participatory spirit. Yet they also must fight a rear-guard action—defending charters against claims that they are selective, unfairly aided by private donors, or no more effective than garden-variety public schools. This pushes charter wonks to engage the old equity logic and comparative indicators of fairness vis-à-vis garden-variety public schools.

Rather than highlighting the particularistic taste of many charter schools, Finn, Manno, and Vanourek (2000) argue that markets will more effectively advance fairness than will the state: "Instead of a government-style enforcement of racial balance, a market-based alternative . . . would leave it to people's good judgment to set checks and balances on charter schools. The marketplace will usually do a decent job, but charter schools should also be vigilant" (p. 164). While not invoking market dynamics, President Clinton's assistant secretary of education, Gerald Tirozzi (1997), expressed similar optimism at a hearing before a congressional committee:

> An important principle [of charter schools] is equity. Sufficiently diverse and high-quality choices among charter schools, and genuine opportunities to take advantage of those choices, must be available to all students. Admission to charter schools must truly be open and accessible to all students. . . . Legisla-

tors, charter authorities, and charter developers should take steps to ensure that such things as the absence of a free lunch program, or a specialized curriculum of a school, do not preclude certain students from attending.

What's notable about both sets of comments is that Finn and the Clinton Administration were talking in the old language of equity, focusing largely on egregious forms of discrimination or barriers to access. Few charter advocates would disagree. But nor would they take seriously affirmative efforts to attract the diverse range of children and families that Tirozzi's comments imply. This would violate the principle of purposeful exclusion in the name of community under the new logic of what's fair. And little empirical work has examined what's being implied: All charter schools may not be created equal, and disparities within the movement across schools have gone unexamined.

Other national advocates simply reject old conceptions of fairness. Listen to Viteritti's (1999) upbeat citation of new evidence from the African American community: "Although a majority of black parents view desegregation as a worthwhile social objective, most do not want to have their children transported out of their communities just to achieve racial balance." Citing recent findings from a Public Agenda Foundation poll, Viteritti summarizes that "80 percent of black parents said that they would prefer schools to focus on achievement rather than integration" (p. 33).

How Researchers Frame Fairness

Empirical studies of charter schools—looking across schools or within their organizational guts—include an important focus on fairness. Two questions dominate this young field: What kinds of parents and children express demand for charters? What are the effects of charter schools on children, parents, or teachers?

Most scholars to date have tacitly worked within the old equity framework as they define their questions and interpret findings. Take, for instance, the question of whether charter schools segregate children (or teaching staffs) along lines of class or ethnicity. Initial empirical work reveals that charter enrollments are similar to the ethnic composition of other public schools overall. About two-thirds of charter schools enrolled a student body that was within 20% of their surrounding district's share of non-White students in the late 1990s. Close to 18% enrolled a higher share of students of color (RPP International, 2000).

Yet charters do tend to isolate Black or Latino students in some states: 69% of all charter students in Michigan are African American, largely situated in the Detroit area, while just 14% of the state's enrollment is Black (Public Sector Consultants Inc., & Maximus, Inc., 1999). Similar statewide patterns have been detailed in Arizona, Connecticut, and Pennsylvania (Bulkley & Fisler, 2002b; Cobb & Glass, 1999; Horn & Miron, 1998; Miron & Nelson, 2000). More comparative work is necessary to determine whether there is less racial or class isolation in neighboring public schools.

Many charter schools have sprouted in low-income neighborhoods. A recent national assessment found that 39% of charter students were eligible for subsidized lunches, compared to 37% of students in all public schools (RPP International, 2000). In 11 of 27 states permitting charter schools, the share of low-income students exceeds statewide enrollment shares by at least 10%. In 17 states the share of charter students designated as English learners (EL) is within 5% of overall enrollment shares. Remaining charter states, including Colorado and Florida, serve low percentages of EL students relative to statewide enrollments. Concerns have been raised about charters possibly discouraging enrollment of children with disabilities. Legal action has been taken by parents against specific schools (Fiore, Harwell, Blackorby, & Finnegan, 2000). Yet state-level analyses to date have not revealed systematic exclusion.

Do Charter Schools Invite Certain Kinds of Families? The case studies briefly reviewed above suggest they do—justified as a means of unifying parents and nurturing like-minded members within an enclosed community.

Even when charter directors attempt to build a more diverse range of students, this effort may be constrained by the school's particular mission. Wells, Jellison Holme, and Vasudeva (2000) detailed how a Los Angeles charter director pursued diversity and preserved magnet school funding by targeting recruitment of Asian American and largely middle-class students of color. "Charter school operators have more power than educators in regular public schools to shape who becomes a part of their school . . . control over recruiting efforts, student academic requirements, and discipline practices" (Wells et al., 1998, p. 42). Another evaluation from California found that three-fourths of all charters required parents to work at the school, perhaps unintentionally excluding certain families (SRI International, 1997).

Are Charter Schools More Effective? The research community seems stuck in the old comparative logic of equity on this topic as well. Movement leaders claim that charter schools will boost children's learning curves, relative to garden-variety public schools, given the dynamics of market competition, a coherent school community, and direct accountability to parents (Finn et al., 2000; Nathan, 1996). But it's not clear that local charter activists worry much about test scores or whether cognitive gains are of paramount importance, relative to shared socialization aims.

Most studies to date have found that charter schools, on average, do not outperform other public schools when it comes to standard achievement measures. In Michigan, Horn and Miron (1998) assessed standardized test scores, comparing charter schools with nearby conventional schools, and found that charter students displayed weaker learning gains than students attending other public schools. No advantage has been detected in schoolwide scores among charter schools in California, compared to other public schools, after taking into account social class, language, and other student characteristics (Brown, in press). In Arizona, researchers tracked student-level scores over a 3-year period; charter students demonstrated slightly higher reading gains across the grade levels, but no significant difference could be detected in math gains (Solmon, Paark, & Garcia, 2001).

More encouraging findings have emerged in Texas, where low-income and "at-risk" students attending charter schools outperformed similar students in other public schools on the Texas Assessment of Academic Skills (Gronberg & Jansen, 2001). Yet for all other students, charter attendees did less well than middle-class students in garden-variety public schools. This research team also found that newly opened charter schools were not as effective in raising achievement as were older ones. Additional evidence on achievement is detailed in Chapter 8 of this volume.

ILLUMINATING SHADES OF FAIRNESS
AMONG CHARTER SCHOOLS

We propose another way to explore the extent to which charter schools are advancing fairness in public education. Our new line of analysis focuses on levels of fairness and equity observed among charter schools themselves. Let's apply these localized conceptions of fairness, advanced by charter advocates, along with conventional conceptions of equity, still emphasized by modernists. Then we can illuminate the extent to which charter schools are created equal—or whether they reflect disparities that persist in garden-variety public schools. We turn next to this empirical analysis.

National Charter School Survey

We are able to study multiple indicators of charter schools' fairness and equity, thanks to the 1999–2000 school survey by the National Center for Educational Statistics. This Schools and Staffing Survey (SASS) included an unprecedented effort to reach all public charter schools that operated during 1998–1999 and 1999–2000, totaling 1,010 known institutions (Gruber, Wiley, Broughman, Strizek, & Burian-Fitzgerald, 2002).

Just over 86% of the schools eventually participated in the SASS, which yielded school-level information reported by the principal or site administrator, a principal survey (90% response rate, $n = 870$), and questionnaires from 79% of a sample of charter school teachers ($n = 2,847$). Data from the 870 participating charter schools were then weighted to provide national estimates pegged to the original universe of 1,010 schools. In the analysis that follows, we report on this weighted sample.[2]

Gauging Fairness Across Diverse School Contexts

Our empirical study examined how multiple indicators of fairness—stemming from the old and new conceptions—varied among charter schools that are situated in highly variable contexts. We could not measure all dimensions of equity and access (along conventional gauges), nor could we fully operationalize localized conceptions of fairness. A portion of the measures do not fit exclusively in one framework. But our analysis shows how the two conceptions of fairness, taken together, more fully illuminate variation among charter schools in their capacity to address fairness and equity concerns.

Conventional Indicators—School Resources. First, we assessed how charters differ in their level of resources and material inputs. We looked at staffing levels by calculating the ratio of students per full- and part-time teacher. We also studied the number of instructional computers available per student, and the midpoint in teacher salaries among incumbent teachers within a school, and the principal's salary. In addition, we constructed a simple index of the relative generosity of health benefits available to staff. A list of all measures, details on constructed indices, and inter-item reliability statistics appear in Appendix A.

Conventional Indicators—Student Attributes and Access. We also reported on basic attributes of students to shed light on who is accessing charter schools, including children's ethnic and linguistic backgrounds, eligibility for Title I and lunch subsidies, and the share of students for whom individualized education plans (IEPs) have been developed, as reported by charter school principals.

Conventional Indicators—Teacher Qualities. We examined important characteristics of teachers, including their qualification levels and tenure in the classroom and the ethnic distribution of the workforce. We calculated the percentage of teachers with incomplete credentials, be they called emergency, probationary, or provisional by their home state (see Chapter 1 of this volume for alternative ways of defining teacher quality). These indicators provide evidence on the kinds of teachers who have joined charter schools and how this may vary systematically among charters situated in differing contexts.

Localized Indicators—Specialized Mission and Autonomy. Next, we described how charter schools differ along the kinds of indicators associated with the new conceptions of fairness. For example, we report on the share of schools that report specialized or "alternative" school missions, discrete classroom innovations aimed at strengthening teacher–student relationships, and the level of influence reported by the principal, as well as the principal's perceived autonomy from state education agencies. We also described variability in teachers' perceived influence and individual autonomy within their charter schools (aggregated to the school level). These facets of social organization capture the new claim that giving teachers and school principals more control and autonomy from the bureaucratic district or state will enhance school-level community and particular missions (Table 5.1).

Localized Indicators—Coherent Community, Parent, and Teacher Participation. Finally, we operationalized direct indicators of each school's cohesive community, as gauged by teachers' reported levels of support from their colleagues and principal, and the extent to which staff expressed shared beliefs. We constructed a simple index of ethnic diversity or homogeneity among students—the number of non-White groups making up at least 10% of the school's enrollment. Under the old conception of fairness, a more integrated student body is desirable. In contrast, we noted above how some charter enthusiasts advocate for the inclusion of particular kinds of children, but not others, to advance a like-minded community.

Two indicators of parent participation were also constructed, measured by the kinds of programs that a school offers to appeal to parents, including parent resource advisers and training for parents on how to help their children with homework.

For each of these indicators of fairness, we examined mean levels across four types of school contexts: the school's *grade level* (elementary, secondary, or combined), charter school *origin* (start-up, converted public school, or converted private school), *community type* (central city, suburb, or rural), and whether the school is managed by a *private company* or not (be it for-profit or nonprofit).

We also began to explore the state policy regimes under which charters operate across the states. For example, some states require charters to employ only credentialed teachers; others provide state aid targeted to charter schools. Yet this line of analysis proved to be complicated—when we found differences associated with state policies, they were difficult to interpret. For instance, are charters with more highly qualified teachers more likely to operate in states that share certain demographic characteristic, which also are associated with more pro-charter state policies? In general, more urban states tend to have more assertive policy regimes (targeted spending and slightly tougher credential requirements). But these dynamics don't necessarily drive differences inside charter schools.

Analytic Overview

Our analysis is exploratory—we set out to illuminate how charter schools varied along the two sets of fairness indicators. We were curious about how conventional indicators of access and equity would be informative, and then about how the new conceptions of school mission, participation, and tight community might also shed light on variability among charter schools. Following a presentation of descriptive statistics, we specify how variations in school contexts help to account for between-school variation along these indicators of fairness and equity.

DESCRIPTIVE FINDINGS: ORGANIZATIONAL CONTEXT AND EQUITY

We would not necessarily expect elementary and secondary schools to exhibit the same levels of fairness and equity. Elementary schools have traditionally been smaller organizations drawing from spatially more confined communities; they have displayed less segmentation internally compared to high schools. But it turns out that this initial dimension of school context was not important in explaining levels of fairness and equity. A few exceptions should be noted.

Charter elementary schools did report having richer teaching staffs: The ratio of students per teacher is significantly lower in elementary charter schools (18:1) compared to secondary charter schools (25:1; $p < .001$).[3] Charter high schools enroll smaller proportions of African American students (22% of their total enrollment) compared to elementary schools (31%; $p < .001$). Yet charter high schools enroll a larger share of Latinos (23%) compared to elementary schools (15%; $p < .001$).

A smaller share of elementary charter teachers reported holding a full credential, just 45% compared to 53% of secondary charter teachers ($p < .05$). That is, 55% of all elementary teachers were working with an emergency, probationary, or provisional certificate. And elementary charters reported more specific programs that encourage parent participation than did high school charters ($p < .001$). This index took into account eight possible programs, including whether the school conducts parent education workshops, requires written contracts between school and parent, and regularly involves parents in budget and governance issues. Beyond these notable differences, elementary and high schools looked similar along our two sets of fairness indicators.

Conventional Indicators of Fairness: Resources, Access, and Teacher Quality

Other dimensions of organizational context proved to better differentiate the extent to which charter schools advance fairness and equity. Turning to Table 5.2, we look at several conventional gauges of fairness, focusing first on the levels of basic resources mustered by charter schools. The three dimensions of school context define the rows: school type, community type, public or private management. We then report weighted means for fairness indicators within these differing contexts.

In column 1 we report on the ratio of students per *full-time teacher*. No significant differences arise that are associated with school context. But reliance on *part-time teachers* (column 2) does vary markedly across different types of charter schools. For example, on average, 103 students are enrolled per part-time teacher in start-up charters compared to a ratio of 249:1 in regular public schools that converted to charter status. That is, start-up charters rely much more on part-time teaching staff. This may allow for a more differentiated curriculum if more specialized teachers are being employed. On the other hand, what are the implications for building a tighter community of fully committed staff? Charters in rural areas also rely more heavily on part-time teachers compared to those situated in central cities or suburban areas.

We see in column 3 that the index of benefits available to teachers is significantly lower in private schools that had converted to charter status. An index value of 2.1 simply means that, on average, private-conversion charters offer just over two of three possible benefits: health coverage, dental, and life insurance. All indices are detailed in Appendix A.

The final two columns in Table 5.2 focus on salary levels, an obvious dimension of school resources. Public school conversions offer significantly higher teacher salaries ($37,103 is the median salary) compared to start-ups ($32,001) or private-conversion charters ($29,985; $p < .001$). These differences may be linked to teacher experience levels, as detailed below. Principal salaries are also considerably higher in public-conversion charters

Table 5.2. Conventional indicators of fairness—variation in school resources among charter schools (n = 1,010 weighted schools; weighted means and significant differences reported)

	Students per full-time teacher	Students per part-time teacher	Health and related benefits (index)	Teacher salaries, mean midpoint ($)	Principal salary($)
Charter school type		***	***	***	***
Start-up	20	103	2.5	32,001	54,530
Conversion—public	22	249	2.5	37,103	62,031
Conversion—private	16	87	2.1	29,985	46,938
Community type		***	***	***	***
Central city	20	116	2.5	32,154	55,980
Suburban	21	173	2.5	32,160	58,397
Rural	18	57	2.3	30,487	44,692
State context— categorical charter funding		***	*	***	
Schools in state without funding	20	103	2.5	30,965	54,354
Schools in state with funding	20	152	2.4	33,171	55,823
Public/private management			*		
Schools under district or state	20	122	2.4	31,907	55,770
Schools managed by private firm	21	133	2.6	31,990	53,459

Note: Significance of mean differences, based on ANOVA or chi-square test, appears above the variable: *, $p < .05$, **, $p < .01$, ***, $p < .001$. Standard deviations and f-values available.

($62,031) compared to start-ups ($54,530, $p < .001$). And suburban charters pay principals more compared to charters in central cities or rural areas ($p < .001$).

Next we focus on traditional indicators of student access: Who do charters enroll across differing school contexts? Charters are clearly serving significant numbers of African American and Latino students, as shown in Table 5.3. Charters that converted from private school status serve the highest proportion of Black children, 33% of their total enrollment, compared to 29% among start-up charters and just 17% among public-conversion charters ($p < .001$). The latter type tends to serve a higher share of Latino students, 22% of total enrollment. Not surprisingly, central-city charter schools serve higher proportions of Black and Latino students compared to suburban and rural charters (both mean differences are significant at $p < .001$). Asian American students are somewhat more concentrated in public-conversion charters, about 4% of total enrollment compared to 1.8% among start-ups ($p < .001$; not shown).

Substantial shares of charter students appear to be eligible for lunch subsidies, as reported by principals. Half of all urban charter students are eligible, falling to 31% among suburban charters ($p < .001$). We also see greater diversity among schools managed by private firms. This begs for further analysis of whether management firms are drawn to states with higher per-pupil spending, including access to categorical aid that may benefit low-achieving students.

But very slight proportions of students actually benefit from Title I compensatory education services. Even in central-city schools, principals estimated that only 5.2% of their students were receiving Title I program support. Nor are charter schools identifying many English learners—just 6.2% of total enrollments in central-city charters. Public-conversion schools identify more English learners, 10.1% of total enrollment, relative to start-ups (4.0%; $p < .001$).

Finally, we report on traditional indicators of fairness that pertain to how teachers are distributed across charter schools. This indicator might also be linked to a localized conception of fairness. For example, a higher percentage of teachers that share ethnic membership with their students could be an indicator of greater community cohesion. With this caveat in mind, Table 5.4 reports on the ethnic composition of teaching staffs, including significant differences between central-city and suburban schools. Just over 18% of all charter teachers are African American in central cities, and about 9% are Latino. This compares to almost 7% Black and 6% Latino in suburban charters ($p < .001$ for Blacks when including rural schools, $p < .05$ for Latinos). Schools managed by private management firms employ a significantly higher share of Latino teachers (11%) compared to

Table 5.3. Conventional indicators of fairness—variation in student attributes and access among charter schools (n = 1,010 weighted schools; weighted means and significant differences reported)

	Student Composition: African American (%)	Student Composition: Latino (%)	Students eligible for reduced-price lunch (%)	Title I students receiving services (%)	English Learners Identified (%)
Charter school type	***	***		*	***
Start-up	29	17	42	5.1	4.0
Conversion—public	17	22	48	2.8	10.1
Conversion—private	33	16	42	2.3	2.2
Community type	***	***	***		*
Central city	39	22	50	5.2	6.2
Suburban	17	13	31	3.9	3.6
Rural	8	12	44	2.9	3.2
State context— categorical charter funding	***	*	***	***	***
Schools in state without funding	22	16	39	5.8	3.3
Schools in state with funding	33	19	47	3.0	6.6
Public/private management	***	*	**	*	
Schools under district or state	25	16	41	3.8	4.6
Schools managed by private firm	32	20	47	5.9	5.6

Note: Significance of mean differences, based on ANOVA or chi-square test, appears above the variable: *, $p < .05$; **, $p < .01$; ***, $p < .001$. Standard deviations and *f*-values available.

publicly managed charters (6%; $p < .001$). Only about 2% of all charter teachers are Asian American.

Large numbers of charter teachers are working without a full credential, comprising 51% of a school's teaching staff in start-ups on average, 28% in public-conversions, and 60% in private-conversion charters ($p < .001$). Teachers who are not fully credentialed are more concentrated in central-city charters (56%), compared to suburban charters (39%; $p < .001$). Private management firms employ significantly higher shares of teachers who are not fully credentialed (55%) compared to publicly managed schools (45%; $p < .001$). The final column of Table 5.4 also shows that private companies employ teachers with 2 years less experience in the classroom, on average ($p < .001$). Future work should examine whether privately managed charters—representing 31% of all charters—intentionally hire low-cost teachers or whether their relatively stronger presence in central cities makes it more difficult to find fully credentialed teachers.

Localized Indicators of Fairness: Mission, Tight Community, and Participation

Next we report on indicators that stem from the new discourse around localized conceptions of fairness. Column 1 of Table 5.5 reports on the percentage of schools reporting that they operated from a "special program focus" or self-identified as an "alternative school." About 44% of all start-up charters designated their school in this way, as did 50% of private-conversion charters. Privately managed schools were significantly less likely to define themselves in this way (35%) compared to publicly managed charters (48%; $p < .001$). This suggests that the rise of private management may moderate the innovative impulse celebrated by early charter advocates.

Principals also reported on classroom innovations that aimed to strengthen social relations, such as having students stay with their teacher for more than a year, relying on block scheduling, or forming children into smaller cohorts or "houses" (6-point innovation scale). Schools reported using an average of 2.8 of 6 such structural innovations (Appendix A).

To gauge levels of perceived autonomy, an identical index was constructed for the perceived influence reported by principals and teachers in each of six domains as well as how principals saw the state's influence in the same domains.[4] For example, principals reported stronger influence in private-conversion schools (4.7 on the 6-point scale) compared to 4.5 in start-up and public-conversion schools on average ($p < .05$). But no other contextual factors were related to the principal's reported influence.

Principals view the state's influence as modest, compared to their own influence, measured along the same six domains. The lowest level of state

Table 5.4. Conventional indicators of fairness—variation in teacher qualities among charter schools ($n = 1{,}010$ weighted schools; weighted means and significant differences reported)

	Teacher Composition: African American (%)	Teacher Composition: Latino (%)	Emergency, probationary, or provisional credential (%)	Tenure (years teaching)
Charter school type	***		***	***
Start-up	12.7	7.4	51	6
Conversion—public	8.0	7.7	28	9
Conversion—private	13.6	7.6	60	6
Community type	***	*	***	
Central city	18.4	9.1	56	6
Suburban	6.7	5.8	39	6
Rural	1.3	5.6	42	7
State context—	***			
categorical charter funding				
Schools in state without funding	15.7	6.3	46	6
Schools in state with funding	9.1	8.9	50	6
Public/private management		***	***	***
Schools under district or state	11.4	6.0	45	7
Schools managed by private firm	13.2	11.1	55	5

Note: Significance of mean differences, based on ANOVA or chi-square test, appears above the variable: *, $p < .05$; **, $p < .01$; ***, $p < .001$. Standard deviations and *f*-values available.

Table 5.5. Localized indicators of fairness—variation in mission and autonomy among charter schools (n = 1,010 weighted schools; weighted means and significant differences reported)[1]

	Alternative schools with specialized mission[2]	Classroom innovations: relationships (index)	Principal's reported influence (index)	Principal's report of the state's influence (index)	Teacher's reported influence (index)
Charter school type			*	**	**
Start-up	44	2.8	4.5	2.6	3.0
Conversion—public	42	2.9	4.5	2.9	3.2
Conversion—private	50	3.1	4.7	2.7	2.9
Community type					**
Central city	46	2.9	4.6	2.7	3.0
Suburban	39	2.8	4.5	2.6	3.0
Rural	46	2.8	4.4	2.7	3.3
State context— categorical charter funding		*			
Schools in state without funding	44	2.7	4.5	2.6	3.0
Schools in state with funding	44	3.0	4.5	2.7	3.0
Public/private management	***				**
Schools under district or state	48	2.9	4.5	2.7	3.1
Schools managed by private firm	35	2.8	4.5	2.6	2.9

1. Weighted principal data, rather than the school survey data, yields different weighted n for selected variables.
2. Percentage of all schools self-reporting as having a "special program focus" or "alternative" instructional mission is reported. This excludes a small number of special education and vocational schools.

Significance of mean differences, based on ANOVA or chi-square test, appears above the variable: *, $p < .05$; **, $p < .01$; ***, $p < .001$. Standard deviations and f-values available.

113

influence was reported by principals in start-up charters (2.6 on the 6-point scale) compared to principals in public-conversion schools (2.9; $p < .01$).

Teachers reported a modest level of influence within the same domains, with higher levels reported by those working in rural charters ($p < .01$) and lower levels by teachers in privately managed schools ($p < .01$). While principals reported higher levels of influence largely independent of their context, teachers do not feel the same level of autonomy or efficacy over these six areas of school policy and practice.

Finally, we examined indicators of community cohesion observed among charter schools. For example, teachers were asked a series of questions regarding the extent to which norms and beliefs about learning objectives were shared and the level of support by the principal around these dominant expectations. An index of "cohesive school beliefs and principal support" was built from five items that emerged from factor analysis. For each item, a 4-point scale indicated the teacher's agreement or disagreement with the statement.

Turning to Table 5.6, we see that teachers' levels of agreement that their fellow teachers shared core beliefs, and that these commitments were reinforced by the principal, were quite high (averaging 3.1 on this 4-point scale).[5] School contexts were not significantly related to levels of perceived cohesion. This suggests that the charter organization itself advances a strong normative consensus, somewhat insulated from the surrounding environment. Direct comparisons with garden-variety public schools would help to confirm this claim.

The school's immediate community obviously affects the mix of students enrolled. The student heterogeneity index did vary systematically by school context. For example, 1.2 non-White groups with at least 10% of school enrollment were observed in central-city charters, on average, compared to 0.5 non-White groups in rural charters ($p < .001$). And privately managed schools were slightly more diverse in their enrollments ($p < .05$).

We constructed two indices of parent participation, as described above. The final column in Table 5.6 reports on the second index, which counts the presence of structured programs and activities for parents, from drop-in centers on site to organized ways for parents to help their children with homework. The average school offered about four of the possible eight programs for parents. Public-conversion schools had created more such programs, on average, as had central-city schools (both significant at $p < .001$).

Which Organizational Attributes Explain Fairness and Equity?

A thorough accounting of the factors that may explain these disparities among charter schools is beyond our scope here. But we did construct sev-

Table 5.6. Localized indicators of fairness—variation in school cohesion and parent participation among charter schools (n = 1,010 weighted schools; weighted means and significant differences reported)[1]

	Cohesive school beliefs and principal support (index)	Student heterogeneity (index)	Homeschooled students (%)	Parent participation programs (index)[2]
Charter school type			***	***
Start-up	3.1	0.9	3.3	4.2
Conversion—public	3.1	0.9	7.1	4.7
Conversion—private	3.2	0.9	0.1	4.6
Community type		***	***	***
Central city	3.1	1.2	0.9	4.5
Suburban	3.1	0.8	6.4	4.4
Rural	3.3	0.5	7.1	3.8
State context— categorical charter funding		***	***	*
Schools in state without funding	3.2	0.8	6.1	4.2
Schools in state with funding	3.1	1.1	6.7	4.5
Public/private management		*	***	
Schools under district or state	3.1	0.9	6.6	4.3
Schools managed by private firm	3.2	1.0	6.1	4.4

1. Weighted teacher data, rather than the school-level data, yield different weighted n for selected variables.

2. One of two parent participation indices detailed in Appendix A. This index pertains to structured programs that invite parent participation or training at the school, as well as structured home-based activities for parent and child.

Significance of mean differences, based on ANOVA or chi-square test, appears above the variable: *, $p < .05$; **, $p < .01$; ***, $p < .001$.

Standard deviations and f-values available.

eral preliminary models to disentangle the effects of differing school contexts. Technical readers may obtain these regression analyses from the authors.

Public-conversion charter schools (making up 16% of sampled charters) look stronger on conventional gauges of equity compared to start-ups and private-conversion schools. For example, the median teacher salary was significantly higher in public-conversion charters (about $4,600 higher than start-ups on average; the β coefficient is significant at $p < .005$), compared to the other two types, after taking into account school grade level, urban or suburban setting, and public or private management.[6] This is partially explained by the fact that the mean public-conversion teacher has 9 years of experience, compared to 6 years for the average start-up teacher (Table 5.4).

The average share of students eligible for lunch subsidies is almost 10% higher in public-conversion charters as a share of total enrollment, compared to start-ups ($p < .001$). And public-conversion schools employ fewer teachers who are not fully credentialed (about 21% fewer than start-ups as a share of the school's mean total teaching staff; $p < .0001$), after taking into account the other covariates.

When we focus on the localized conceptions of fairness, public-conversion and elementary charters report more discrete programs aimed at parent participation ($p < .002$ and $p < .0001$, respectively), again after taking into account the other aspects of school context. Private school conversions tend to be more innovative in creating methods for strengthening student–teacher relationships, again compared to start-ups (the base; $p < .06$).

Central-city charters, not surprisingly, serve more diverse children and families, as we saw in the descriptive analysis. The share of students eligible for lunch subsidies is 18% higher in central-city charters compared to suburban charter schools ($p < .0001$). These more urban schools also report about 12% more teachers who are not fully credentialed compared to suburban and rural schools ($p < .002$). And central-city teachers report less convergence in staff beliefs and less consistent support from their principal than do teachers in suburban or rural schools ($p < .02$).[7]

CONCLUSIONS: CHARTER SCHOOLS
ARE NOT CREATED EQUAL

These findings reveal wide variability among charter schools in their interest in, or capacity to, advance fairness and equity. The organizational history of a charter school—especially whether it is a converted public school rather than a start-up—makes a large difference in the resources it has mobilized, quality of teachers, salaries paid to teachers and principals, and the school's propensity to serve children from lower-income families, especially Black children.

Public-conversion charters tend to be better resourced but not always more equitable along old conceptions of equity. They are more vigilant in identifying English learners yet, overall, serve a lower share of African American students. Public-conversion charters also display more numerous efforts to involve parents compared to start-ups.

This more resourceful character of public-conversions may stem from stronger funding streams, or perhaps from an a priori spirit of public schooling—manifest before and after conversion to charter status. Or it may be that public-conversion charters display a greater survival rate, compared to poorly resourced start-ups that may suffer from higher mortality. Survival of the fittest may benefit conversion charters that do not sever their ties with home districts and the resources these interdependencies yield.

Attending to Low-Performing Students

One troubling finding is that charter schools overall rarely draw Title I funds to serve eligible children, even though 43% are reportedly eligible for subsidized lunches. Even charters in central cities reported that just 5% received services supported by Title I. The average public-conversion charter identified just 10% of its students as limited in English proficiency. It could be that charters are disproportionately serving middle-class Latino families where Spanish is no longer students' home language. More likely, charter schools appear to be uninterested in identifying children's language proficiencies. More research should look into why support efforts are not being mounted for children from lower-income families.

The disparate quality of charter school teachers is another important issue to explore further. Credentials are not the only valid gauge of teacher quality (see Chapter 1, this volume). But 51% of all charter teachers in start-ups are not fully credentialed. This share drops to 28% among public-conversion charters and rises to 60% among private school conversions.

Charter schools managed by private companies rely more heavily on teachers who are not fully credentialed (55% of their staff on average) compared to schools operating under district boards (where 45% are not fully credentialed). Privately managed charters do serve higher shares of Latino students and children from poor families, offer slightly stronger benefit packages, pay principals slightly less, are less likely to have specialized educational missions, and employ teachers who report lower levels of influence within their schools.

Generally, low levels of teacher resources and benefits may stem from the fact that privately managed schools are more frequently found in lower-income communities compared to the typical location of publicly managed schools. Why privately managed schools report less commitment to alternative programs, employ teaches who feel less influence, and rely on less experienced teachers are questions that cry out for further research. On balance, the resource flows that conversions experience may outweigh the claimed efficiencies pursued by privately managed charters. On the other hand, *if* the latter can boost student performance levels at lower costs, then lessons about cost-effectiveness may abound.

Who Will Equalize Charter School Opportunities?

We are left with a broader, more troubling question: Do public authorities possess the political will or legitimacy to address the disparities observed among charter schools as revealed by this analysis?

The charter movement is founded in part on the assumption that excessive state authority and the bureaucratic organization of schooling must be surrounded and confined. And in many quarters—from state legislatures to local school boards—there's an attitude that charter schools asked for autonomy, so let's allow them to sink or swim on their own accord.

Two problems arise, however, if public authorities choose to ignore questions of fairness and equity across charter schools. First, charters may be reproducing structured forms of inequality based on unequal levels of resources and insufficient attention to low-performing and non-English-speaking students. We have detailed how start-up charters in particular display weaker resources, less qualified and lower-paid teachers, and even less attention to engaging parents. Start-ups comprise the bulk of all charter schools—three-fourths of all schools in the national sample. Privately managed charters, to their credit, serve disproportionately higher numbers of low-income communities. But similar to start-ups, they are serving central-city neighborhoods with lower levels of resources compared to suburban charters. So, unless the state steps in—or charter associations seriously raise fairness and equity concerns—the movement will reproduce the very inequalities that charter advocates claim they will erase.

Second, charter advocates have shifted the modern discourse around equity and fairness down to very local levels of civil society. Rhetoric around options and community are replacing the old conceptions of equal access, equal inputs, and comparable measures of teacher quality. This conceptual shift is shaking how we think about fairness in the radically decentralized pockets of the education sector. This debate is important and may open up discussion on how to define what's fair in garden-variety public schools. But as the old conceptions of fairness erode, charter advocates inadvertently subvert the state's legitimacy in trying to make all segments of public schooling more fair. As some charter advocates have recognized in recent years, they occasionally need a strong and active state—when it comes to education funding and regulatory standards—not a weak and diminished political structure.

Future Work on Fairness

The research community has been slow to explore how charter schools may be advancing fairness in their own terms, offering organizational alternatives, tighter school communities, and participatory social rules for teachers and parents alike. We found that charters vary less along these new conceptions of fairness, under differing school contexts, compared to wider inequities when it comes to material resources, staff qualities, and which students gain access. Future research, however, might build from both logic and concrete indicators when it comes to assessing fairness and equity—both among charters and when charters are compared to garden-variety public schools.

Focused work on start-up charters—which continue to make up the bulk of all charter schools—might ask whether they are advancing teacher well-being and advancing student achievement with fewer resources compared to conversion charters. The ability of the latter to hire more experienced teachers and pay them more does not necessarily lead to higher student performance. In fact, many charter advocates argue that it's a different spirit and social commitments, not school inputs, that power their success. Let's test this claim empirically, looking at different kinds of charter schools. The life cycles and mortality rates of start-ups and conversions also deserve more research. It may be that conversion charters are more robust, compared to start-ups, because only the strong survive.

Finally, we know almost nothing about how state policies aid, subvert, or simply ignore the health of charter schools. Certain state policies may be moderating the between-school disparities that we have illuminated. Conversely, certain state policies may exacerbate how charters are reproducing unequal outcomes for children and teachers.

This leads to a dilemma for charter advocates: Their minimalist instincts, when it comes to state activism, may act to reinforce the resource gaps that appear to be dragging down start-up and privately managed charter schools. Put another way, inaction by the state may advantage public-conversion charters that are disproportionately serving suburban families. And if state policymakers elect to ignore such disparities, they again forfeit political authority and, inadvertently perhaps, undercut the charter movement's own legitimacy over time.

NOTES

1. Authors are listed alphabetically. Gordon Gibbings helped in reviewing earlier literature. Special thanks to Luis Huerta for his plentiful contributions to our thinking over the years. This work is supported by the Hewlett Foundation and the Spencer Foundation's research apprenticeship program at Berkeley's Graduate School of Education.

2. The original list of charter schools provided by the Office of Educational Research and Improvement (OERI) included 1,122 that were operating during the 1998–1999 schoolyear. By the following year, when the SASS survey was conducted, 112 schools had shut down, resulting in 1,010 schools included in the sampling frame. Methodological details appear in the Technical Notes of Gruber and colleagues (2002, p. 195ff).

3. All significance levels are derived from ANOVA or chi-square tests unless otherwise mentioned. F or χ^2 values are available.

4. Principals and teachers reported on their perceived levels of influence (along a 4-point scale) on each of six items, including influence over student performance standards, evaluating and hiring new teachers, setting discipline policies, establishing a curriculum at the school, the content of in-service professional development, and deciding how the school budget will be spent.

5. These items included "The school administration's behavior toward the staff is supportive and encouraging" and "The principal knows what kind of a school he/she wants and has communicated it to the staff." Appendix A includes details and inter-item reliability statistics.

6. All regression findings stem from weighted least-squares analyses. Standard error terms are not adjusted for possible design effects resulting from the nesting of units within particular states; marginal significance levels should be interpreted cautiously. Regression statistics are available.

7. Weaker relationships and larger error terms were observed when estimating coefficients for central-city, suburban, and rural schools with alternative bases for the weighted least-squares models.

CHAPTER 6

Balancing Act: Educational Management Organizations and Charter School Autonomy

Katrina E. Bulkley

All things considered, you can go from one school to the next and essentially see the same type of program in place. . . . A teacher from one of those schools [in another state] could come to one of our schools here and still, you know, be able to function quite well.
    —Representative of Educational Management Organization

What we did is we stressed to all of our people that we give them the car. We give the destination, with the parameters . . . we don't choose the road for them.
    —Representative of Educational Management Organization

What we can do, if need be, we can go in and assist a school in developing their own curriculum for a particular discipline. . . . There is really no area that we can't assist them in, but again, we sit back and wait until we are asked to do it as opposed to imposing it.
    —Representative of Educational Management Organization

As charter schools have flourished nationally over the last decade, one of the most intriguing—and controversial—aspects of their growth has been the increasing use of contracts with both for-profit and nonprofit companies, often called education management organizations (EMOs), that take responsibility for a wide range of school-related activities.[1] EMOs, including large companies (such as Edison Schools, Mosaica Advantage, and Chancellor-Beacon) and a growing number of smaller companies, offer a range of services to schools. Services offered by EMOs include administrative services such as payroll, budgeting, and personnel management as well as educational services/programs such as curricula, assessments, and teacher training. A school district or the board of a charter school can choose to contract with an EMO to provide specified services (e.g., payroll) or overall comprehensive management services. In some cases, EMOs are involved from the early development stages of new charter schools. In theory, charter school boards or school districts that are dissatisfied with the services provided by an EMO can simply choose to end the relationship.

The number of EMO-operated schools has increased within both the charter and district-run public school sectors. In this chapter, I focus on for-profit EMOs, which are estimated to manage about 15% to 20% of charter schools (Molnar, 2001).[2] The use of EMOs appears likely to increase over the next few years; as one report put it, "The education management industry is in its infancy, but clearly growing" (Arsen, Plank, & Sykes, 1999, p. 54). While the growth and potential impact of EMOs has been noted in the media and education magazines (Dykgraaf & Lewis, 1998; Furtwengler, 1998; Schnaiberg, 1999; Symonds, Palmer, Lindorff, & McCann, 2000), there has been little research on this new phenomenon (cf. Rhim, 1998; Scott, 2001).

The link between EMOs and charter schools creates a new experiment in hybridizing public and private forces to provide education and has significant implications for public education more broadly and for the role of government in funding versus providing education (Hill, Pierce, & Guthrie, 1997; Lyons, 1995). The dearth of research on EMOs means that policymakers have little good information about EMO approaches to core issues, including the role of school stakeholders.

The existence of EMOs creates a new set of questions as to the use and impact of the autonomy granted to charter schools. On the one hand, charter founders use their autonomy to select an EMO to provide services to the school, while on the other hand, they give up some of their own control over decisions in the school. According to Horn and Miron (2000), "While charter schools are intended to have their own boards with decisions made locally, the growing involvement of EMOs has had an impact on the level of local control" (p. 48). The quotes at the beginning of this chapter demonstrate the variety of views that EMO central office staff express about the role of the individual school in decision making.

After examining research on site-based management, Jane David (1995) asked, "How can site-based management be structured to balance school autonomy and flexibility with certain centralized operations that require consistency, coordination, and legal constraints" (p. 9)? EMOs must respond to this same issue in structuring their relationships with schools they operate. EMO central office staff must address issues around local/organizational autonomy, determining how to balance the need for central control with local autonomy in the areas of the educational program (mission, curriculum, pedagogy, assessment, and professional development), school structure, fiscal issues (including budgeting and facilities acquisition), and hiring/selection practices. Those employed by the EMO may work at either the school site or the central office, and the primary issues around autonomy in these areas are not necessarily between EMO and non-EMO stakeholders, but between those operating at the school and corporate levels. As is the case with districts, the schools that EMOs operate are, to some extent, a part of the larger entity, not distinct from it.

The following section discusses the issues for charter school autonomy that are raised by the growth of EMO involvement. This is followed by a review of the research on EMOs, privatization, and school autonomy, drawing at times on literature on site-based management. After admission of methods, the next section offers a brief description of the 15 companies that provide comprehensive services (including administrative and educational services) included in this study, followed by an analysis of school-level autonomy across a range of areas. In conclusion, the implications of the varying approaches to autonomy adopted by EMOs, and the need for further work in this area, are considered.

CHARTER SCHOOL AUTONOMY AND EMOS

As EMOs have become more involved in charter schools, the role of local stakeholders has become less clear. Autonomy for charter schools was originally conceived of as a mechanism for bringing decision making closer to the "consumer" and giving those with direct involvement in children's lives more opportunities to alter and adapt to address different needs. However, charter school boards that have used their autonomy to turn control in some areas over to a corporate office have implicitly decided that some decisions are *not* best made locally.

From the company perspective, EMOs must deal with tensions between their needs for efficiency, control, and some level of "brand-name" consistency and the wishes of members of the school community. The presence of EMOs has important implications for autonomy at the school site, as schools exchange more site-based control for the potential financial, technical, and educational benefits of corporate support. EMOs need to balance school-level autonomy with their own company vision in each of four main areas: the educational program (including mission, curriculum, assessment, professional development, and instructional practices), fiscal policies, personnel hiring, and school governance.

In terms of the educational program, a critical decision is whether or not to have a common educational mission or vision for schools operated by the company. Earlier research suggests that some school personnel may resist a company's attempt to put in place a particular educational vision. For example, a number of schools in a Michigan study "expressed concern with the management companies, primarily due to the issue of control over the curriculum and focus of the school" (Horn & Miron, 2000, p. 47). A shared mission and a shared educational program are not synonymous; several schools could share a mission but implement it with different "specifics" (e.g., curriculum, materials and instructional practices) or could share some of these specifics in pursuit of at least moderately different missions.

For EMOs, there are a number of different ways to provide schools with a "program," and the choices made about what to include in the program have important implications for the autonomy, or number of "choices" that school stakeholders are able to make. One part of this program may be a shared curriculum, either for some or for all of the subjects taught in the school. Another part involves assessment; while many states require schools (including charter schools) to participate in state-level assessments, EMO educational programs can also include other assessments, such as placement exams and lesson-based classroom assessments. A company may also have particular ideas about the pedagogy that teachers should use to be consistent with the mission and curriculum of the program. Implementing any combination of curricula, assessments, and instructional techniques requires some level of professional development, which might include a summer program, in-service workshops, and in-class support. While not explicitly "educational," the internal governance structure of a school can help to support an educational program.

Fiscal autonomy incorporates school-site control over budgeting decisions (including how many and what type of staff to hire) and facilities. For site-based managed schools, district-driven finance systems often guide budgeting in ways that limit flexibility for individual schools (Wohlstetter, Mohrman, & Robertson, 1997), and EMOs may act similarly. Obtaining appropriate facilities is often cited as one of the most significant obstacles in the start-up of charter schools (RPP International, 2000). This is an area where EMOs can offer some assistance by providing capital or financing opportunities not readily available to individual schools (Horn & Miron, 2000).

Control over personnel decisions—including the selection of school leaders and other staff—is often pointed to as an essential issue affecting school quality. Companies that contract with schools recognize this: "Almost all contracts provide contractors with some kind of control over personnel. Contractors apparently believe they can yield higher performance if they control the selection, training, and assignment of personnel, particularly teaching personnel" (Hannaway, 1999, p. 7). The selection of a school leader is also a critical hiring decision for a charter school, since leadership appropriate to a school's mission can be crucial to a school's success. Thus, both schools and companies have a strong interest in influencing staffing decisions.

EVIDENCE FROM THE LITERATURE: EDUCATIONAL MANAGEMENT ORGANIZATIONS AND CHARTER SCHOOLS

Development of charter school legislation has been accompanied by a growing interest among policymakers and businesspeople in increasing the role of the for-profit sector in the provision of education. Attention to options such as EMOs has increased as the American public has become disenchanted with other efforts to improve public education; according to one report, "Public interest in contracting clearly reflects Americans' desperation about fixing schools now. Many are demoralized that the rash of school reform efforts launched over the last decade has failed to turn the tide" (Richards, Sawicky, & Shore, 1996, p. 49).

Charter schools have proven appealing to entrepreneurs interested in operating schools, including some who are wary of contracting directly with school districts. The charter school movement provides an ideal alternative for education management companies to gain contracts to operate publicly funded schools in a context where the company has greater autonomy than in the district-run sector across the three areas discussed in the introduction—from higher levels of government, at the organizational level, and to the level of individual "consumers." As one report noted:

> The legal structure of public education presents numerous stumbling blocks to schools that want to consider private management. . . . Charter school legislation removes some obstacles to more diverse participation in managing publicly financed schools. (Richards et al., 1996, p. 52)

From the perspective of charter advocates, EMO interest in operating charters can increase the supply of schools—and thus competition—and bring new investors into public education.

From an economic standpoint, the principal rationale for privatization is that the private sector can produce more efficiently than the public sector and, thus, either reduce costs or offer more "product" for the same cost (Pack, 1987; Starr, 1989). Because the private sector is motivated by competition and rewarded with profits, there are incentives for efficiency that do not exist amidst the bureaucracy and regulation of the public sector. Proponents of privatization intend to bring greater efficiency and innovation to public services as firms produce in the most cost-efficient way in order to gain and keep contracts. One proponent argued that "the education marketplace desperately needs more competition" and that it will "improve instruction by rewarding providers that perform well and weeding out those that don't" (quoted in Walsh, p. 1).

EMOs can offer a variety of services to charter schools, including limited services in specific areas such as bookkeeping and reporting, payroll, special education, and personnel. However, this chapter focuses on those that provide comprehensive services. Lin and Hassel (1999) define comprehensive management companies as those that offer "'soup-to-nuts' educational programming and management for schools" (p. 1). Such companies are also called "full-service operators" (Horn & Miron, 2000).

STUDY METHODS

This is an exploratory comparative case study (Yin, 1994) that analyzes the responses of company representatives in an effort to discern patterns in EMO approaches to school management, particularly around issues of decision making. The sample, data collection, and approach to analysis are described in this section.

Sample of Educational Management Organizations

A significant challenge for this study was developing a list of for-profit EMOs that offered "comprehensive management" services (defined as companies that work with all aspects of a charter school's program, including staffing, budgeting, and the educational program) and that worked with at least three charter schools. Part of the difficulty lay in the fact that these companies vary, particularly regarding their approach to a school's educational program, the aspects they seek to control, and the level of specificity within those areas.

In order to develop the list, we contacted representatives of state charter school associations and state departments of education in every state with a charter school law and requested names of companies corresponding to our definition. The resulting list was then combined with one generated by the Center for Educational Research and Analysis at the University of Wisconsin (Molnar, Morales, & Wyst, 2000) and reviewed by several people working in organizations that have closely followed the growth of EMOs. When each company was contacted, the description of comprehensive management was offered and the representative was asked whether the company's services fit this description. In several cases, companies were removed from the list after they offered a clear explanation for how they did not fit the description.

Two special challenges emerged in generating the list. The first involved companies operating in Arizona, where they can obtain charters directly and, thus, may not manage charter schools for a third party. These companies were not included unless they also operated schools in other states. The second challenge involved two cases where one company purchased another during the course of the data collection (Edison Schools purchased LearnNow, and Mosaica Education purchased Advantage Schools). Since these four companies were each distinct entities at the beginning of the study, we treated them as four separate organizations for purposes of data collection and analysis. The final list included 21 companies that comprehensively manage 309 schools serving more than 125,000 students in 20 states and the District of Columbia.

In total, we conducted telephone interviews with representatives of 15 companies (71% of the total of 21) that manage 276 schools (89% of the total of 309). The companies operated between 3 and 70 charter schools each, with each EMO serving between 900 and more than 30,000 students. Six companies were classified as "regional" (operating in only one state), while the remaining were "national companies" that operated in 3 to 17 states and/or the District of Columbia. Six of the 15 companies worked only with charter schools, while 9 offered other education-related services, ranging from operating other public or private schools (5 companies) to providing specific services such as professional development.

Data Collection and Analysis

Data collection involved conducting interviews with as many company representatives as possible from the "universe" of comprehensive management EMOs described above. Letters, phone calls, e-mails, and personal contacts were used in seeking to arrange interviews with representatives from each of the 21 companies (general descriptions of the companies are provided below). Gaining access to company personnel was a significant challenge, as many companies are wary of speaking with researchers amid concerns about their own work, or their industry, being portrayed negatively. At each EMO, we asked to speak with someone at the central office who had sufficient breadth of knowledge about company operations to answer a broad range of questions; in most cases, this was somebody near the top of the organization's management structure or the head of the organization.

The response rate for companies operating relatively large numbers of charter schools (21 or more schools) was better (6 out of 6 companies, or 100%) than for those operating small numbers (3 to 10 schools, response rate of 58%, or 7 out of 12 companies) or medium-sized numbers of schools (11 to 20 schools, response rate of 67%, or 2 out of 3 companies). Interviews followed a semistructured interview guide (Patton, 1990) and focused on four areas: general information about the company's structure, history, and work with charter schools; roles of the central office and school staff in decision making; descriptions of the educational program; and experiences of the company with accountability issues and variations across authorizers and states. Interviews were conducted between May and October of 2001. When needed, brief follow-up interviews were conducted with respondents or other company central office staff. The primary interviews lasted between 30 and 120 minutes, averaging 75 minutes.

All interviews were taped and transcribed, and transcriptions were coded thematically using NUD*IST qualitative data analysis software (Miles & Huberman, 1994). This coding was then used to analyze each area of autonomy and generate ratings in different areas of autonomy.[3] Appendix B lists the codes used to generate the ratings. A researcher who did not participate in conducting the interviews originally created the ratings based on interview transcripts; the author then reviewed these ratings. Uncertainty about ratings was resolved by recontacting the company representative or examining company websites.

Company websites were reviewed and information was organized around the primary research questions (14 of the 21 companies had websites that were used for this purpose). The websites proved most useful for general information about the company (size, states in which schools are operated, etc.) and the company's educational approach, including mission and curriculum. Websites and other documents were used to supplement information from interviews and to verify representatives' statements about the company. These documents and websites are not explicitly used in the analysis to protect the confidentiality of the participating companies.

Cross-case analysis, drawing on qualitative themes and the autonomy ratings, was used to discern patterns that could be used to distinguish among approaches or types of comprehensive EMOs (Miles & Huberman, 1994). As discussed below, this analysis resulted in the classification of companies into three general approaches.

RESULTS: AUTONOMY AND THE EDUCATIONAL PROGRAM

We identified three general ways in which comprehensive management EMOs approach issues directly related to the educational program, including the mission/vision of the schools; the curriculum, materials, instructional/ pedagogical approaches; student assessment; and school structure in the schools they operate (while the literature on site-based management does not focus on governance as a part of the educational program, EMO central office staff often see them as closely intertwined). (See Table 6.1.) These three approaches were the "all-purpose," "mixed-autonomy," and "high-influence" strategies. Most company representatives said that their organization had a single approach to issues of autonomy versus company influence (although relationships with particular schools likely vary within these patterns). However, for two companies, two distinct approaches were used; for these companies, the two approaches were separated in the analysis, creating 17 approaches across 15 companies.[4]

In general, the missions of the companies varied considerably. The most common mission or curricular emphasis was a rigorous, "traditional," or "back-to-basics" program with a focus on "high standards" for academic success. Specifically, three respondents said that their company uses the "Direct Instruction" curriculum and materials for at least a part of their educational program. Three programs were aimed specifically at high school students who had not been succeeding in their previous schools or had already dropped out of school. Five respondents specifically mentioned "individualized learning," but the meaning of the term varied. Other themes included close attention to brain development, a focus on schools within the community, technology, hands-on learning, and close relationships with parents. Several companies relied heavily on prepackaged curriculum and educational programs, such as "Success for All."

Decision making about the amount and source of professional development varied across companies. Some companies chose to provide professional development "as needed," while others had very prescribed programs in which all teachers participated. Ten companies had specific, intensive (2 to 4 weeks) summer programs for teachers newly hired by a school they operated; in six of these cases, continuing teachers also participated in the program. One company central office did not provide formal training but rather worked on an "apprenticeship" model, where newly hired teachers were given up to 3 months of learning alongside a mentor prior to operating independently.

Companies took quite different approaches to school-level assessments and pedagogy. Almost every person interviewed discussed state testing as an important form of assessment, but only some companies had particular classroom assessments that they expected or encouraged teachers to use. Similarly, while some EMOs had very specific ideas about instructional practices (ranging from highly scripted direct-instruction approaches to more constructivist, teacher-as-facilitator modes), other companies said little about specific pedagogical techniques to be used in classrooms.

Finally, companies also varied considerably in both the extent to which they prescribed a school structure and the specifics of that structure. The most common structure involved what company representatives described as a

Table 6.1. School influence on educational program and school structure

	School influence on mission	School influence on curriculum	School influence on classroom assessment	School influence on instruction	School influence on school governance/ organizational structure	School influence on professional development
All-Purpose EMOs						
Company 1	High	High	High	High	High	High
Company 2A	High	High	High	High	High	High
Company 3A	High	High	High	High	High	High
Mixed-Autonomy EMOs						
Company 3B	Low	Medium	High	High	Medium	High
Company 4	High	Medium	High	High	Medium	Medium
Company 5	High	Medium	High	Low	Low	Medium
Company 2B	Low	Medium	High	Low	High	Low
Company 6	Low	Medium	High	Medium	Low	Low
Company 7	Low	Low	High	Low	Medium	Low
Company 8	Low	Medium	Low	Medium	Medium	Low
High-Influence EMOs						
Company 9	Low	Low	Low	Low	High	Low
Company 10	Low	Low	Low	Medium	Low	Low
Company 11	Low	Low	Low	Low	Medium	Low
Company 12	Low	Low	Low	Low	Medium	Low
Company 13	Low	Low	Low	Low	Low	Low
Company 14	Low	Low	Low	Low	Low	Low
Company 15	Low	Low	Low	Low	Low	Low

Note: Companies 2 and 3 used multiple approaches to management, as reflected by the "A" and "B" designation.

"strong principal" model. In most cases, this meant that the principal was given considerable discretion in terms of structuring school governance, including whether and how to incorporate parents and teachers in formal and informal decision making. Some educational programs, however, created specific roles for different stakeholders; two companies mandated a role for "teacher teams," and several formalized parental influence through parent organizations.

Companies with an All-Purpose Approach

A small portion of the companies studied fell into the "all-purpose" category, where EMOs provide educational services, but on a "customer-driven" model; for example, a school may wish to select a new science curriculum, and the EMO provides assistance through researching available alternatives or identifying consultants who can assist. Of the fifteen companies studied, one provided only an all-purpose approach, while two others offered some schools these more flexible services while providing others with a more defined model. The all-purpose EMO sits somewhere between a truly comprehensive approach and a company that focuses on back-office support.

All-purpose EMOs have no predetermined educational program and leave staff in each school to decide mission, curricula, assessment strategies, instructional approach, and professional development needs. In the words of one company representative (also cited above):

> We can go in and assist a school in developing their own curriculum for a particular discipline. . . . There is really no area that we can't assist them in, but, again, we sit back and wait until we are asked to do it as opposed to imposing it.

One representative from an all-purpose EMO contrasted his company with one that provides a complete program:

> They do everything, they have their own curriculum . . . so we are not like that at all. . . . What we do is we provide business and personnel services to people who want to run charter schools and we don't particularly care too much about what philosophy they espouse.

Companies with a Mixed-Autonomy Approach

Seven companies (or parts of companies) provide a "mixed model," where the educational program is prescribed in some areas but quite flexible in others. The two companies that provide more than one approach offer some services in this category. For all but one of the seven, the general mission is consistent across schools (or the portion of schools included in this category). A staff member at one of these companies likened its central office function to a river:

> We supply what might be characterized as the banks of the rivers. That is, here are some guidelines that are fairly permanent, but not immutable. . . . The mission we also supply. And like a river—and the river's mission is get to the sea—the individual components of the river upon encountering an obstacle do not seek higher authority before figuring out how to get around the obstacle. . . . What we do is try to give our people as much knowledge of the truths of the basic mission, and then, "You guys figure it out."

While these EMOs maintain a consistent mission across schools, they vary as to where they prescribe behavior and where they allow or encourage variation. The most flexible of these companies offers a particular program for education and a small amount of professional development in that program but does not specify curricula, assessments, or instructional approach. At times, the flexibility of the program has created tensions between the EMO and the boards of individual schools. A representative commented that one challenge was ensuring that school leaders followed the company's model, "while at the same time giving them the autonomy they want and need to have." Since the company central office must rely on individual schools to interpret the general mission without a more prescribed program, there is more potential for them to shift away from it.

Another company does not require specific curricula, materials, or assessments but does have a very clearly defined mission that incorporates explicit ideas about student learning and school governance. For this company's schools, professional development is at the core of the educational program. As a company representative described it, "We provide continuous training, really. Most Friday afternoons are free for training every week in every school. We have intensive week-long training three times throughout the schoolyear." At the start of the year, she added, "we have opportunities for selected staff to visit other schools to receive specialty training." This focus on training is combined with a well-defined structure for democratic school governance.

At the more fixed end of the mixed-autonomy spectrum, one company central office does not prescribe a particular curriculum or the use of specific materials but does have an intensive assessment system that monitors student learning.

We don't get into the minutia of what they're doing on a day-to-day basis, but through quizzes, tests, lessons, standardized tests, assessment programs, we know exactly how the kids are doing and we hold the teacher accountable for the performance of the student. . . . We have a very sophisticated software program that allows us to monitor student performance on a daily basis.

For this company, the focus is on outcomes rather than processes. The curricula vary between schools, but the assessments are used as the primary tool for ensuring consistency across sites.

In each of these cases, companies have determined that providing autonomy in some areas—whether it be curricula and materials, assessments, or professional development—but not others allows individual schools to "personalize" an educational vision while still maintaining some "corporate identity."

Companies with a High-Influence Approach

Representatives of seven EMOs described a management approach that involved true soup-to-nuts management, with program designs that included the mission, curricula, assessments, instructional approaches, professional development, and school organization. While each of these companies offers what it considers a focused program, the content and styles of the programs vary.

The most highly structured educational approaches incorporate very specific ideas about how a school can best succeed academically. Still, EMOs varied as to the amount of decision making they encourage at the classroom level, with EMOs that rely on very teacher-directed approaches being more likely to minimize teacher decisions. One representative argued that, for her company, "There's total quality control . . . which comes from implementing the exact same approach and curriculum . . . all things considered, you can go from one school to the next and essentially see the same type of program in place." Another spokesperson said, "We have a fairly structured notion of what we think makes for an outstanding educational experience, and there's not a lot of deviation around that." In cases where the approach of the company is independent study, very specific materials and curricula for courses—developed centrally or purchased "off the shelf"—provide this type of focus. In other cases, programs such as "Success for All" or "Direct Instruction" are used to provide consistency across school sites.

One important difference between most high-influence and mixed-autonomy EMOs is the emphasis on very specific approaches to instruction.

In some cases, particularly with companies that focus on a back-to-basics approach, the purpose of this specificity is to "teacher-proof" the educational program, as exemplified by these statements from representatives of two different companies:

> If you just openly . . . create an environment where individuals are expected to be creative in how they implement something, then you're essentially surrendering or risking the possibility that a particular school will either succeed or fail depending on the ability of that particular group of individuals.

> So it's—we try to make it individual-free, if you will. Or try to minimize the risk that a bad team could screw things up. So very simply, we believe that with our population [of mostly minority, urban students] that at the primary grade levels, an inventive, creative teacher is a disaster. Because that assumes the kids have a minimum level of academic skills upon which you can build the creativity.

Not all of the high-influence companies adopt this particular viewpoint. However, they all do see themselves as creating educational programs that—with proper training and careful hiring—can be "scaled up" in ways that do not rely heavily on the skills or propensities of specific individuals.

Assessment is another tool for developing consistency across sites. In some cases, high-influence EMOs rely heavily on tests provided with prepackaged programs. Other companies have developed their own assessments that can be administered as often as weekly; one representative noted that "we can test kids weekly on what they've learned for that week. And we're able to pinpoint exactly where particular gaps may be forming." EMOs that rely on independent study have assessments built into the materials that students complete.

High-influence EMOs also see professional development as essential, particularly around introducing and maintaining fidelity to the educational program. In each of these companies, new teachers (and sometimes continuing teachers) participate in extensive training prior to operating independently; this occurs mostly in summer programs, but one company uses an extensive "apprenticeship" model.

While such formal professional development programs continue throughout the year, these EMOs also rely on more informal approaches—including curriculum support staff in schools who observe classes and review assessments, and gatherings of school leaders and/or staff across school sites. One person interviewed argued that such meetings can be more effective than traditional professional development conferences; he said that, for teachers:

The interesting thing about [our interschool meetings], and how that's different from the typical professional development conference, is that people come together not only around their subject area but around a common program . . . They all have the same kind of issues or problems and they know that when they go back home, they're gonna be trying to improve a program with a principal who understands what they're trying to do.

Overall, high-influence EMOs are more likely than other companies to have given some attention to the governance structure within individual schools. One respondent said that, for his company, "We have a very clear understanding of the management of the schools." One example of prescribed governance involves the role of school leaders; all seven of these companies had particular ideas about the role of the school leader in one of their schools. In two companies, school leaders (sometimes but not always called principals) are viewed as administrative leaders, and there is another formal role or roles for educational leaders within the school structure. Two other companies focus on more collaborative governance; one respondent reported that his company expects principals to act "in an open, collegial, consulting way so that decisions will not be arbitrarily made." The remaining three companies explicitly espouse a "strong principal" model. One company representative argued that this is important for accountability purposes: "If you want to attract people who are willing to be held to those standards, then . . . you have to give them broad discretion with respect to staffing and budgeting and program supervision or you're tying their hands." Governance extends beyond the role of the principal, and five of the seven high-influence companies specify other structures, ranging from leadership teams to required committees to student government.

RESULTS: AUTONOMY IN FISCAL AND HIRING DECISIONS

Two areas identified as critical to school autonomy in the site-based management literature—budgeting/ fiscal control and personnel hiring—are either quite similar across EMOs or vary in ways only somewhat related to decision-making the educational program. The high-influence companies tend to have more overall control in these areas but to prioritize different decisions. Table 6.2 summarizes the findings in these areas.

Fiscal Issues

Two of the most prominent fiscal issues for charter schools are determining the overall school budget and deciding how to finance the school's

Table 6.2. School influence over fiscal and personnel issues

	School influence on school budget	School control of facilities	School influence on teacher hiring	School influence on principal selection
All-Purpose EMOs				
Company 1	Low	High	Medium	Medium
Company 2A	Low	High	High	Medium
Company 3A	Medium	High	High	Medium
Mixed-Autonomy EMOs				
Company 3B	Low	Medium	High	Low
Company 4	High	High	High	Medium
Company 5	Low	High	Medium	Medium
Company 2B	Low	High	Medium	Medium
Company 6	Low	Medium	Medium	Low
Company 7	Medium	Medium	High	Medium
Company 8	Medium	Low	Medium	Medium
High-Influence EMOs				
Company 9	Low	Medium	Low	Medium
Company 10	Low	Medium	High	Medium
Company 11	Low	Medium	High	Low
Company 12	Medium	Medium	High	Medium
Company 13	Medium	Low	Medium	Low
Company 14	Low	Low	Medium	Low
Company 15	Low	Medium	High	Low

Note: Companies 2 and 3 used multiple approaches to management, as reflected by the "A" and "B" designation.

facility. Interviewees cited three basic approaches to school budgeting: writing the budget at the school level (perhaps with some suggestions by the EMO); writing it as a "collaborative effort" between school personnel and the company, with the board and/or principal actively involved in ensuring that the budget reflects fiscal priorities; and having the EMO take the primary role in creating a budget that would then need to be approved by the local board. The most common approach (11 out of 15 companies) was the last, described by one respondent as: "We draft a budget [to be] presented to the board as a recommendation that they approve or disapprove. But they're not crafting the budget."

Where budgeting is described as a more collaborative effort, it is difficult to determine how much influence each actor has in the process. One respondent reported that boards, as they become more accustomed to working with budgets, also become more assertive, even hiring separate accountants to review the budget. Only one company gave its schools primary authority over creating their budget. One of the mixed-autonomy EMOs said that schools had control over their budgets within company guidelines:

> They make a case for what they want to do, how they want to do it, and if it can be managed within their budget; they have the latitude to do it. . . . We are not so participative that we are going to let them do something we think is innately stupid, but rarely is that going to happen.

Once the budget is made, the discretionary spending at the school level also varies. While some companies report that schools have some budgetary control throughout the year, others argue that there is little discretionary money to be spent at any level. According to one interviewee, discretionary money is raised in their schools in ways similar to other public schools: "Fundraising, picture days, book fairs. Whatever money they raise that way reverts back to the school to spend anyway they want."

As noted earlier, the issue of acquiring (and often renovating) appropriate facilities is a significant challenge for charter schools. One of the attractions of EMOs is that they can often provide assistance in this area by providing capital, purchasing buildings or land, building new facilities, or arranging financing. Of the EMOs studied here, six did not purchase any facilities (although, in some cases, they did help to arrange financing). In three cases, the company (or an affiliated company) owned or leased all of the buildings used by the managed schools. In the remaining cases, there was a mix of situations for each company. Two representatives noted that short-term ownership by the EMO was more common than long-term because of concerns about limiting the availability of capital for other purposes. As one interviewee put it:

> For [the company] to actually own a facility on a long-term basis is pretty unusual. We might do that temporarily to get a facility bought and fixed and open, but we will almost immediately look to finance it or to sell it and then lease it back ourselves because we don't want to be in the real estate business with our capital tied up in buildings.

On the one hand, EMO ownership of facilities allows schools access to buildings that might otherwise be unavailable to them. On the other hand, EMO ownership raises concerns about school autonomy, especially the ability of schools to end a relationship with a company (Horn & Miron, 2000; Molnar, 2001). One company representative (whose company owns some facilities) cited cases where charter boards have decided to take on ownership of their buildings:

> I think that's a very strong statement. If they own the building, if they decide to fire us at some point, they've got the building, they're in a much stronger position. And in some ways, that's better for us 'cause it's a very good answer to the charge that the charter groups are just straw groups that do our bidding.

Once a facility is acquired, there can also be continuing tensions around its use. One respondent described a difficult situation where school stakeholders resisted the company's plan to expand the school enrollment and reduce the amount of space available for "extra" activities.

Personnel

In the literature on site-based management, control over hiring is often seen as central to school-level autonomy. Hiring of teaching staff is one area where—with the exception of one company—school-level staff (especially the principal) have a moderate to significant amount of influence; this is true across all three approaches to comprehensive management of education. While the EMO central office is often involved in recruiting candidates, and in some cases doing initial screening, most companies allow school staff to take an active role in the selection of new teachers. Also, in many cases, the board of the charter school makes the final decision about teacher hiring.

Perhaps not surprisingly, EMO staff consistently demonstrated much more concern about the selection of school leaders than the selection of teachers. This reflects a widely held belief that, as one company representative put it, the principal "is the most important job on the campus, without any question." EMOs want school leaders to share the company's vision of schooling and to act on this vision and its components when making decisions about such issues as hiring staff, professional development, and budgeting. Some companies maintain a high level of control over principal selection, screening candidates and recommending one for board approval, if required. Others attempt to strike a balance with the school, focusing on selecting a leader in keeping with the needs and philosophy of the company. As one representative described the process:

> Nobody can get to be the principal unless both the charter board and the [company] are thumbs up on that person. In terms of the charter board, they've got the authority and the ultimate accountability for the school. Plus it's their community and it's their kids. We're making a substantial investment and it's our reputation. So neither one of us can be in the position of having to accept a principal sort of over our better judgment.

She went on to argue that charter board participation in the principal selection process is an important factor in local support for the school:

> I don't think it's right to expect the board not to have a say. And frankly, it's the board that lends local legitimacy to what we do. We can quickly be painted as folks from out of town. So it's very important, I think, for the principal to have credibility and for the school to have a good standing in the community.

For both personnel and fiscal issues, EMOs were willing to vary the level of input from schools—including giving more control over areas that school districts have traditionally dominated (especially teacher hiring) as long as the overall goal was consistent with the company's purposes—both financial and educational.

CONCLUSION

One of the most important findings in this exploratory study of EMOs is that all EMOs are not created alike, either in terms of the educational substance of the programs they offer or in terms of the way they balance school and corporate autonomy. Thus, some EMOs focus on working with the preferences of individual school sites around educational and administrative matters, while others present a highly prescriptive program.

For charter schools that work with educational management organizations, the level of organizational autonomy offered in a state law is likely to be altered by the relationship with an EMO. From the perspective of EMO central office staff, specifics of school autonomy vary considerably between companies, even among EMOs that fall into the category of "comprehensive management." Company staff view the removal of some autonomy as critical to developing quality charter schools and, often, to maintaining fidelity to EMO ideals.

While the original charter school concept placed a strong emphasis on autonomy as a critical predecessor to innovation, there are still many questions to be answered about how much autonomy, and in what areas, seems most related to school quality. Beliefs about that autonomy "mix" are quite different from the perspectives of those interviewed for this study, although all believe that an outside organization can provide some level of valuable guidance and assistance to charter schools that might otherwise be more isolated.

Future research in this area (both qualitative and quantitative) might look not only at autonomy but also at internal school structures, the role of different decision makers at a school site, and the content and outcomes of different EMOs' educational programs. Another ripe area for research is comparing implementation of EMO models with experiences in non-EMO-operated charter schools and with other types of schools (charters and district-run) that are attempting to follow a "whole-school" model—especially those adopting school designs. Interviews with EMO staff reveal only the intentions of program designers and are limited in their ability to provide information about fidelity to the model in the classroom. This can help to address another area not covered in this study—the differences between schools that operate with and without EMO involvement.

One of the goals of the charter school movement was to allow for increased innovation at the school level, with both autonomy and accountability offering opportunities and pressure for change (Nathan, 1996). From the perspective of EMO central office staff, there is a need to limit that autonomy in a variety of ways if companies are to offer multiple schools with consistent offerings and of consistent quality, and maintain some control over school spending. The "success" of the different ways in which EMOs have sought to balance company control and school autonomy is an open question. As the number of schools operated by EMOs (charter and noncharter public schools) expands, it is essential that both researchers and policymakers develop a clearer understanding of how such companies influence the process of public education.

NOTES

1. Funding for this research was provided by the U.S. Department of Education's National Institute on Educational Governance, Finance, Policymaking and Management (Grant #OERI-R308A60003). The opinions expressed in this research are those of the author and do not necessarily reflect the views of the Consortium for Policy Research in Education (CPRE); the National Institute on Educational Governance, Finance, Policymaking and Management; the Office of Educational Research and Improvement; the United States Department of Education; or the institutional partners of CPRE. The author would like to thank Jennifer Fisler, Richard Birdsall, and Elisabeth Gordon for their valuable assistance on this project.

2. In some states, this percentage is likely much higher—for example, in Michigan, where about 70% of schools contracted for some level of service from either a for-profit or nonprofit EMO (Arsen, Plank, & Sykes, 1999; Horn & Miron, 2000).

3. These ratings follow a similar logic to those used by Wohlstetter and her colleagues to examine autonomy in state charter school legislation (Wohlstetter, Wenning, & Briggs, 1995).

4. Appendix B provides the codes used in Tables 6.1 and 6.2. The approaches for the companies with two modes are listed as Company 2A and 2B, and Company 3A and 3B.

CHAPTER 7

Balancing Disparate Visions: An Analysis of Special Education in Charter Schools

Lauren Morando Rhim
Eileen M. Ahearn
Cheryl M. Lange
Margaret J. McLaughlin

Charter school advocates regularly portray special education policies and procedures as a burdensome carryover from the traditional public school structure that they are attempting to escape. Yet, at their core, charter schools and special education are philosophically similar in that both are committed to matching a particular educational model with students' unique needs. The disconnect between special education and charter schools arises due to their vastly dissimilar approaches to an individual education. Charter schools have been characterized as "schools without rules" (Heubert, 1997, p. 1) that grow and flourish in a competitive market environment that rewards effectiveness and punishes ineffectiveness (Chubb & Moe, 1990; Hill et al., 1997). One factor used to assess state charter laws is the degree to which the laws liberate charter schools from higher levels of government (i.e., state and local regulations), which are perceived to hinder innovation and effectiveness (Center for Education Reform, 2001a). In contrast, special education is highly regulated by federal, state, and, in some districts, local regulations aimed at protecting the civil rights of students with disabilities.

In reality, charter schools are not fully without rules. They are public schools and required to abide by all federal laws aimed at protecting students' civil rights and basic health and safety. Absent from most discussions regarding charter schools is the challenge to autonomy posed by federal and state mandates, such as special education, that cannot be waived.

 ISBN 0-8077-4393-3 (paper), ISBN 0-8077-4394-1 (cloth).

A complex, interrelated set of federal, state, and district policies govern special education programs. These policies are founded on the civil rights principles articulated in the 1954 Supreme Court decision in *Brown* v. *Board of Education* that guarantees all children access to public education. Several federal statutes share certain fundamental characteristics. The federal Individuals with Disabilities Education Act (IDEA), Section 504 of the Vocational Rehabilitation Act, and the Americans with Disabilities Act (ADA) all protect the right of children with disabilities to attend public schools. The IDEA further entitles each eligible student to a free appropriate public education (FAPE) in the least restrictive environment (LRE).

The federal laws are more than civil rights declarations. While neither Section 504 nor the ADA provides resources to schools to implement them, the IDEA provides funds annually to states to defray the costs of special education. The IDEA designates state education agencies as the entity responsible for implementing the federal provisions. State agencies in turn delegate this responsibility to local school districts. This results in a complex interdependent network of federal → state → local mandates that challenge the concept of an autonomous local school.

Prior to the emergence of charter schools, the delegation of authority and distribution of special education funds were relatively straightforward. Charter schools introduced a new twist to the definition of a local education agency (LEA): a single school that carries the legal status of a district. Operating as an autonomous school district is appealing to charter advocates because it provides schools with the desired freedom to determine their curricula and develop their own policies. However, charter schools are public schools, even if they are autonomous, and they carry the same legal responsibility to adhere to civil rights statutes such as the IDEA. This responsibility includes providing services to students with a wide range of disabilities that may range in severity from mild to profound.

The IDEA outlines specific procedures that must be implemented by schools. The procedures are designed to ensure that students with disabilities receive FAPE. What constitutes an "appropriate" education is defined in law through a student's individualized education program (IEP). IEPs are developed by a team of general and special education teachers, parents, and school psychologists, and they specify the special education and related services that students require to succeed in school. There is ongoing discussion, reflected in years of litigation and policy debates, regarding what constitutes a "free appropriate public education" and "least restrictive environment" for an individual student.

Research suggests that educating students with disabilities as stipulated by the principles of Section 504, the ADA, and the IDEA is one of the more complex challenges facing public charter schools. Specifically, charter schools struggle to comprehend the plethora of regulations governing special education and to amass the human and fiscal capacity needed to provide a diverse array of special education and related services (Fiore, Harwell, Blackorby, & Finnegan, 2000; Lange, 1997; McKinney, 1996; McLaughlin & Henderson, 1998; Rhim & McLaughlin, 2001).

In this chapter, the findings of Project SEARCH—a multistate study that examined how states, districts, and charter schools are negotiating the interplay among state charter school laws and federal, state, and, in some cases, local special education rules and regulations—are discussed.[1] Project SEARCH identified state policies that influence charter schools' capacities to deliver special education. The research revealed that the manner in which individual state charter school laws define autonomy from a local district is critical to charter schools' capacities to deliver special education. To provide a context for our discussion of some of the findings, a summary of current literature on special education in charter schools is required.

RESEARCH ON SPECIAL EDUCATION IN CHARTER SCHOOLS

Research on special education in charter schools is limited, but the literature to date reveals a few common themes regarding enrollment and capacity that are relevant to our research. A number of research studies have examined the proportion of students with disabilities in charter schools and have reported mixed findings. McKinney's (1996) research in Arizona found that charter schools enrolled notably fewer students with disabilities than their public school peers, yet research in Minnesota found that charter schools actually enrolled more students with disabilities than conventional public schools in the first years of operation (Lange, 1997). The National Study of Charter Schools documented that while some states enroll higher percentages of children with disabilities than traditional public schools, nationwide charter schools enroll a smaller percentage of students with disabilities than do conventional public schools (Nelson et al., 2000).

Horn and Miron's (2000) evaluation of Michigan charter schools documented that these schools (referred to as public school academies) generally enroll fewer students with disabilities than traditional public schools and enroll children who have mild or "high-incidence" disabilities such as specific learning disabilities. This is in contrast to children with more severe or "low-incidence" disabilities, such as deafness/blindness, who require extensive services. Fiore, Harwell, Blackorby, and Finnegan (2000) also found that charter schools are generally attracting children with mild to moderate disabilities who can be served in inclusive classroom environments. While their sample of

32 charter schools is not generalizable to the universe of charter schools, they documented that once enrolled in charter schools, most students with disabilities attend inclusive classrooms as opposed to more restrictive settings in which they are separated from peers who do not have disabilities.

Given the high degree of variability in the research, a question that begs further investigation is whether charter schools are in fact enrolling a different proportion of children with disabilities than their conventional public school peers, or whether they are enrolling the same proportion but not identifying them as having a disability (Fiore et al., 2000; Rhim & McLaughlin, 2000). Anecdotal data collected through Project SEARCH suggest that some charter schools may enroll but not identify students with disabilities. Quantitative data are needed to test this hypothesis. Fiore and colleagues (2000) found that parents of students with disabilities enroll their children in charter schools for reasons related both to the attractive features of the charter school and to their negative experiences with the child's previous school. These reasons loosely parallel the reasons that founders start charter schools and parents in general select charter schools (Berman, Nelson, Ericson, Perry, & Silverman, 1998).

Related to the question of who enrolls in charter schools is "counseling-out," whereby parents are advised against enrolling their child with a disability in a particular school. Fiore and colleagues (2000) concluded that charter schools "counsel" parents of some students with disabilities against enrolling in charter schools and that a number of issues contribute to the counseling-out. For instance, charter operators noted that lack of adequate funding and staff, poor facilities, their school's particular academic approach, and the high costs of transportation contributed to counseling-out students with disabilities. Along these lines, Finn, Manno, and Vanourek's (2000) multistate study of charter schools found that some charter schools are not meeting the needs of their students with disabilities. They attribute service inadequacies to "lack of experience, expertise, or resources" on the part of charter schools (p. 159). Because of legal implications, it is difficult to collect the quantitative data needed to determine the degree to which the practice of counseling-out of children with disabilities occurs.

Research indicates that the relationship that a charter school maintains with a local district contributes to its ability to deliver special education. Fiore and colleagues (2000) documented that while strained relationships with local districts can hinder special education, a positive relationship can foster students' success. An early General Accounting Office (GAO) study of charter schools also documented that the relationship between charter schools and local districts can be critical to charter schools' success, including developing special education programs that depend on federal, state, and local infrastructures (USGAO, 1995). The study concluded that ambiguity regarding who is responsible for delivering special education services in a charter school hindered delivery of services. The study recommended that the federal government clarify who is responsible for special education in charter schools. The U.S. Department of Education responded to the GAO recommendations with a number of policy papers regarding special education in charter schools and additional language in the 1997 amendments to the IDEA and subsequent regulations. The IDEA regulations stipulate that "Children with disabilities who attend public charter schools and their parents retain all rights under this part" (Assistance to States, 34 CFR§300.312 (a), 1999). IDEA also addresses the responsibilities of charter schools in terms of their legal identity as separate autonomous local education agencies or as schools in an LEA.

Case law regarding charter schools' roles and responsibilities related to special education is still evolving and is far from definitive (O'Neill, Wenning, & Giovannetti, 2002). The recent reauthorization of the Elementary and Secondary Education Act (the No Child Left Behind Act of 2001) and the pending reauthorization of the IDEA will most likely raise additional questions regarding how charter schools provide special education and how these autonomous and semi-autonomous schools will be held accountable for educating students with a wide range of disabilities.

PROJECT SEARCH STUDY METHODS

Much of the research previously noted examines the operational aspects of serving students with disabilities in charter schools (e.g., how many enrolled). The purpose of Project SEARCH was to identify the larger policy issues that emerge when charter schools open and are required to fulfill federal laws and regulations. The study methods for Project SEARCH were state-level exploratory case studies. The well-documented variability in state charter school laws positions the state as the primary actor in implementing special education in charter schools. Consequently, the state is the appropriate unit of study for an inquiry regarding policies and practices that influence charter schools' capacity to deliver special education.

Exploratory case study methods were appropriate for this inquiry because exploratory cases serve to answer the question of "what" and aim to "develop pertinent hypothesis and propositions for further inquiry" (Yin, 1994, p. 5). Within the parameters of acceptable practice for case study research (see Merriam, 1998; Yin, 1994), we conducted a pilot study of 15 states and then conducted exploratory case studies of seven states. In addition to the 7 state case studies, we conducted a case study of the District of Columbia because it was the first district to develop a special education cooperative for charter schools. The D.C. case served as an example of a strategy charter schools can implement to fulfill their special education obligations.

The case studies drew on data from state-, district-, and school-level sources. In order to examine states that represent the full array of charter school issues, we drew a "purposeful sample" of "information-rich cases" (Patton, 1990, p. 169). The 7 case study states are Arizona, California, Colorado, Connecticut, Florida, Minnesota, and North Carolina. The sample was purposeful in that it reflects maximum variation based on (1) the number of charter schools operating in the state, (2) the length of time charter schools have been operating in the state, and (3) the relationship or linkage between charter schools and their LEA for the purposes of special education as dictated by the state charter school law.[2] The sample states provide rich information regarding unique issues that stem from particularities in state special education and charter school policy and practice. Table 7.1 describes the states according to our selection criteria.

We also purposefully selected charter schools within each case study state to represent maximum variation according to (1) population density (i.e., rural, urban, and suburban), (2) grades served, (3) size, and (4) instructional program. We selected local school districts that were in proximity to the charter schools.

The three primary Project SEARCH field researchers collected data over the course of an 18-month period beginning in the spring of 1999 and ending in the fall of 2000. Data-collection strategies included reviewing documents and conducting individual face-to-face and telephone interviews, focus groups, small-group meetings, and charter school site visits. We selected state and district personnel to be interviewed or to participate in the focus groups based on their knowledge of special education or charter schools, or special education in charter schools. The individuals were selected based on their title and/or on recommendation by knowledgeable informants (i.e., snowball or chain sampling). Documents reviewed included state charter schools laws, state and district special education policy memoranda, and other relevant policy documents identified by informants.

Data were coded and sorted according to the charter school operational concepts that emerged from the initial 15-state analysis and that guided the data collection. Examples of the thematic codes were state law, charter school application process, and technical assistance. Using the codes, we developed lengthy case study reports for each of the states and Washington, D.C. The case studies served as the database for the cross-state analysis. We used the constant comparative method (Glaser & Straus, 1967) to compare all the data from the case studies in order to establish patterns and document themes. We identified, explored, and synthesized cross-cutting themes to produce comprehensive study findings and recommendations. Due to the purposeful

Table 7.1. State characteristics

Case Study Site	Number of Charter Schools[1]	Year First Charter School Opened[2]	Relationship Between Charter Schools and LEAs for the Purpose of Special Education[3]
Arizona	High	Second Generation	No link
California	High	First Generation	Partial link
Colorado	Medium	First Generation	Total link
Connecticut	Low	Third Generation	Total link
Florida	High	Second Generation	Partial link
Minnesota	Medium	First Generation	Partial link
North Carolina	Medium	Third Generation	No link

1. *High* = 100 or more charter schools; *Medium* = 26-99 charter schools; *Low* = 0–25 charter schools, as of 11/98.

2. *First Generation*: Prior to 1994; *Second Generation*: Between 1994–1997; *Third Generation*: After 1997.

3. *Total Link* = Formal linkage established in statute or through application that links charter school and LEA (or equivalent) in all areas of special education. *Partial Link* = Charter school is legally independent, but there is a legislated requirement for a negotiated relationship with the traditional LEA (or equivalent), or a legislated protection for special education responsibilities at the LEA level; *No Link* = Charter school is legally independent and operates autonomously from LEA (or equivalent) control. Any relationship with the LEA is entirely voluntary for both the charter school and the LEA.

nature of the study sample, the value of this exploratory study is the identification of issues rather than the generalizability of these issues to all charter schools nationwide.

FINDINGS: CHARTER SCHOOL LEGAL IDENTITY AND THE SIGNIFICANCE OF LINKAGE

Project SEARCH documented that, with few exceptions, charter schools in the case study states are struggling to amass the capacity to deliver special education. As with many policies, there are multiple, often complex intervening and overlapping, factors that influence special education implementation in charter schools. Nevertheless, a central finding across all the state case studies is the critical importance of a charter school's legal identity and the degree to which it is connected or "linked" to a local school district or other educational entity for the purposes of special education. The cases revealed that both legal identity and linkage influence charter schools' capacity to deliver special education services. Yet legal identity and linkage are separate constructs.

A charter school's legal identity and, consequently, degree of autonomy are specified in state charter law. A higher level of government than individual charter schools generally determines legal identity. Individual state laws classify charter schools as part of an LEA or an autonomous LEA. Legal identity is important because, under federal special education law, an LEA has more responsibilities than an individual school within an LEA. The critical component of legal identity involves who is ultimately responsible for providing students with disabilities with an appropriate education. LEAs are wholly responsible for special education whereas individual schools within an LEA share responsibility.

Linkage to an LEA for the purposes of special education is dictated by law but can be negotiated by contract between a charter school and an LEA. In contrast to legal identity, charter schools have some, albeit in some cases limited, control over the type of linkage they establish with an LEA.

While charter schools generally strive to maximize their autonomy from local districts, linking with a district for the purposes of special education can bolster charter schools' ability to meet obligations stemming from the IDEA. In particular, linkage to an LEA can assist charter schools in addressing the pronounced special education knowledge gap that emerged in all of the case study states.

Both legal status and the linkage the charter school has to a traditional district or sponsoring district must be known to fully understand the charter school's role and responsibilities regarding the implementation of special education laws. The SEARCH team developed a typology of linkage—"total link," "partial link," or "no link"—to describe how charter schools relate to local districts for the purposes of special education. Total-link charter schools (e.g., charter schools in Connecticut and Colorado) are part of an LEA, and the LEA is responsible for providing special education to children enrolled in the charter school. Partial-link schools (e.g., charter schools in Florida) may or may not be part of an LEA, but they share responsibility for providing special education to children enrolled in the charter school. Or, in the case of Minnesota, they share financial responsibility for the student although the charter school has programmatic responsibility. No-link charter schools (e.g., charter schools in Arizona or North Carolina) are typically legally autonomous LEAs and are wholly responsible for delivering special education to all their students with disabilities (Ahearn, Lange, Rhim, & McLaughlin, 2001, Rhim & McLaughlin, 2000). The following sections explore the issues associated with each type of linkage documented in the case study states.

Issues Associated with Total-Link Status

A total-link charter school has a formal linkage, established in statute, regulation, or a negotiated charter contract, that connects the charter school to an LEA in all areas of special education (Ahearn et al., 2001; Rhim & McLaughlin, 2000). Within the study sample, total-link charter schools were most prevalent in Colorado and Connecticut. These states specifically dictate that charter schools be part of an LEA and that the authorizing entity (the LEA in the case of Colorado) or the student's LEA of residence (in the case of Connecticut) retain all responsibility for special education. In practice, these charter schools typically work closely with an LEA to identify and deliver services to students with disabilities but operationalize the total-link status differently.

Connecticut charter schools either provide special education services and receive reimbursement from the district, or the district directly provides special education services to its students enrolled in charter schools. In either case, Connecticut state law places the responsibility for seeing that services are delivered on the charter school. The responsibility to provide or pay for the provision of those services rests with the student's home district.

In Colorado, charter schools in many districts purchase services through the district using a risk-pooling model in which they pay the local district a standard per-student price for all students enrolled in charter schools. In return, the district provides special education and related services to children with disabilities who enroll in the charter school.

Charter schools in both Colorado and Connecticut experienced benefits and challenges associated with total linkage. For example, total-link charter schools reported that they benefit from districts' depth and breadth of human and fiscal resources but must negotiate with district personnel regarding special education services. As a result, these charter schools are likely to conform to district special education policies. Charter school operators in total-link schools also expressed concerns that district-hired special education teachers working in charter schools might not support or "buy into" charter schools' unique instructional programs.

The gap between what charter school operators know and what they need to know regarding special education was a recurring challenge across all three types of linkage. In total-link schools, charter school operators' lack of knowledge is readily apparent to district personnel responsible for working with charter schools. A district liaison who is responsible for supporting special education in charter schools explained: "Generally, charters are aware of special education but not knowledgeable about specific requirements that are very important. The schools want assistance with compliance." Another district liaison noted: "Lack of special education knowledge on the part of charter schools is a huge issue."

While imperfect and at times challenging due to the need to negotiate with the district regarding special education, charter operators in the total-link schools noted that by linking with a district, charter schools can enjoy the benefits of its special education infrastructure. The benefits include technical assistance, a financial safety net, and the multiple specialized instructional personnel charter schools require to deliver appropriate special education programs.

Issues Associated with Partial-Link Status

Partial-link status is defined by the fact that while the charter school is legally independent, there is a legislated requirement for some type of a negotiated relationship between the charter school and an LEA for the purposes of special education. Charter schools in California, Florida, and Minnesota are generally partial-link schools, although the manner in which the linkage manifests itself differs within these states.

Florida charter schools are responsible for hiring special education staff and delivering all special education services. The local district assigns a staffing specialist to supervise the individual charter schools. Local districts pay for these supervisory staff using an administrative fee that they retain from charter schools' budgets. In contrast, charter schools in Minnesota receive all federal and state special education dollars directly and are responsible for hiring their special education staff and delivering all services. However, the Minnesota law contains a provision whereby charter schools may bill a student's local district of residence for excess costs associated with delivering special education services. As a result, while most Minnesota charter schools are substantively independent, nearly all have a financial relationship with local districts. In California, yet another variation of partial-linkage status exists: The law allows a charter school to become its own LEA for special education, although, without that election, the charter school is linked to the LEA in which it is located for purposes of special education.

Similar to total-link schools, partial-link schools in states such as Florida and California must negotiate with their local district regarding how the responsibility to deliver special education is distributed. Given the greater autonomy generally extended to partial-link schools relative to total-link schools, the negotiation process can be awkward. On the one hand, the charter school is autonomous from the district while, on the other hand, it is seeking assistance from the district. In the words of a principal of a partial-link charter, "It is a weird dynamic, the relationship between the charters and the districts." Furthermore, there is tension associated with the negotiations between districts and partial-link charter schools due to charter schools' desire to be independent yet simultaneously rely on the district. A district liaison explained, "If you can be a better grown-up, you can't turn around and be a child [for the purposes of special education]."

The tension between partial-link charter schools and their local districts is exacerbated by the marked gap between what charter operators actually know and what they need to know about special education. Illustrating the lack of knowledge, a charter school special education teacher candidly commented:

> When I first got hired and realized what I was doing, I was really psyched that I got the job. But then I realized as I walked in that I don't have what it takes to do this. I don't know enough. I'm not experienced enough for this. I was really scared to be in the position that I was in. We were dealing with state and federal laws, and if I mess up—I am messing up—I can really be vulnerable in a situation.

In an effort to share responsibilities for special education, charter schools and districts must negotiate their roles and responsibilities. A district liaison who works closely with partial-link charter schools explained that shared responsibility raises challenging issues around who is ultimately responsible for special education.

The oversight and the responsibility to assure that the child is adequately served rest with the district, but the implementation rests with the charter. So if the charter does it poorly, incompletely, not to the satisfaction of the parents, not to the letter of the IEP, the responsibility lies with the district to make sure that it's being done well, but the district isn't actually empowered to make that happen. And that leads to problems sometimes, because it's not well defined in the law.

Approaching the issue from the perspective of autonomy, a district special education administrator who oversees charter schools posed the question, "If a charter school is autonomous but the district still retains some responsibility stemming from IDEA, how does the LEA fulfill its responsibility without impeding the charter school's autonomy?"

Total-link and partial-link charter schools share common characteristics in that they require some degree of negotiation between charter schools and districts, which may or may not be receptive to charter schools. In cases where the district is not receptive to charter schools, the district can use the negotiation process as a means to limit the school's autonomy by adding additional regulations. In the words of a resource center director, "Special education can be the 'gotcha' for the district" to impair charter schools. In state or district environments that may not be particularly supportive of charter schools, special education is one program that districts can use to limit charter schools' autonomy.

Issues Associated with No-Link Status

The third type of linkage, no-link, is defined as a charter school which is legally independent from an LEA and for which any relationship with an LEA for the purposes of special education is entirely voluntary on the part of both entities. Charter schools in the states of Arizona and North Carolina can be described as no-link. The schools are also generally considered legally independent LEAs. As noted previously, LEA status introduces significant responsibilities arising from the guarantees established in the IDEA. Total- and partial-link charter schools are required to some degree to share responsibility for special education with an LEA. No-link charter schools are wholly responsible for providing and financing a full continuum of placements for all children enrolled in their school regardless of the type of disability. These responsibilities range from classroom accommodations and modifications, to related services, and even to financing private residential placements for students with significant disabilities when the no-link charter school cannot meet the child's needs.

The case studies of Arizona and North Carolina documented that while no-link charter schools enjoy the autonomy from higher levels of government associated with their LEA status, the added responsibilities associated with the independence can be challenging. In particular, no-link charter schools struggle at times to amass the financial and human capacity to develop a comprehensive special education program. A special education teacher in a charter school located in a no-link state described the challenge of a single small school functioning as an LEA in the following manner:

> We are not really an LEA. Funding is an issue; it is not enough. We should be in cooperation with a [traditional] LEA. The LRE issue, how can a single school be an LEA and serve all students? The question of reasonable accommodations . . . the reason for charters yet [now charter schools are] changing for the children with disabilities.

Complying with the myriad regulations articulated in the IDEA requires a significant depth of knowledge regarding special education procedures as well as specialized instructional practices. The previously cited knowledge gap among charter schools is particularly troublesome in schools that are autonomous LEAs and thereby responsible for all aspects of special education. As a result, many no-link schools operate in continual ambiguity. They are frequently unsure whether decisions made for a specific student with a disability are indeed legal or appropriate.

A key component of the knowledge gap is that many charter school administrators and teachers are not educators by training and therefore may not be aware of the purposes and practices within special education. Further, neither state or district special education nor charter school administrators may be aware of how little charter school personnel know. A charter school principal explained, "Special education is the most confusing area. If you don't know what questions to ask and [the people] on the other side don't know what people don't know, how can you bridge the gap?"

In order to provide an appropriate special education program, no-link charter schools need to build special education capacity by hiring qualified staff or contracting with third-party providers. However, the more charter schools introduce new professionals into the school or modify their program to fit students with disabilities, the greater the perceived risk of losing sight of the goal or focus of the charter school. For instance, which modifications and accommodations are appropriate in a small, experiential learning–based charter school that tries to utilize the rural landscape for its academic program and which entail significant independent learning? In this type of situation, charter schools must balance their commitment to their mission with their obligations stemming from the IDEA. Securing fiscal, human, and organizational resources that enable them to address their knowledge gap is critical to developing special education capacity.

The evidence from the case studies suggests that to develop the capacity to deliver special education, charter schools may fare better if they affiliate with a special education infrastructure (e.g., an LEA, special education or charter school cooperative, or other service-delivery structure, such as a local nonprofit). In addition, and especially for autonomous, no-link charter schools, regardless of how they affiliate, they require significant early and ongoing technical assistance to meet the multiple complex administrative and instructional requirements stemming from federal disability statutes.

DISCUSSION: BALANCING CHARTER SCHOOL AUTONOMY AND SPECIAL EDUCATION REGULATIONS

The basic bargain of the charter school movement is that schools are granted autonomy and consumer sovereignty in exchange for accountability. In contrast, special education is highly regulated by nature of the fact that the last 30 years have been dedicated to ensuring equal access for *all* students to *all* educational opportunities. The case studies revealed that charter schools' legal identity and linkage to a local district can influence their capacity to deliver special education. Project SEARCH also documented what Heubert (1997) predicted: There is tension associated with complying with special education rules and regulations in an environment perceived to be deregulated. At the district and school level, the tension manifests itself in resistance to special education and sometimes even anger at the fact that special education regulations hinder charter school operators' decision-making autonomy. In the words of a charter school principal, "special education is regulatory reloading" of the requirements presumed to be waived under state charter school laws. A district liaison described charter school operators' reaction to special education paperwork in the following terms: "Charter operators are frustrated. They are looking at the [special education] forms and thinking this is what the charter freed them of."

Beyond the basic misperception regarding the degree to which charter schools are deregulated and autonomous are more subtle incursions into charter schools' independence associated with administering special education programs. For instance, in total- and partial-link charter schools, operators questioned the degree to which they are granted autonomy in light of the continued regulation and, at times, perceived overregulation of charter schools by local districts. District personnel involved with total- and partial-link schools expressed frustration with having to walk the fine line of providing charter schools with operational autonomy yet ultimately being accountable for the special education programs charter schools provide.

Balancing autonomy and regulation also arose regarding the issue of teacher certification. A number of the case study states waive teacher certification requirements for charter schools. The waiver does not extend to special education teachers, who must abide by the federal guidelines requiring that "qualified personnel" educate students with disabilities, which translates into the highest state-level credentials or certification. Charter operators were frustrated that while state law releases them to develop their own hiring qualifications, federal law essentially mitigates this autonomy. The frustration is exacerbated by the practical reality that there is a particularly dire shortage of qualified special education teachers nationwide.

Finally, there is a built-in conflict underlying special education decision making and charter school decision making. To ensure that decisions regarding students' IEPs are made in the best interest of the student, the IEP is developed by a team of school personnel and parents who meet as equal members. The team process ideally ensures that school personnel and parents collaborate to determine what is best for the student based on each one's potentially unique knowledge of the student's needs. In contrast to this team decision-making process, the charter school movement is built on a commitment to consumer sovereignty (i.e., parental choice) and providing parents the opportunity to select a school based on what they alone, or in consultation with their children, perceive is the best choice. Charter schools may liberate parents to make unilateral decisions regarding their children's education. However, by enabling parents to act outside of the traditional IEP team decision-making structure, charter schools simultaneously remove checks and balances in the special education system that are designed to meet children's needs.

CONCLUSIONS AND SUGGESTIONS FOR FUTURE RESEARCH

Charter schools seek autonomy, yet that autonomy can be limited by federal and state mandates regarding the education of students with disabilities. Charter school autonomy raises a host of issues regarding the manner in which new, small, independent schools can amass the human and fiscal capacity necessary to meet the plethora of requirements mandated by the IDEA. Ultimately, the major challenge is how to bridge or integrate the somewhat disparate visions of how charter schools and special education address students' individual educational requirements.

Project SEARCH documented and illustrated that states, districts, and individual charter schools are collectively struggling to comply with the federal disability requirements in charter schools. Regardless of their autonomy, charter schools have the same duties and responsibilities as traditional public schools to provide a free appropriate public education to all students with disabilities. This requirement compels charter school advocates and operators to work with state- and district-level policymakers to find a balance between charter schools' desire to be autonomous and the unique challenges associated with potentially having to provide a comprehensive special education program within a single school. Policymakers must acknowledge that, as the charter school movement grows nationwide, states and districts must develop appropriate infrastructures to support the new and generally unique administrative, fiscal, instructional, and technical assistance requirements of these fledgling autonomous public schools for which states, and in some cases districts, are ultimately responsible.

The linkage typology provides a means for understanding the three key types of relationships existing between charter schools and local districts. It also provides a framework for understanding how state charter school laws and local practices converge to influence charter schools' ability to deliver FAPE to students with disabilities. Additional research analyzing special education in charter schools is necessary. Specifically, questions regarding access, identification policies and procedures, and the manner in which special education and related services are provided in charter schools need to be addressed.

The charter school movement—not unlike the traditional public schools— has viewed special education as a separate program and addressed it after the profusion of other operational details have been addressed. Charter school policymakers and operators need to acknowledge that special education and decisions shaped by special education policies and practices are an integral part of any public school. Furthermore, policymakers and practitioners should give closer attention to special education during the charter school planning, application, and start-up stages in order to integrate students with disabilities in their unique programs. At their best, charter schools hold the potential to introduce new alternatives to the larger menu of strategies to address the unique educational requirements of students with disabilities. Conversely, at their worst, charter schools have the potential to further separate children with disabilities from their peers without disabilities and limit the access of students with disabilities to a free appropriate education in the least restrictive environment. While charter schools may be able to address their knowledge gap and augment their capacity by linking with a district, the policy tension between regulation and autonomy appears to be far more intractable. Future research needs to investigate how autonomous charter schools are building special education capacity and determine to what degree these schools can operate as incubators for innovative general and special education practices.

NOTES

1. This research, entitled Project SEARCH: Special Education as Requirements in Charter Schools, was funded by the Office of Special Education Programs, U.S. Department of Education (Grant #H324C980032). Views expressed in this paper do not reflect the position or policy of the U. S. Department of Education, and no official endorsement by the department should be inferred.

2. The notion of linkage was relatively fluid in some of the case study states. Consequently, while each of the states was categorized by its predominant linkage for the purposes of developing our sample, these categorizations do not necessarily represent the type of linkage documented in each individual school visited within these states.

PART IV

The Impact of Charter Schools on Students

CHAPTER 8

Student Achievement in Charter Schools: What We Know and Why We Know So Little

Gary Miron
Christopher Nelson

Central to the charter school theory of action has been the idea that, through various mechanisms, charter schools would lead to improved student achievement.[1] Education is largely a nonroutine, nonrepetitive task (Rowan, Raudenbush, & Cheong, 1993). Thus, the enhanced autonomy granted to charter school teachers, administrators, and other stakeholders might allow them to better craft educational interventions appropriate for students' unique needs and learning styles, while accountability to markets and government might provide the motivation to improve achievement.

Citing both the relative newness and small number of charter schools, many researchers and oversight agencies have avoided the question of achievement altogether. Recently, with the maturing of the movement, a number of studies have taken up the question of charter schools' impact on student learning and achievement, examining whether or not attending charter schools is leading to improved student learning relative to comparable schools. In this chapter we attempt to summarize what is currently known about the impact of attendance at charter schools on student achievement. We find that evaluations of student achievement in many states offer both evidence of success and disappointments. Our examination of some of the most obvious reasons for variations in the impact of charter school attendance on student achievement does not provide a clear explanation. One important goal of this chapter is to highlight how studies of student achievement (and the data used in them) might be strengthened in future research.

In presenting this synthesis of research on student achievement in charter schools, we are mindful of four important limitations. First, a full assessment of charter schools' effectiveness and overall desirability must examine nonachievement outcomes, such as equity, customer satisfaction and market accountability, the schools' legitimacy in the eyes of key stakeholders, and so on. Moreover, even if student achievement were the only goal of charter schools, standardized test results are only one of many ways to assess it. Few, if any, measurement experts would endorse evaluating a school or student on the basis of standardized tests alone. Second, the research and evaluation literature has not yet produced clear and unambiguous statements of fact about achievement in charter schools. This, in turn, requires stakeholders to weigh the strengths and weaknesses of the evidence.

Third, like any review or meta-analysis, our portrayal of the existing literature is colored by the selection of studies for examination. In this chapter, we have made explicit the rules that guided our search for and selection of studies, and where possible we sought to test our findings' sensitivity to these assumptions. Generally, we have been somewhat surprised at the paucity of studies of student achievement in charter schools and the difficulty we had in obtaining some of the studies. Finally, in the spirit of full disclosure, we must point out that we authored three of the studies covered in this chapter. As readers will see in the next section, we attempted to set out clear evaluative criteria and to apply them fairly to all studies reviewed.

Before presenting our synthesis, the following section outlines expectations for student achievement by reviewing states' testing, reporting, and evaluation requirements for charter schools. The expectations, as noted in state charter school laws, are then contrasted with actual practices. Next, we move to a summary of methodological issues, such as how one should measure student achievement, which studies should be included, how one should evaluate the quality of studies, and how one should combine findings into a "bottom-line" statement of overall charter school impact. The fourth section presents our findings regarding the current knowledge base about student achievement in charter schools. The chapter then closes with a discussion of some preliminary explanations for variations in charter schools' achievement impacts across states and for the dearth of knowledge about student achievement in charter schools.

EXPECTATIONS FOR ACCOUNTABILITY IN CHARTER SCHOOLS

Before summarizing what we know about student achievement in charter schools, we describe the expectations for charter school accountability, particularly as these relate to student achievement. We examine the extent to which charter schools are required to meet state standards and administer state assessments, whether state laws require independent evaluations of charter school performance, and how many states' charter schools have been subject to evaluations or other research studies that include findings on student achievement. This provides the context for the research synthesis.

Standardized Testing

In the spring of 2002, 34 out of 38 charter school laws required charter schools to meet the same standards as noncharter public schools. These 34 laws also required charter schools to administer the same tests as those required by noncharter public schools in these states. All but three states specified the test(s) that must be used. Sixteen percent of the states required both criterion-referenced and norm-referenced tests. In 77% of the states, only a criterion-referenced test was required, and in 6.5% of the states only a norm-referenced test was required.

Evaluations of Charter School Reforms

The testing requirements noted above suggest that there is the potential for many evaluations of charter schools' impact on achievement. However, our review of documentation and literature turned up some surprising findings. First of all, few states actually require independent evaluations. In total, we found reference to required independent evaluations in only 3 states. In 15 states, however, the state board of education or the state department of education is expected to submit an annual descriptive report to the state's legislature regarding the status of the charter schools. In some states such reports are completed only irregularly. Most descriptive reports prepared by state education agencies contain only brief profiles of the schools with little or no reference to the academic progress of students.

Legal requirements notwithstanding, we found that 19 states plus the District of Columbia conducted evaluations. At least 4 additional states have evaluations under way. Eight of the 19 state evaluations were excluded either because they did not consider student achievement, were quite dated and/or of limited scope, or have not yet released completed evaluation reports. In total, 11 states and the District of Columbia had 17 evaluations or studies that considered student achievement in charter schools that are included in our analysis (the selection criteria we used is detailed in the next section).

Other things being equal, one would expect to see evaluations in states with long-standing charter school laws and/or a large number of charter schools in operation. However, we found a number of states with such characteristics but with no evaluations of student achievement across schools, including Florida, Massachusetts, Minnesota, and Wisconsin. While the latter three states have conducted evaluations of charter schools, they have not produced any comprehensive evaluation that examines charter schools' impact on student achievement. Delaware, Hawaii, Kansas, New Mexico, and South Carolina are examples of other states where we expected—and failed—to find an evaluation of charter schools, since these states had laws in place by 1996 or earlier and have 6 or more schools in operation.

STUDY METHODS

Attempts to synthesize existing research are usually sensitive to a number of key methodological decisions. For this reason, we clearly describe the criteria we use for *selecting* studies as well as the methods we have used for *summarizing* each study's key findings in this section and assigning a *quality weight* to each. Finally, we describe how we combined the impact and quality ratings given to each study into a synthesis of findings. Quality ratings are especially important in a synthesis of charter school research given the wide variety of methodological rigor across studies. Our approach has been to include studies with substantial limitations but to give them less weight than other studies. In this way, our approach differs from that of a recent research synthesis by RAND (Gill, Timpane, Ross, & Brewer, 2001), which considered only three relatively high-quality studies of charter schools' achievement impact and did not weight the studies based on quality.

Selecting Studies

In deciding which studies to include, we applied six criteria:

- Clear description of analytical procedures used
- Presence of aggregate analysis and conclusions
- Use of standardized tests to measure student achievement
- Use of comparison groups (if multiple analyses, used methodologically strongest findings)
- Quality of sample/scope of study
- Recency (include most recent version of serial reports)

First, we included only studies that provide a clear account of the analytical procedures used. Because such descriptions facilitate replication, they add credibility to the findings. Second, we excluded studies that did not *analyze* student achievement data (e.g., studies that include only tables of scores, not aggregate analysis). Third, our synthesis is restricted to studies that analyze standardized test results, as they often provide the only way to compare achievement in a wide range of charter and noncharter schools. Fourth, we selected studies that used comparison groups, as any attempt to assess charter schools' achievement impact requires some understanding of what student achievement of those students in charter schools might have looked like in the absence of these schools (in other words, the impact of charter schools on student achievement). While randomized experiments with control groups are the best way to determine impact, practical considerations have limited charter school researchers to observing "naturally" occurring comparison groups of noncharter schools.[2] Many studies include analyses based on a variety of research designs. In each instance, we have included only the methodologically strongest findings (later in this section we explain the ratings of methodological quality).

The last two criteria for the selection of studies concern the quality of the sample and recency of the studies. Available studies of achievement in charter schools have been largely restricted to single states. (The lack of cross-state comparisons of student achievement is most likely due to the difficulty of making comparisons across schools subject to different state testing regimes. See Miron and Applegate [2000] and Nelson and Applegate [2002] for methods for studying charter schools' achievement impact *across* states.) We have focused on studies conducted on entire states or significant portions thereof. Quite simply, studies that focus on only a handful of "case" schools are unlikely to produce findings that can be generalized to the larger population of schools in a state.[3]

Finally, in cases where a report by a given author or group has been updated or superseded by a more comprehensive analysis with the same study design, we have included only findings from the most recent study. In four states we included two or more studies in the analysis because they used different methodologies or substantially different sources of data.[4]

Summarizing Key Findings

For our purposes, the key finding in each study was an assessment of charter schools' *impact* on student achievement. It is important to bear in mind that impact is not necessarily synonymous with absolute achievement *levels*. For example, a charter school with low absolute scores might still add a significant amount of value if its students are gaining at a faster rate than noncharter public schools with similar students. Conversely, a charter school with high absolute scores might not be adding value to its students if student gains are not as large as (or are growing at a slower rate than) noncharter public schools with similar students.

In this analysis, we have given each study a rating according to the scale shown in Table 8.1, with positive values indicating that charter schools serve to increase student achievement and negative values indicating that they decrease student achievement.[5] Table 8.2 includes summaries of the findings that were the basis for our impact ratings. Due to the wide variety of measures and methods employed across the studies, it would be difficult, if not impossible, to derive an overall "effect size" (see, e.g., Hedges & Olkin, 1985; Light & Pillemer, 1984).

Quantifying findings in this way is a useful but imperfect tool. As such, readers should not read too much meaning into small differences in average ratings. Instead, the quantitative methods used here help supplement "eyeballing" of the data by allowing us to systematically combine information about both the studies' findings and aspects of their design quality.

Assessing the Quality of the Studies

Once selected, studies were rated on four dimensions of overall quality: (1) design quality (as shown in Table 8.2), or the quality of the study's quasi-experimental design (e.g., construction and use of comparison groups); (2) the number of years in which student achievement was observed; (3) the proportion of charter schools included from a state; and (4) the range of grade levels for which achievement data are analyzed. All four attributes were combined into a rating of overall study quality.

Generally speaking, the strongest studies employ a combination of these strategies. Solmon, Paark, and Garcia's (2001) analysis of Arizona charter schools, for instance, tracks individual test score gains over 3 years *and* includes a comparison group of traditional public school students matched on

Table 8.1. Scale for impact ratings of studies of student achievement in charter school

Scale Value	Description
2	Positive overall impact
1	Mixed to slightly positive overall impact
0	Mixed impact
-1	Mixed to slightly negative overall impact
-2	Negative overall impact

prior test score, grade level, and a number of other factors.[6] In addition, the study employs a number of rigorous statistical controls, including fixed and random effects models that control for unmeasured student-level differences. The weakest studies, by contrast, simply make cross-sectional comparisons between charter and noncharter schools, often without controls for pre-existing differences among charter and noncharter students.

In order to combine information on findings regarding both impact and study quality, we calculated an average impact rating weighted by the quality criteria outlined above.

THE IMPACT OF CHARTER SCHOOLS ON STUDENT ACHIEVEMENT

Table 8.2 provides brief details about the studies selected for review and analysis. Careful inspection of the table reveals extensive variation in the scope and quality of the studies and in the nature of the findings. For each study, the table includes information used in the analysis, including grade levels covered, the number of years included in the study, a brief summary of key findings, the impact rating (according to the criteria shown in Table 8.1), and a design quality rating. Close examination of the table reveals a wide range in both impact and quality.

Overall, the charter school impact on achievement is mixed (–0.18 on the impact rating scale in Table 8.1). A few studies provide evidence of a substantial positive charter school effect. Solmon, Paark, & Garcia's (2001) analysis of Stanford Achievement Test (SAT9) scores in Arizona, for instance, found that charter schools had a significant positive impact on SAT9 scores in reading and a mixed to positive impact in math. At the other end of the spectrum, all three studies of achievement in Michigan charter schools are, for the most part, negative. Eberts and Hollenbeck (2002), for instance, found that Michigan charter schools scored between 2% and 4% lower than comparable host districts on state criterion-referenced examinations. The Miron and Nelson (2002) study was slightly less negative, finding that charter school trends were either indistinguishable from or lower than those of their host districts in all grades and areas except fifth-grade science. Similarly, Bettinger (1999) reported generally negative findings; however, he found weak evidence that charter schools had moved some students out of the "low" category on the state examination. Findings from Texas by Gronberg and Jansen (2001) and the Texas Education Agency (2002) represent the middle of the spectrum. These studies found that while charter schools showed smaller gains on the state test than noncharter schools, schools classified by the state as "at risk" outgained comparable noncharter public schools.

Table 8.2. Summary of studies included in this synthesis

State	Citation	Design Quality Rating*	Years Covered	Proportion of Schools†	Grade Levels	Impact Rating	Summary of Findings
AZ	Mulholland (1999)	3	1996/97–1997/98	2	2-11	Mixed (0)	Mixed, with nonsignificant gains in some grades and subjects. No difference overall.
AZ	Solmon, Paark, & Garcia (2001)	4	1996/97–1998/99	2	2-11	Positive (2)	Positive in reading; slightly positive in math.
CA	Rogosa (2002)[7]	3	1998/99–2000/01	3	2-11	Mixed Negative(-1)	Charter school students gained less on the API index than noncharter schools. Same finding when matching only socially disadvantaged students in both groups.
CO	Andras (2002)	1	2001/02	2	3, 4, 5	Mixed (0)	Mixed results. Most differences with matched schools were less than 0.5 percent.
CO	Colorado Department of Education (2002)	1	2000/01	2	4, 5, 7, & 9	Mixed/ Positive (1)	Mildly positive at grades 4 and 5, stronger positive at grade 7.
CT	Miron & Horn (2002)	3	1997/98–2001/02	3	4, 6, 8, & 10	Mixed/ Positive (1)	On average, charter schools gained more than comparison groups, and by the end of 5 years they have matched or surpassed absolute scores of comparison groups.
DC	Henig, Holyoke, Lacireno-Paquet,& Moser (2001)	2	1999/00–2000/01	2	1-11	Negative (-2)	Charter schools less likely to have improved, more likely to have declined than host district schools.
GA	Georgia Department of Education (2001)	2	1998/99–2000/01	2	4, 6, 8, 11	Mixed/ Positive (1)	10 out of 14 schools decreasing relative to comparison group; 4 out of 14 increasing.
MI	Bettinger (1999)	3	1996/97–1998/99	1	4 & 7	Negative (-2)	Generally negative, though charter schools show some success (nonrobust) in moving students out of the "low" category.

168

State	Study		Years		Grades	Rating	Findings
MI	Eberts & Hollenbeck (2002)[8]	3	1996/97–2000/01	3	4 & 5	Negative (-2)	Negative charter schools score 2% to 4% lower than comparable noncharter public schools.
MI	Miron & Nelson (2002)	2	1995/96–1999/00	3	4, 5, 7, & 8	Mixed/Negative (-1)	Slightly positive for math 4; slightly negative for math 7, science 5 & 8; negative for reading 4 & 7, write 5 & 8.
NC	Noblit & Corbett (2001)	3.5	1997/98–2000/01	1	3-8	Mixed/Negative (-1)	Most charter school students had higher initial scores but lost ground against noncharter students.
NJ	KPMG (2001)	2	1998/99–1999/00	1	4 & 8	Mixed/Positive (1)	Positive in math 4 and language 8: negative in language 8, science 4, and math 8.
OH	LOEO (2002)	1	1999/00	1	4 & 6	Mixed/Negative (-1)	Most differences not significant, but of those that were significant 22 favored traditional public schools and 8 favored charter schools.
PA	Miron, Nelson, & Risley (2002)	3	1997/98–2001–02	3	5, 8, & 11	Mixed/Positive (1)	Fifty-seven percent of the charter schools outgained demographically similar public schools.
TX	Gronberg & Jansen (2001)	4	1996/97–1999/00	2	3-8	Mixed/Positive (1)	Negative for all schools (-.909 on TLI) and non-at-risk schools (-1.56 on TLI). Positive for at-risk schools (+.759 on TLI)[9]
TX	Texas Education Agency (2002)	1	1998/99–2000/01	2	3-10	Mixed/Negative (-1)	Over three years charter schools had negative change scores while noncharter public schools showed gains on the TAAS.

* Design quality ratings are based on the quasi-experimental design used in the study (the highest quality of design received a 4). Ratings were based on the following scale: 4 = Analysis of individual-level change scores along with inclusion of strong statistical controls and/or bloc king; 3 = Analysis of consecutive cohorts with comparison group and statistical controls; 2 = Analysis of consecutive cohorts with a comparison group but no statistical controls; 1 = Analysis of consecutive cohorts or cross-sectional analysis with comparison group.

† Studies with 67% or more of the schools considered in the analysis received a 3, studies with between 33% and 66% received a 2, and studies with less than 33 percent of the schools considered in the analysis received a 1.

To provide some sense of how strong a "positive" effect is, it is useful to consider the effect sizes reported in a handful of the studies. Some of the most strongly positive findings come from Solmon and colleagues' (2001) study of Arizona charter schools. In this study, however, the average gain among charter school students was a tenth of a standard deviation. As a point of comparison, research on class size reductions has suggested effect sizes of a third of a standard deviation. On the other side of the spectrum, Eberts and Hollenbeck's (2002) more negative findings from Michigan suggest that charter schools lag behind by 9% to 10%.

As noted above in Table 8.1, we found that the unweighted average across all studies was –0.18. In substantive terms, this suggests that, as a group, the studies provide a mixed picture of the charter school effect; three studies were strongly negative, five were mixed/negative, two were mixed, six were mixed/positive, and one was strongly positive. Mixed/positive, mixed, and mixed/negative ratings may reflect one of two scenarios. In one, large gains (losses) in some charter schools are offset by losses (gains) in other charter schools, yielding a mixed-achievement impact. In the other scenario, the achievement effect is consistent across charter schools but small in magnitude. Overall, the impact ratings are widely dispersed, if very weakly negative. Due to the importance of considering study quality as well as findings, we turn now to a discussion of the quality of the studies examined and how this affects our bottom-line assessment of charter schools' impact on student achievement.

As discussed above, these findings were generated by studies of varying methodological quality. Overall, the sum of the four quality ratings ranged from a low of 5 to a high of 20, with an average overall quality rating of 12.5. It is important to note that even studies earning the highest rating may suffer from methodological limitations.

As it turns out, introducing weights for quality changes the overall picture very little. Whereas the average *unweighted* impact rating was –0.18, the average *weighted* impact rating was –0.16 (when we used alternative weighting schemes and tested the effect of eliminating lower-quality studies, the findings remained essentially the same). Thus, irrespective of study quality, the main finding is that charter schools appear to have a negligible (if slightly negative) aggregate net impact on student achievement. As discussed above, however, there also appears to be considerable variations across states.

EXPLAINING VARIATIONS ACROSS STATES

As noted earlier, states vary in significant ways in how they have put the charter school idea into practice, with differences including the laws themselves, the process of implementation, and resources provided to charter schools. These variations create an opportunity for researchers to identify the policy-related and other conditions under which charter schools can have a positive (or negative) impact on student achievement. In the spirit of states as the "laboratories of democracy," researchers might be able to identify "policy levers" in some states that could be used to guide reforms in other states.

While a thorough investigation of the reasons for success among charter schools is well beyond the scope of this chapter, we did investigate a number of fairly straightforward explanations for variations in observed charter impact across the states, including "strength" of law and the frequency with which charter schools have been closed. Neither variable appears to explain variations in charter schools' impacts on student achievement. As for strength of law, one finds low and high performers (e.g., Michigan and Arizona) among the ranks of states receiving a grade of A in the Center for Education Reform's (CER) rating system. (In the CER rating system, the laws most supportive of charter schools receive an A, while less supportive laws receive Bs, Cs, Ds, and Fs.) The same holds for the frequency of closures, where both high- and low-performing states (e.g., Arizona and the District of Columbia) have closed a relatively high proportion of their schools (Table 8.3 presents data on these background factors). Clearly, there are other variables at work. These might include indicators of the extent and nature of oversight other than school closures. In Michigan, for instance, there is little evidence that most university authorizers (who hold the lion's share of charters in the state) provide effective oversight of the schools they authorize (Michigan Office of the Auditor General, 2002; Miron & Nelson, 2002). Other possible correlates might include teacher quality, funding, class size, and availability of support and technical assistance.

WHY WE KNOW SO LITTLE ABOUT STUDENT ACHIEVEMENT IN CHARTER SCHOOLS

This chapter set out to answer two questions about charter schools' impact on student achievement. First, what do we know about it? Second, why do we know so little? Indeed, perhaps more striking than the substantive findings of the studies is how few studies there are and how few states these studies cover. In this section we briefly speculate about some of the reasons for the paucity of good empirical evidence.

One set of reasons revolves around limitations in the availability of achievement data. First, some states (e.g., New Hampshire) have only a few charter schools, limiting the utility of statewide evaluations of charter school

Table 8.3. Summary of findings, study quality, and explanatory factors by state

State	CER Rating	Year of Law	Number of Schools in 2001	Percent Schools Closed	Number of Studies	Average Design Quality Rating	Average Impact Rating
AZ	A	1994	419	4.7%	2	3.5	1.0
DC	A	1996	41	5.0%	1	2.0	-2.0
MI	A	1993	187	3.1%	3	2.7	-1.7
CA	B	1992	358	2.1%	1	3.0	-1.0
CO	B	1993	89	0.5%	2	1.0	0.5
NC	B	1996	96	8.2%	1	3.5	-1.0
NJ	B	1996	55	3.5%	1	2.0	1.0
OH	B	1997	68	2.8%	1	1.0	-1.0
PA	B	1997	77	1.5%	1	3.0	1.0
TX	B	1995	214	5.9%	2	2.5	0.1
CT	C	1996	16	11.1%	1	3.0	1.0
GA	C	1993	46	0.0%	1	2.0	1.0

Note: Source of information regarding ratings for charter school law is from the Center for Education Reform (CER). Data on other background data are from CER and respective state education agencies.

achievement. Second, even in states with large numbers of charter schools, a large portion of them have been open for only a few years, leaving many schools with little or no student achievement data to report. Third, many states test students at only a few grade levels. As a consequence, in a state that does not test students until the fifth grade, there will be no broadly comparable student achievement data from charter schools offering only lower elementary grades. Fourth, student confidentiality policies often prohibit reporting scores from small schools (e.g., with fewer than 10 students taking any given subject and grade-level test), many of which are charter schools. Finally, a few states have recently changed testing regimes, thus severely limiting evaluators' ability to make reliable comparisons in student achievement over time.

Data limitations notwithstanding, in some states charter schools apparently collect student achievement data but do not report it to a centralized source. This leaves evaluators with the difficult task of collecting data—sometimes based on different tests—from schools scattered across large geographical areas. Furthermore, in a few states charter schools report accountability data to local authorities or sponsoring agencies, not the state education agency. Once again, this dramatically increases data-collection costs for would-be evaluators. We have sought in many of our own statewide evaluations to collect norm-referenced test data directly from schools. However, a combination of reluctance on the part of charter school officials and the sheer scale of the task yielded little usable data.

Finally, political factors may discourage state officials and others from commissioning, sponsoring, and funding statewide evaluations of charter school achievement. Similar to Levin's (2001) discussion of cost-effectiveness analyses, high-profile, statewide evaluations of charter schools' impacts on student achievement may appear threatening to policymakers since unexpected findings might diminish the credibility of popular policy approaches. Officials, in short, might decide that commissioning a high-profile, statewide evaluation is not worth the risk. Similarly, many core policy questions related to charter schools are imbued with fundamental value questions, such as the intrinsic value of choice, the moral weight one gives to the often competing goals of equity and efficiency, and so on (Godwin & Kemerer, 2002; Miron & Nelson, 2002). Since such fundamental value judgments are not grounded in empirical knowledge, evaluation studies about charter schools and student achievement may seem beside the point to policymakers and stakeholders attempting to grapple with these issues.

CONCLUSION

This chapter sought to summarize what is currently known about charter schools' impacts on student achievement. The question is of paramount importance given that at the heart of the charter school concept lies a bargain whereby the schools received enhanced autonomy in exchange for greater accountability for student outcomes. As we have stated, student achievement is not the only relevant student outcome, but certainly it is among the most important outcomes of charter schools.

Overall, we find that the existing body of research on charter schools' impacts on student achievement reveals a mixed picture, with studies from some states suggesting positive impacts, studies from other states suggesting negative impacts, and some providing evidence of both positive and negative impacts. Of the methodologically strongest studies, the strongest positive findings come from Arizona, while the strongest negative findings come from Michigan. The inclusion of relatively lower-quality studies does little to change this mixed view of charter schools' impact on student achievement.

In spite of the topic's importance to the debate over charter schools and school reform, it is striking how little we currently know about charter schools' impact on student achievement. As discussed above, we found usable independent evaluations of achievement impacts in only 11 states plus the District of Columbia. Leaving aside the recently enacted state laws, as well as the states with laws but no currently operating charter schools, this amounts to less than a third of the states with charter school laws. If we restrict our view to relatively high-quality studies, there are such studies for only five states. Thus, any conclusions drawn from the body of existing research on charter schools must be treated with an appropriate degree of skepticism. The reasons for the lack of evidence—as discussed in the previous section—include limitations in state testing regimes, charter schools' failure to report data, state agencies' failure to collect such data centrally, and political motivations.

Given the available data, we cannot yet identify any clear explanations for variations in charter school performance among states. Exploring such explanations is important because the ways in which the charter school concept is operationalized and implemented varies substantially across the states. Identifying the factors behind such variations might yield important insights about what types of conditions are most likely to support successful charter schools.

During the next few years, we expect to see many more studies. Also, we can expect the overall quality of studies to continue to improve as there will be more years of data and larger numbers of charter schools considered in the studies. We can also expect better test data to become available as states strengthen their accountability systems and as new policies, such as the No Child Left Behind Act, force states to test students at more grade levels.

In summary, our knowledge of charter schools' impacts on student achievement is still in its infancy, in spite of the fact that the movement is now 10 years old. Indeed, state policymakers need to consider ways to improve the "evaluability" of charter schools through improvements in data-collection and testing practices.[10] Policy decisions, however, usually cannot wait for the emergence of scientific certainty. Thus, in the meantime evaluators and researchers should seek out new data sources and reanalyze data from existing studies in order to learn more about charter schools' impacts on student achievement. Without such efforts by both policymakers and researchers, the charter concept's promises about performance accountability might eventually ring hollow.

NOTES

1. This chapter is based on an occasional paper prepared for the National Center for the Study of Privatization in Education (www.ncspe.org). This occasional paper contains a more thorough description of the methods used and describes in great detail the various weighting schemes used. Revisions and updating of the work have been supported by a field-initiated activities grant (84.282F) from the U.S. Department of Education.

2. Inasmuch as many charter schools are oversubscribed and most state laws require schools to select students at random from their waiting lists, randomized experiments of the sort used to evaluate voucher programs ought to be possible, in principle. However, our fieldwork in charter schools suggests that charter school waiting lists are often insufficient for the construction of a good randomized experiment, since they are often out of date, contain a cumulation of names over a number of years, and sometimes cannot be produced for review when requested.

3. It should be pointed out that there were very few studies left out due to this criterion. Two examples are evaluations of California charter schools by SRI International (1997) and WestEd (1998), which examined student achievement in a handful of schools (the latter in the Los Angeles area only).

4. For example, in Michigan, we excluded the earlier evaluations by Horn and Miron (1999, 2000) since they were superseded by the analysis reported in Miron and Nelson (2002), which considered more years of data than the 1999 evaluation and applied a more sophisticated methodology than the 2000 evaluation. We also excluded two evaluations conducted by Public Sector Consultants (Khouri, Kleine, White, & Cummings, 1999; Kleine, Scott, & White, 2000) since they used a similar design but included fewer years of data and only covered half the charter schools in the state. At the same time, two other studies were included because they used different study designs.

5. Readers should bear in mind that our 5-point scale might understate the variation in impacts found across studies.

6. As Nelson and Hollenbeck (2001) pointed out, however, this unusually strong sampling design is not reflected in the authors' interpretation of their statistical results.

7. The Rogosa (2002) study was prepared in response to a study conducted by researchers at California State University, Los Angeles (Slovacek, Kunnan, & Kim, 2002). Because of errors in coding the data and flaws in the data analysis, we chose not to include the Slovacek and colleagues study, even though it received substantial national media coverage. The Rogosa study used the same data and came up with slightly different results (slightly negative rather than slightly positive for charter schools). In addition to replicating the analyses conducted by Slovacek and colleagues, the Rogosa study also utilized more rigorous designs and comparison groups.

8. While this chapter uses individual-level student data, by and large it cannot trace individual changes over time. Thus, we have given this study a design quality rating of 3 rather than 4.

9. An important caveat about the design quality ratings is that the scale implicitly assumes that movement from one level to the next is equal across the levels. For instance, it is assumed that the quality advantage of a 4 study over a 3 study is exactly the same as the advantage of a 3 over a 2 and a 2 over a 1. This assumption is somewhat arbitrary. Having issued this caution, we proceed with the analysis in the absence of a clearly superior alternative.

10. We provided some preliminary recommendations for improving state data collection and testing practices in Horn and Miron (2000) and Miron and Nelson (2000).

Lighting Out for the Territory: Charter Schools and School Reform Strategy

David N. Plank
Gary Sykes

But I reckon I got to light out for the territory ahead of the rest, because Aunt Sally she's going to adopt me and sivilize me, and I can't stand it. I been there before.

—*Huckleberry Finn*, Mark Twain

There are a number of stories that have a permanent resonance in American politics. Among the most familiar is the one in which the virtuous people struggle to defend the public good against an array of powerful special interests. In another, the valiant sheriff stands tall against a host of villains and restores decency and order to the community. These stories echo through our political life, in debates over issues ranging from estate taxes to missile defense.

Perhaps the most powerful of all these stories, however, is the founding American story, the story about leaving the corruption and complexity of the Old World behind and creating a better, simpler, freer life beyond the frontier. This story has animated pioneers and reformers since the Pilgrims landed at Plymouth Rock to build their city on a hill. The opportunity to start over, to dispense with entanglements, to shake off the burden of past mistakes and "light out for the territory" and a new life is the essential American story. It is repeated over and over again, in sermons, folk songs, novels, and movies. It is a recurrent theme in our politics as well.

In education policy debates, the founding American story finds its clearest recent expression in the movement to establish charter schools. The prospect of starting over with a clean slate, freed from school codes and union rules, is as irresistible to contemporary reformers as was the prospect of settling a New World to the Pilgrims in 1620. Rather than struggling with the bitter and frustrating work of improving the public schools we have, reformers see in charter schools the tantalizing prospect of creating new schools, untainted by the corruption and complexity of the current system. The persistent appeal of this story attracts advocates and defenders for charter schools from nearly all points on the political spectrum, from the communitarian left to the fundamentalist right.

CHARTER SCHOOLS AND SCHOOL REFORM STRATEGY

The founding American story is really two stories. First, of course, it is a story about leaving the Old World behind. In addition, though, it is a story about creating a New World, freed from the "sivilizing" constraint of Europe (or Hannibal, Missouri). The move to create charter schools relies on both of these stories. On the one hand, charter schools offer parents a way out, an opportunity to escape from schools they dislike and enroll their children in new schools, beyond the boundaries of the regular public school system. At the same time, reformers look to charter schools as pioneers, exploring new possibilities and offering inspiration and guidance to those left behind in traditional public schools.

The fundamental bargain behind the creation of charter schools is the exchange of increased autonomy for enhanced accountability. Charter schools are released from some of the rules and red tape that are believed to constrain the performance of traditional public schools. In return, they agree to be held to account for the accomplishment of specific outcomes, which are often spelled out in the schools' authorizing documents. The idea behind this bargain is that charter schools should be held accountable for the results that they achieve, rather than for the means that they use to achieve them. Relief from the obligation to comply with the myriad regulations in the school code provides charter schools with greater administrative flexibility and frees them to experiment with new and perhaps better ways of educating young people.

Like the Puritans' city on a hill, charter schools are expected to make the world better in two distinct ways. First of all, they are supposed to be successful schools in their own right, for their own students. Relieved of the burden of regulation and focused on results, charter schools are expected to provide better schooling for their students than those youngsters could obtain in the Old World of regular public schools. Beyond this, the advent of charter schools is supposed to encourage improvement in the traditional public school system. By taking advantage of their enhanced autonomy to experiment and innovate, charter schools should provide examples to traditional public schools of new and different ways of organizing schools and delivering instruction. In addition, competition from charter schools is expected to provide a powerful incentive for traditional public schools to improve their own performance in order to protect their claims on students and revenues.

WHAT DO WE KNOW ABOUT CHARTER SCHOOLS?

What do the preceding chapters tell us about the efficacy of charter schools as a strategy for school reform? Is the strategy working? Are charter schools better than traditional public schools? Are traditional public schools improving as they compete with charter schools? The authors of the preceding chapters deliver mixed reviews.

On the bright side, charter schools are often different—and sometimes very different—from traditional public schools in the ways in which they are organized and managed. As both Chapters 4 and 6 show, the administrative flexibility extended to charter schools by state legislatures has produced a widely varied assortment of schools. Some charter schools remain an integral part of traditional school districts, but many operate independently. Some charter schools have been founded by groups of teachers seeking a more productive or congenial work environment. Others have been founded by community groups aiming to create a more supportive learning environment for their children. For-profit private companies manage a growing number of charter schools under a variety of contractual arrangements. Charter school administrators have introduced a variety of innovations including alternative schedules, nontraditional hiring, and differential pay for teachers (Podgursky & Ballou, 2001). Many of these experiments remain local, but they nevertheless offer valuable examples of new ways of organizing schools.

Whether charter schools are developing promising new instructional practices is less certain. On the one hand, Chapter 3 suggests that charter schools use their autonomy to implement effective literacy practice. In contrast, Chapter 4 raises theoretical and empirical doubts about whether much innovation in instruction has occurred or will occur in charter schools. Chapter 1 shows that charter school teachers are generally less qualified and less experienced than their counterparts in traditional public schools, while Chapter 2 suggests that the professional opportunities provided for charter school teachers look very much like the professional opportunities available to teachers in traditional public schools.

According to the evidence presented in this volume, charter schools look very much like traditional public schools in terms of teacher qualifications and professional commitment, student achievement, and instructional practice. So far, at least, flexibility and diversity in administration and governance do not seem to have produced generalized improvements in the education that charter schools provide for their students. Some charters are extraordinarily good and others are astonishingly bad—but this is equally true of traditional public schools. In the absence of generalized improvements in the academic performance of charter schools, however, there is little reason to believe that competition from charter schools will encourage general improvements in the academic performance in the rest of the public school system.

WHAT DON'T WE KNOW ABOUT CHARTER SCHOOLS?

The original charter school is barely a decade old. Most charter schools have been in operation for only a few years. Because they are still a relatively new feature of the educational landscape, it is still too early to draw firm conclusions about how charter schools are doing or about how they are affecting the traditional public school system. In our view, three lines of research can begin to provide answers to some of the big questions about the long-term impact of charter schools on the American education system.

Charter Schools and the Emerging Market for Schooling

Charter schools mark an important first step toward the creation of a competitive market for schooling. Understanding how this market works is critically important for evaluating the performance of charter schools and for designing effective strategies for school improvement. At present we know relatively little about this market on either the demand side or the supply side. Additional research can help us to answer two key questions. First, how do parents choose schools? Second, how do traditional public schools respond to competition from charter schools?

On the demand side, understanding how charter schools will affect the education system requires us to understand how parents make choices among the schools available for their children. Markets produce what consumers want. If parents demand high-quality schooling for their children, then that is what charter schools will seek to produce. Parents who choose charter schools may base their choices on other considerations, however. If parents are seeking schools that are closer to home or that reflect and honor their own culture and values, the hope that charter schools will provide schooling of higher quality than that available in the traditional public schools is unlikely to be realized.

On the supply side, we need to know more about how charter schools compete with traditional public schools and how traditional public schools respond to the new competitive pressures introduced into the education system by charter schools. Do charter schools aspire to compete on the basis of academic performance or something else? For example, do they seek to target niche markets defined by communal affinities or shared values? If they seek to compete on quality, then we might expect to see charter schools leading the way toward the identification of new and better strategies for delivering instruction. If they seek to compete on other factors, however, there is little reason to suppose that charter schools will develop effective new instructional strategies or practices, or that they will achieve academic results that are generally superior to those observed in traditional public schools.

We also need to learn more about how traditional public schools respond in the newly competitive market for schooling. School-choice advocates often assume that public school educators will respond aggressively to competition, improving the performance of their schools in order to retain their claims on resources (Chubb & Moe, 1990; Hoxby, 2001). Other responses are also possible, however. As Hirschman (1970) observed many years ago, the way in which organizations respond to decline depends on a variety of factors, including the perceived character of the competitive challenge (i.e., why are parents leaving?) and the availability of organizational "slack" (i.e., does the organization have the capacity to reallocate resources and do things differently?). Some schools may indeed seek to improve their performance in order to attract prospective students, but others may respond differently. Some may deal with competition like Hirschman's "lazy monopolist," who is content to let troublesome students leave in order to minimize conflict and disruption. Still others may lack the capacity to mount an effective response; competition may launch these districts on an accelerating spiral of decline (Arsen, Plank, & Sykes, 1999). For now, we know too little about the distribution of these responses and about the likely consequences of increased competition for the performance of the traditional public school system.

Diversity and Difference in Charter Schools

The observed diversity among charter schools may provide valuable leverage for researchers seeking to understand "what works" (and what doesn't) in efforts to improve school performance. Considered as a class, the performance of charter schools when compared with traditional public schools is mixed, as the chapters in this volume show. There is nevertheless a growing body of anecdotal evidence from charter schools in several states which suggests that some schools may be quite effective at raising achievement for poor students, developing promising instructional practices, involving parents in community formation, and other desirable outcomes. The next generation of studies should begin to disaggregate the population of charter schools on criteria including curricular choices, management status, governance arrangements, and so on in order to systematically explore the differences among schools that are associated with effective operation and successful outcomes.

The Rules Matter

From the point of view of school reform strategy, the wide variation in state laws governing charter schools provides a remarkable opportunity to examine how different policy choices affect the character and performance of charter schools across states. Different rules create different incentives for authorizers, educational management organizations (EMOs), educators, and parents, and different incentives are likely to produce different outcomes. Research that focuses on the relationship between the policy choices made by legislatures and the populations of charter schools produced by these choices promises important new insights into the efficacy of charter schools as a strategy for accomplishing specific reform objectives. In addition, of course, such research can offer valuable guidance for legislators and others engaged in the task of developing or revising charter school policies at the state level.

WHAT'S NEXT FOR CHARTER SCHOOLS?

Having left Aunt Sally and the NEA behind, can charter school educators—at large beyond the frontier—resist the encroachments and blandishments of the civilization that they ostensibly left behind? Can they encourage general improvement in the American education system? What does the future hold for charter schools? In our view, the answers to these questions are likely to feature two complementary trends—social differentiation and institutional domestication.

First, charter schools reflect a response to a continuing trend toward social differentiation in the education system. As Chapter 5 suggests, the creation of charter schools can be interpreted as an effort to revive and protect "premodern" and "tribal" ideals of community, which can help to rescue their members from the homogenizing constraint of the modern secular state. In keeping with the founding American story, charter schools offer parents an opportunity to escape *from* the educational mistakes of the 20th century (Ravitch, 2000) by moving beyond the public school frontier. They simultaneously provide an opportunity to escape *to* a safer and more comfortable world, in which schools better reflect the culture and values of the parents and students who patronize them. In this version of the charter school story, the traditional American ideal of the common school is discredited and abandoned in favor of providing a variety of schools that are better adapted to the values and interests of particular groups.

Second, policy and administrative realities are creating pressures for the institutional domestication of charter schools. The fundamental bargain that motivated the move to charter schools—increased autonomy in exchange for improved outcomes—is shifting decisively against autonomy and toward closer regulation of charter schools (Mintrom & Plank, 2001). As Chapter 4 points out and several other chapters echo, charter schools are coming to look more and more like regular public schools. The move to hire EMOs often has a standardizing effect, because charter schools subject to the profit-maximizing goals of EMOs may focus on the goal of attracting as many students as possible at the expense of a distinctive mission. The pressure to maximize enrollments and revenues introduces the same kinds of homogenizing pressures that oblige traditional public school systems to try to satisfy all the diverse preferences expressed by their clients and constituents. In addition, as Chapter 7 concludes, the federal rules that govern special education also limit the opportunities available to charter schools to look very different from traditional public schools.

One need not attribute the trend toward domestication to the malevolence of teachers unions or the cowardice of legislators; charter schools are public schools spending public money, and it is not surprising that citizens and taxpayers want to know where it goes. Moreover, state legislators now find themselves under intense and increasing pressure to demonstrate improvement in the performance of public schools, according to standardized criteria. The federal No Child Left Behind legislation reflects the recognition that leaving choices about schooling up to communities and states, let alone families and "tribes," may not satisfy public expectations for student achievement. These pressures leave legislators disinclined to rely on local communities or the market to improve school performance.

CHARTER SCHOOLS ARE HERE TO STAY

After a decade, charter schools are already an established part of the American educational system. In states including Arizona, California, and Michigan they enroll a significant share of all public school students, and the number of states adopting charter school legislation continues to grow. There is no reason to suppose that these trends will be reversed. Virtually all the available data indicate that charter school parents are considerably happier with their schools than traditional public school parents are with theirs. Parents like having choices, and they like the schools that they choose for their children. Charter schools provide educational options that many parents value, and it is hard to imagine circumstances in which these options might be withdrawn.

It is nevertheless increasingly unlikely that early hopes that charter schools will transform or revivify public education will be realized. Charter schools are free to experiment with new ways of organizing and managing schools, but the evidence presented in this volume suggests that they continue to resemble traditional public schools in most important respects, including the academic performance of their students. The authors offer no reason to suppose that dramatic improvements are in prospect.

At the end of the day, though, Americans like having choices. They like knowing that they can get away if they need to—or at least their children can. Lighting out for the territory will never lose its appeal, but by itself it is not likely to prove an effective strategy for improving American education.

Constructs, Measures, and Statistical Properties

Constructs for gauging fairness and school context	Measure	National mean (sd)
I. BASIC SCHOOL ATTRIBUTES		
	Student enrollment (median = 169)	264 (297)
	Number of teachers (median = 12)	17.3 (17.6)
II. FAIRNESS—TRADITIONAL INDICATORS (TABLES 5.2, 5.3, AND 5.4)		
School resources		
Teacher resources	Students per full-time teacher	20 (22)
	Students per part-time teacher	125 (184)
	Students per classroom computer	8.1 (8.2)
Teacher/principal compensation	Benefits index: additive of availability of general medical, dental, and life insurance	2.5 (0.8)
	Teacher salaries: midpoint between lowest- and highest-paid teacher currently employed	31,939 (6,672)
	Current principal's salary	55,073 (18,824)
Student attributes and access		
Ethnic and composition	Percentage enrolled: Asian American (2.2%), African American (27.1%), or Latino (17.5%)	47
Access by diverse children	Percentage enrolled, receiving Title I services (median = 0)	4.5
	Percentage enrolled, eligible for lunch subsidies	43
	Percentage enrolled, identified English learners (median = 0)	4.9
	Percentage enrolled with IEPs	11

Teacher qualities

Basic attributes	Age in years	37.6 (7.9)
	Percentage school's teachers, Asian or African American, Latino	21
Qualifications and experience	Percentage working under an emergency, provisional, temporary, or probationary credential	48
	Years of teaching experience	6.1 (5.6)

III. FAIRNESS—LOCALIZED INDICATORS   (TABLES 5.5 AND 5.6)

Specialized mission	Percentage of principals reporting that school has a "special program emphasis" or is an "alternative" school (excluding special education and vocational schools)	44
	Classroom innovations linked to quality of student–teacher social relations: additive index of six possible innovations	2.8 (1.6)
Autonomy	Principal's reported influence within seven domains (alpha = .83)	4.5 (0.5)
	Reported influence of the state on charter operations within seven domains (alpha = .80)	2.7 (0.8)
	Teacher's reported influence within seven domains (alpha = .86)	3.0 (0.8)
	Percentage of enrolled students who were homeschooled	3.6
Coherent community	Teacher reports of cohesive beliefs and principal's support within five domains (alpha = .85)	3.1 (0.6)
	Student homogeneity index: number of non-White groups with at least 10% of the enrollment	0.9 (0.7)
Parent participation	Specific opportunities for parent participation, including open house, written contracts with parents, volunteer opportunities, parents involved in budget planning and governance (8-point additive index)	6.4 (2.1)
	Affirmative programs involving parents, including parent drop-in center, log of parent participation, specific requirements, and involvement of parents in homework activities	4.3 (2.0)

IV. CHARTER SCHOOL CONTEXT

School origin	Percentage of schools, start-ups	74
	Percentage of schools, converted from a conventional public school	16
	Percentage of schools, converted from a private school	10
Community type	Percentage of schools in central city	53
	Percentage of schools in suburb	32
	Percentage of schools in rural area	15
Private management	Percentage of schools managed by a private company (for-profit or nonprofit)	31
State policy regime	Percentage of schools in states requiring that charter teachers be credentialed	56
	Index score (0–3) indicating state provides fiscal support for start-up funds, facilities, and/or student transportation (median = 1.0)	1.5 (0.5)

Note: All measures are further described in Gruber, Wiley, Broughman, Strizek, & Burian-Fitzgerald (2002). Indicators of state policies are from Education Commission (2002).

Rating System Used in Tables 6.1 and 6.2

Codes Used in Table 6.1

School influence on mission

> High = mission determined primarily by school
>
> Low = mission determined primarily by EMO

School influence on curriculum

> High = little influence
>
> Medium = company provides standards but not curriculum/basic guidelines and standards
>
> Low = company provides specific curriculum and materials

School influence on classroom assessments

> High = assessments in addition to standardized or state tests
>
> Low = assessments in addition to standardized or state assessments provided by company

School influence on instruction/pedagogical approaches

> Medium = some influence
>
> Low = specific instructional approach required/strongly encouraged

School influence on school governance/organizational structure

> High = no organizational or governance structure recommended or required by company
>
> Medium = suggested structure for either governance or organization
>
> Low = clearly stated structure for either governance or organization

School influence on professional development

> High = school primarily determines professional development needs and selects providers
>
> Medium = mix of school and EMO determined needs and provider selection
>
> Low = EMO primarily determines professional development needs and selects providers

---

Codes Used in Table 6.2

School influence on school budget

    High = board primarily with some EMO advice

    Medium = EMO and board jointly

    Low = EMO designs—gets board approval

School ownership of facilities

    High = EMO does not own/lease any facilities

    Medium = mix of school and EMO ownership/leasing

    Low = EMO owns/leases most of the facilities

School influence on teacher hiring

    High = school staff/board primarily responsible for teacher selection

    Medium = school staff/board and EMO jointly select teachers

    Low = EMO primarily responsible for teacher selection

School influence on principal selection

    High = school staff/board primarily re sponsible for principal selection

    Medium = school staff/board and EMO jointly select principal

    Low = EMO primarily responsible for staff selection

References

Abell Foundation. (2001). *Teacher certification reconsidered: Stumbling for quality.* Baltimore, MD: Author.

Ahearn, E., Lange, C., Rhim, L. M., & McLaughlin, M. J. (2001). *Project SEARCH: Special education as requirements in charter schools. Final report of a research study.* Alexandria, VA: National Association of State Directors of Special Education.

American Federation of Teachers. (1998). *Building on the best: Learning from what works.* Washington, DC: Author.

American Federation of Teachers. (1999, June). *Charter schools update* (Educational Issues Policy Brief 9). Washington, DC: Author.

Anderson, L., & Marsh, J. (1998, April). *Early results of a reform experiment: Charter schools in California.* Paper presented at the American Educational Research Association, San Diego, CA.

Andras, R. (2002). *Analysis of grades 3, 4, and 5 2002 CSAP results.* Unpublished report. Denver: RBC Dain Rauscher, Denver Public Finance.

Arizona Department of Education. (n.d.). Charter schools [website]. Retrieved March 26, 2002, from http://www.ade.state.az.us/CharterSchools.

Arsen, D., Plank, D., & Sykes, G. (1999). *School choice policies in Michigan: The rules matter.* East Lansing, MI: Education Policy Center at Michigan State University.

Ashton, P., & Crocker, L. (1987). Systemic study of planned variations: The essential focus of teacher education reform. *Journal of Teacher Education, 38*(3), 2–8.

Ballou, D. (1996). Do public schools hire the best applicants? *Quarterly Journal of Economics, 111*(1), 97–134.

Ballou, D., & Podgursky, M. (1997). *Teacher pay and teacher quality.* Kalamazoo, MI: Upjohn Institute.

Ballou, D., & Podgursky, M. (2000). Reforming teacher preparation and licensing: What is the evidence? *Teachers College Record, 102*(1), 5–27.

Barr, R., & Dreeben, R. (1991). Grouping students for reading instruction. In R. Barr, M. L. Kamil, P. B. Mosenthal, & P. D. Pearson (Eds.), *Handbook of reading research* (Vol. 2; pp. 885–910). New York: Longman.

Becker, H. J., Nakagawa, K., & Corwin, R. G. (1997). Parent involvement contracts in California's charter schools. *Teachers College Record, 98*(3), 511–536.

Bennett, W. J., Fair, W., Finn, C. E., Flake, F. H., Hirsch, E. D., Marshall, W., & Ravitch, D. (1998). A nation still at risk. *Policy Review, 90*, 23–29.

Berman, P., Nelson, B., Ericson, J., Perry, R., & Silverman, D. (1998). *A national study of charter schools: Second year report.* Washington, DC: Office of Educational Research and Improvement, U.S. Department of Education.

Bettinger, E. P. (1999). *The effect of charter schools on charter students and public schools* (Occasional Paper No. 4). New York: National Center for the Study of Privatization in Education. Retrieved September 9, 2001, from //www.ncspe.org/.

Bimber, B. A. (1993). *School decentralization: Lessons from the study of bureaucracy.* Santa Monica, CA: RAND.

Bobrow, D., & Dryzek, J. (1987). *Policy analysis by design.* Pittsburgh: University of Pittsburgh Press.

Bomotti, S., Ginsberg, R., & Cobb, B. (1999). Teachers in charter schools and traditional schools: A comparative study. *Education Policy Analysis Archives,* 7(22). Retrieved March 7, 2002, from http://epaa.asu.edu/epaa/v7n22.html.

Borcherding, T. (1977). *Budgets and bureaucrats.* Durham, NC: Duke University Press.

Brown, R. (in press). *Which California schools are improving? A four-year analysis of performance growth.* Berkeley and Stanford: Policy Analysis for California Education.

Buchanan, J. M., Tollison, R. D., & Tullock, G. (1980). *Toward a theory of the rent-seeking society.* College Station: Texas A&M University.

Buechler, M. (1996, July). *Charter schools: Legislation and results after four years* (PR-B13). Bloomington: Indiana Education Policy Center.

Bulkley, K. (2001). Charter school authorizers: A new governance mechanism? *Educational Policy,* 13(5), 674–699.

Bulkley, K., & Fisler, J. (2002a). *A decade of charter schools: From theory to practice* (CPRE Policy Briefs). Philadelphia, PA: Consortium for Policy Research in Education, University of Pennsylvania.

Bulkley, K., & Fisler, J. (2002b). *A review of the research on charter schools* (CPRE Web Paper Series, WP-01). Philadelphia: Consortium for Policy Research in Education, University of Pennsylvania, Graduate School of Education. Retrieved July 1, 2002, from http://www.cpre.org/Publications/WP-01.pdf.

Caldwell, B. J., & Spinks, J. M. (1992). *Leading the self-managing school.* Washington, DC: Falmer.

Calfee, R., & Hiebert, E. (1991). Classroom assessment of reading. In R. Barr, M. L. Kamil, P. B. Mosenthal, & P. D. Pearson (Eds.), *Handbook of reading research* (Vol. 2; pp. 281–309). New York: Longman.

Cardenas, J. (2002, June 25). Sowing Home-Grown Education. *Los Angeles Times,* p. B1.

Center for Education Reform. (2000). *Charter schools today: Changing the face of American education.* Washington, DC: Author.

Center for Education Reform. (2001a). *Charter school laws: Scorecard and rankings.* Retrieved March 10, 2002, from http://www.edreform.com/charter_schools.

Center for Education Reform. (2001b). Charter school statistics. Retrieved November 1, 2001, from www.edreform.com/press/2001/ranking.htm.

Chubb, J. E., & Moe, T. M. (1990). *Politics, markets, and America's schools*. Washington, DC: Brookings Institution.

Clayton Foundation. (1997). *The Colorado charter schools evaluation, 1996*. Denver: Colorado Department of Education.

Clayton Foundation. (1998). *1997 Colorado charter schools evaluation study*. Denver: Colorado Department of Education.

Clayton Foundation. (1999). *1998 Colorado charter schools evaluation study*. Denver: Colorado Department of Education.

Clune, W., & White, P. A. (1988). *School-based management: Institutional variation, implementation, and issues for further research*. Madison, WI: Center for Policy Research in Education.

Cobb, C. D., & Glass, G. V. (1999). Ethnic segregation in Arizona charter schools. *Educational Policy analysis Archives*, 7(1). [Retrieved February 1, 2002, from http://epaa.asu.edu/epaa/v7n1/]

Code of Federal Regulations. Assistance to states for the education of children with disabilities and the early intervention program for infants and toddlers with disabilities: Final regulations. 34 CFR§300.312 (March 12, 1999).

Coleman, J. S. (1990). Choice, community and future schools. In W. H. Clune & J. F. Witte (Eds.), *Choice and control in American education* (pp. ix–xxii). London: Falmer.

Colorado Department of Education. (2001). *The state of charter schools in Colorado 1999–2000*. Denver: Author.

Colorado Department of Education. (2002). *The state of charter schools in Colorado: 2000–01: The characteristics, status, and performance record of Colorado charter schools*. Denver: Author.

Corwin, R. G., & Flaherty, J. F. (Eds.). (1995). *Freedom and innovation in California's charter schools*. Los Alamitos, CA: Southwest Regional Laboratory.

Cunningham, A. E., & Stanovich, K. E. (1998). What reading does for the mind. *American Educator*, 22(1–2), 1–8.

Curriculum Development and Supplemental Materials Commission. (1999). *Reading/language arts framework for California public schools: Kindergarten through grade twelve*. Sacramento: California Department of Education.

Daft, R. L., & Becker, S. W. (1978). *Innovation in organizations: Innovation adoption in school organizations*. New York: Elsevier.

Darling-Hammond, L. (2000). Teacher quality and student achievement. *Educational Policy Analysis Archives*, 8(1). Retrieved May 9, 2001, from http://epaa.asu.edu/epaa/v8n1.html.

Darling-Hammond, L., Berry, B., & Thoreson, A. (2001). Does teacher certification matter? Evaluating the evidence. *Educational Evaluation and Policy Analysis*, 23(1), 57–77.

David, J. L. (1995). The who, what, and why of site-based management. *Educational Leadership*, 53(4), 4–9.

DiMaggio, P. J., & Powell, W. W. (1983). The iron cage revisited. *American Sociological Review*, 48(2), 147–160.

Dimmock, C. (1993). School-based management and linkage with the curriculum.

In C. Dimmock (Ed.), *School-based management and school effectiveness* (pp. 1–21). London: Routledge.

Doyle, D. P. (1994). The role of private sector management in public education. *Phi Delta Kappan, 76,* 128–132.

Dykgraaf, C., & Lewis, S. (1998, October). For-profit charter schools: What the public needs to know. *Educational Leadership,* pp. 51–53.

Eberts, R. W., & Hollenbeck, K. M. (2002). *Impact of charter school attendance on student achievement in Michigan* (Staff Working Paper No. 02-080). Kalamazoo, MI: W.E. Upjohn Institute for Employment Research.

Education Commission of the States (2002). *State notes: Charter school teachers and finance.* Denver: Author.

Education Commission of the States, & Nathan, J. (1995). *Charter schools: What are they up to?* Denver, CO: Author.

Everston, C. M., Hawley, W. D., & Zlotnik, M. (1985). Making a difference in educational quality through teacher education. *Journal of Teacher Education, 36*(3), 2–12.

Ferguson, P., & Womack, S. T. (1993).The impact of subject matter and education coursework on teaching performance. *Journal of Teacher Education, 44*(1), 55–63.

Ferguson, R. F., & Brown, J. (2000). Certification test scores, teacher quality, and student achievement. In W. Grissmer & J. M. Ross (Eds.), *Analytic issues in the assessment of student achievement* (NCES No. 2000-050). National Center for Education Statistics. Washington, DC: U.S. Government Printing Office.

Ferguson, R. F., & Ladd. H. F. (1996). How and why money matters: An analysis of Alabama schools. In H. F. Ladd (Ed.), *Holding schools accountable: Performance-based reform in education* (pp. 265–298). Washington, DC: Brookings Institution.

Fetler, M. (1999). High school staff characteristics and mathematics test results. *Education Policy Analysis Archives 7*(9). Retrieved March 22, 2002, from http://epaa.asu.edu/epaa/v7n9.html.

Finn, C. (1997, June 2). Education: The era of big government is still here. *The Weekly Standard,* 5–7.

Finn, C., & Gau, R. L. (1998). New ways of education. *Public Interest, 130,* 79–92.

Finn, C., Manno, B. V., & Bierlein, L. A. (1996, November/December). The empire strikes back: Sensing a threat, public education's monopolists are sandbagging charter schools. *The New Democrat, 8,* 11–13.

Finn, C. E., Manno, B., & Vanourek, G. (2000). *Charter schools in action: Renewing public education.* Princeton, NJ: Princeton University Press.

Fiore, T. A., Harwell, L. A., Blackorby, J., & Finnegan, L. A. (2000). *Charter schools and students with disabilities: A national study.* Washington, DC: U.S. Department of Education, Office of Education Research and Improvement.

Fitzgerald, J. (1995). *Charter schools in Colorado.* Denver: Colorado Children's Campaign.

Fitzgerald, J. (2000). *1998–99 Colorado charter schools evaluation study*. Denver: Colorado Department of Education.

Flaherty, J. F. (1995). Innovations: What are the schools doing? In R. G. Corwin & J. F. Flaherty (Eds.), *Freedom and innovation in California's charter schools* (pp. 63–73). Los Alamitos, CA: Southwest Regional Laboratory.

Fulford, N., Raack, L., & Sunderman, G. (1997). Charter schools as change agents: Will they deliver? In North Central Regional Education Laboratory (Ed.), *Charters in our midst: The impact of charter schools on school districts* (pp. 34–36). Oak Brook, IL: National Central Regional Educational Laboratory.

Fuller, B. (2000). The public square, big or small? Charter schools in political context. In B. Fuller (Ed.), *Inside charter schools: The paradox of radical decentralization* (pp. 12–65). Cambridge, MA: Harvard University Press.

Fuller, B., & Elmore, R. F. (1996). *Who chooses? Who loses? Culture, institutions and the unequal effects of school choice*. New York: Teachers College Press.

Fuller, B., & Rubinson, R. (Eds.). (1992). *The political construction of education: The state, school expansion, and economic change*. New York: Praeger.

Furtwengler, C. (1998, October). Heads up! The EMOs are coming. *Educational Leadership*, pp. 44–47.

Garn, G. A. (1998). The thinking behind Arizona's charter movement. *Educational Leadership, 56*, 48–51.

Gauri, V. (1998). *School choice in Chile: Two decades of educational reform*. Pittsburgh: University of Pittsburgh Press.

Gee, J. P. (2001). Identity as an analytic lens for research in education. In W. Secada (Ed.), *Review of research in education, 2000–2001* (Vol. 25; pp. 99–125). Washington, DC: American Educational Research Association.

Georgia Department of Education. (2001). *Charter schools evaluation*. Atlanta: Author.

Gifford, M., Phillips, K., & Ogle, M. (2000). *Five year charter school study*. Phoenix, AZ: Center for Market-Based Education, Goldwater Institute.

Gill, B. P., Timpane, M., Ross, K. E., & Brewer, D. J. (2001). *Rhetoric versus reality: What we know and what we need to know about vouchers and charter schools*. Santa Monica, CA: RAND.

Glaser, B., & Straus, A. (1967). *The discovery of grounded theory: Strategies for qualitative research*. Chicago: Aldine.

Glassman, J. K. (1998). Class acts. *Reason, 29*, 24–30.

Godwin, R. K., & Kemerer, F. (2002). *School choice tradeoffs: Liberty, equity, and diversity*. Austin: University of Texas Press.

Goebel, S. D., Ronacher, K., & Sanchez, K. S. (1989). *An evaluation of HISD's alternative certification program of the academic year: 1988–1989*. Houston: Houston Independent School District Department of Research and Evaluation. ERIC Document No. 322103.

Goldhaber, D. D., & Brewer, D. J. (1997). Why don't schools and teachers seem to matter? Assessing the impact of unobservables on educational productivity. *Journal of Human Resources, 32*(3), 505–523.

Goldhaber, D. D., & Brewer, D. J. (2000). Does teacher certification matter? High school teacher certification status and student achievement. *Educational Evaluation and Policy Analysis, 22*(2), 129–145.

Good, T. L., & Braden, J. S. (2000). *The great school debate: Choice, vouchers, and charters.* Mahwah, NJ: Erlbaum.

Greene, J. D. (1996). How much privatization? A research note examining the use of privatization by cities in 1982 and 1992. *Policy Studies Journal, 24*(4), 632–641.

Greenwald, R., Hedges, L., & Laine, R. (1996). The effect of school resources on student achievement. *Review of Educational Research, 66,* 361–396.

Gronberg, T., & Jansen, D. W. (2001). *Navigating newly chartered waters: An analysis of Texas charter school performance.* Austin: Texas Public Policy Foundation.

Gruber, K., Wiley, S., Broughman, S., Strizek, G., & Burian-Fitzgerald, M. (2002). *Schools and staffing survey, 1999–2000: Overview of the data for public, private, public charter, and Bureau of Indian Affairs elementary and secondary Schools (2002–313).* Washington, DC: U.S. Government Printing Office.

Halpern, K., & Culbertson, E. R. (1994). *Blueprint for change: Charter schools.* Washington, DC: Democratic Leadership Council.

Hannan, M. T., & Freeman, J. H. (1977). The population ecology of organizations. *American Journal of Sociology, 82*(5), 929–964.

Hannaway, J. (1993). Decentralization in two school districts: Challenging the standard paradigm. In J. Hannaway & M. Carnoy (Eds.), *Decentralization and school improvement* (pp. 135–162). San Francisco: Jossey-Bass.

Hannaway, J. (1999). *Contracting as a mechanism for managing education services* (Policy Brief RB-28). Philadelphia: Consortium for Policy Research in Education.

Hanushek, E. A. (1971). Teacher characteristics and gains in student achievement: Estimation using microdata. *American Economic Review, 61*(2), 280–288.

Hanushek, E. A. (1989). The impact of differential expenditures on school performance. *Educational Researcher, 18*(4), 45–51.

Hassel, B. C. (1998). Charter schools: Politics and practice in four States. In P. E. Peterson & B. C. Hassel (Eds.), *Learning from school choice* (pp. 249–271). Washington, DC: Brookings Institution Press.

Hassel, B. C. (1999a). *The charter school challenge: Avoiding the pitfalls, fulfilling the promise.* Washington, DC: Brookings Institution Press.

Hassel, B. C. (1999b). Charter schools: A national innovation, an Arizona revolution. In R. Maranto, S. Milliman, F. Hess, & A. Gresham (Eds.), *School choice in the real world: Lessons from Arizona charter schools* (pp. 68–95). Boulder, CO: Westview.

Hawk, P., Coble, C. R., & Swanson, M. (1985). Certification: It does matter. *Journal of Teacher Education, 36*(3), 13–15.

Heck, R. H., Brandon, P. R., & Wang, J. (2001). Implementing site-managed educational changes: Examining levels of implementation and effect. *Educational Policy, 15*(2), 302–322.

Hedges, L., & Olkin, I. (1985). *Statistical methods for meta-analysis.* Orlando, FL: Academic Press.

Henig, J. R., Holyoke, T. T., Lacireno-Paquet, N., & Moser, M. (2001). *Growing pains: An evaluation of charter schools in the District of Columbia: 1999–2000.* Washington, DC: Center for Washington Area Studies, George Washington University.

Hentschke, G. C. (1997). Beyond competing school reforms: A redefinition of *public* in public schooling. *Education and Urban Society, 29*(4), 474–489.

Heubert, J. P. (1997). Schools without rules? Charter schools, federal disability law, and the paradoxes of deregulation. *Harvard Civil Rights–Civil Liberties Law Review, 32,* 301–353.

Hill, C. W. L., & Jones, G. R. (1989). *Strategic management theory: An integrated approach.* Boston: Houghton Mifflin.

Hill, P., Pierce, L., & Guthrie, J. (1997). *Reinventing public education: How contracting can transform America's schools.* Chicago: University of Chicago Press.

Hirschman, A. O. (1970). *Exit, voice, and loyalty: Responses to decline in firms, organizations, and states.* Cambridge, MA: Harvard University Press.

Hoffman, J. V. (1991). Teacher and school effects in learning to read. In R. Barr, M. L. Kamil, P. B. Mosenthal, & P. D. Pearson (Eds.), *Handbook of reading research* (Vol. 2; pp. 911–950). New York: Longman.

Horn, J., & Miron, G. (1998). *First annual report of the evaluation of the charter schools and the charter school initiative in the state of Connecticut.* Kalamazoo: The Evaluation Center, Western Michigan University.

Horn, J., & Miron, G. (1999). *Evaluation of Michigan public school academy initiative.* Kalamazoo: The Evaluation Center, Western Michigan University.

Horn, J., & Miron, G. (2000). *An evaluation of the Michigan charter school initiative: Performance, accountability, and impact.* Kalamazoo: The Evaluation Center, Western Michigan University.

Hoxby, C. M. (1994). *Do private schools provide competition for public schools?* (Working Paper No. 4978). Cambridge, MA: National Bureau of Economic Research.

Hoxby, C. M. (2000). *Would school choice change the teaching profession?* (NBER Working Paper No. 7866). Cambridge, MA: National Bureau of Economic Research.

Hoxby, C. M. (2001). Rising tide: New evidence on competition and the public schools. *Education Next, 1,* 68–75.

Huerta, L. (2000). Losing pubic accountability: A home schooling charter. In B. Fuller (Ed.), *Inside charter schools: The paradox of radical decentralization* (pp. 177–202). Cambridge, MA: Harvard University Press.

Ingersoll, R. (1996). Teachers' decision-making power and school conflict. *Sociology of Education, 69,* 159–176.

Ingersoll, R. M. (1999). The problem of underqualified teachers in American secondary schools. *Educational Researcher, 28*(2), 26–37.

Johnson, S. M., & Landman, J. (2000). "Sometimes bureaucracy has its charms": The working conditions of teachers in deregulated schools. *Teachers College Record, 102*(1), 85–124.

Kalt, J. P., & Zupan, M. A. (1984). Capture and ideology in economic theory of politics. *American Economic Review, 74*(3), 279–300.

Keegan, L. G. (1999). The empowerment of market-based school reform. In R. Maranto, S. Milliman, F. Hess, & A. Gresham (Eds.), *School choice in the real world* (pp. 189–197). Boulder, CO: Westview.

Khouri, N., Kleine, R., White, R., & Cummings, L. (1999). *Michigan's charter school initiative: From theory to practice*. Lansing, MI: Public Sector Consultants.

Kleine, R., Scott, C., & White, R. (2000). *Issues in Michigan's public school academy initiative phase II*. Lansing, MI: Public Sector Consultants.

Klitgaard, R. E., & Hall, G. R. (1974). Are there unusually effective schools? *Journal of Human Resources, 10*(3), 90–106.

Knight, B. (1993). Delegated financial management and school effectiveness. In C. Dimmock (Ed.), *School-based management and school effectiveness* (pp. 114–142). London: Routledge.

Kolderie, T. (1990). *Beyond choice to new public schools: Withdrawing the exclusive franchise in public education*. Washington, DC: Progressive Policy Institute.

Kolderie, T. (1998, February). *What does it mean to ask: Is "Charter Schools" working?* St. Paul, MN: Charter Friends National Network. Retrieved March 1, 2002, from www.charterfriends.org/working.html.

KPMG. (2001). *The evaluation of New Jersey's charter school program*. New York: Author.

Krashen, S. (1993). *The power of reading: Insights from the research*. Englewood, CO: Libraries Unlimited.

Lake, R. J., & Millot, M. D. (1998). *Accountability for charter schools: A comparative assessment of charter school laws*. Seattle, WA: Center on Reinventing Public Education.

Lane, B. (1999). *Choice matters: Policy alternatives and implications for charter schools*. Portland, OR: Northwest Regional Educational Laboratory.

Lange, C. (1997, March). *School choice, charter schools, and students with disabilities*. Paper presented at the meeting of the American Educational Research Association, Chicago.

Lauder, H., & Hughes, D. (1999). *Trading in futures: Why markets in education don't work*. Buckingham, UK: Open University Press.

Lee, V., Bryk, A., & Holland, P. (1993). *Catholic schools and the common good*. Cambridge, MA: Harvard University Press.

Lee, V., Dedrick, R., & Smith, J. (1991). The effect of the social organization of schools on teachers' efficacy and satisfaction. *Sociology of Education, 64*, 190–208.

Levin, B. (1997). The lessons of international education reform. *Journal of Education Policy, 12*(4), 253–266.

Levin, H. (2000). *A comprehensive framework for evaluating educational vouchers* (Occasional Paper No. 5). New York: National Center for the Study of Privatization in Education.

Levin, H. (2001). Waiting for Godot: Cost-effectiveness analysis in education. *New Directions for Evaluation, 90*, 55–68.

Lieberman, A., Darling-Hammond, L., & Zuckerman, D. (1991). *Early lessons in restructuring schools*. New York: National Center for Restructuring Education, Schools, and Teaching, Teachers College, Columbia University.

Light, R., & Pillemer, D. (1984). *Summing up: The science of reviewing research.* Cambridge, MA: Harvard University Press.

Lin, M., & Hassel, B. (1999). *Charting a clear course: A resource guide for charter schools contracting with school management organizations.* Minneapolis: Center for Policy Studies.

Link, J., Gordon, H., & Khanna, R. (1999, April). *Urban seedbeds for charter schools: A thousand flowers blooming.* Paper presented at the American Educational Research Association, Montreal.

Little, J. (1990). The persistence of privacy: Autonomy and initiative in teachers' professional relations. *Teachers College Record, 91,* 509–536.

Little Hoover Commission. (1996). *The charter movement: Educational reform school by school.* Sacramento, CA: Author.

Legislative Office of Education Oversight. (2002). *Community schools in Ohio: Preliminary report on proficiency test results, attendance, and satisfaction.* Columbus, OH: Legislative Office of Education Oversight.

Louis, K. S. (1998, Fall). "A light feeling of chaos": Educational reform and policy in the United States. *Daedalus,* pp. 13–40.

Louis, K. S., Kruse, S. D., & Associates. (1995). *Professionalism and community: Perspectives on reforming urban schools.* Thousand Oaks, CA: Corwin.

Louis, K. S., Marks, H. M., & Kruse, S. (1996). Teachers' professional community in restructuring schools. *American Educational Research Journal, 33*(4), 757–798.

Loveless, T. (2002, September). *The 2002 Brown Center report on American education: How well are american students learning?* Washington, DC: Brookings Institution.

Lubienski, C. (2001a). Redefining "public" education: Charter schools, common schools, and the rhetoric of reform. *Teachers College Record, 103*(4), 634–666.

Lubienski, C. (2001b). *The relationship of competition and choice to innovation in education markets: A review of research on four cases* (Occasional Paper No. 26). New York: National Center for the Study of Privatization in Education.

Lubienski, C. (2001c). *Institutionalist and instrumentalist perspectives on "public" education: Strategies and implications of the school choice movement in Michigan* (Occasional Paper No. 39). New York: National Center for the Study of Privatization in Education, Teachers College, Columbia University.

Lyons, J. (1995). Contracting out for public school support services. *Education and Urban Society, 27*(2), 154–167.

MacGillivaray, L., & Rueda, R. (2001). *Listening to inner city teachers of English language learners: Differentiating literacy instruction.* Ann Arbor, MI: Center for the Improvement of Early Reading Achievement.

Malen, B. (1994). Enacting site-based management: A political utilities analysis. *Educational Evaluation and Policy Analysis, 16,* 249–267.

Malen, B., Ogawa, R. T., & Kranz, J. (1990). What do we know about school-based management? A case study of the literature—A call for research. In W. H. Clune & J. F. White (Eds.), *Choice and control in American education: The practice of choice, decentralization and school restructuring* (Vol. 2; pp. 289–342). London: Falmer.

Malloy, C. L., & Wohlstetter, P. (2003). Working conditions in charter schools: What's the appeal for teachers? *Education and Urban Society, 35*(2), 219–241.

Manno, B. V., Finn, C. E., Bierlein, L. E., & Vanourek, G. (1998a). Charter schools: Accomplishments and dilemmas. *Teachers College Record, 99*(3), 537–558.

Manno, B. V., Finn, C. E., Bierlein, L. A., & Vanourek, G. (1998b, March). How charter schools are different: Lessons and implications for a national study. *Phi Delta Kappan, 79*, 489–498.

Mansfield, E. (1970). *Microeconomics: Theory and applications.* New York: Norton.

Manzo, K. K. (2001). Anxious educators await details of Bush reading initiative. *Education Week, 20,* 30.

Maranto, R. (1999). The death of one best way: Charter schools as reinventing government. In R. Maranto, S. Milliman, F. Hess, & A. Gresham (Eds.), *School choice in the real world: Lessons from Arizona charter schools* (pp. 39–57). Boulder, CO: Westview.

Marks, H., & Louis, K. S. (1997). Does teacher empowerment affect the classroom? The implications of teacher empowerment for instructional practice and student academic performance. *Educational Evaluation and Policy Analysis, 19,* 245–275.

Marks, H., & Louis, K. S. (1999). Teacher empowerment and the capacity for organizational learning. *Educational Administration Quarterly, 35* (Supplemental, December), 707–750.

Masten, S. (1984). The organization of production: Evidence from the aerospace industry. *Journal of Law and Economics, 27,* 402–417.

McKinney, J. R. (1996). Charter schools: A new barrier for children with disabilities. *Education Leadership, 54*(2), 22–25.

McLaughlin, M. J., & Henderson, K. (1998). Charter schools in Colorado and their response to the education of students with disabilities. *Journal of Special Education, 32,* 99–107.

Medler, A. (1996). Promise and progress. *American School Board Journal, 183*(3), 26–28.

Merriam, S. B. (1998). *Qualitative research and case study applications in education.* San Francisco: Jossey-Bass.

Meyer, J. W. (1992). Innovation and knowledge use in American public education. In J. W. Meyer & W. R. Scott (Eds.), *Organizational environments: Ritual and rationality* (updated ed.; pp. 233–260). Beverly Hills, CA: Sage.

Michigan Office of the Auditor General. (2002). *Performance audit of the office of education options, Michigan Department of Education.* Lansing, MI: Author.

Miles, M. B., & Huberman, A. M. (1994). *Qualitative data analysis: An expanded sourcebook* (2nd ed.). Thousand Oaks, CA: Sage.

Miller, G. (1992). *Managerial dilemmas: The political economy of hierarchy.* New York: Cambridge University Press.

Mintrom, M. (2000). *Leveraging local innovation: The case of Michigan's charter schools.* East Lansing: Michigan State University.

Mintrom, M., & Plank, D. N. (2001). School choice in Michigan. In P. E. Peterson & D.E. Campbell (Eds.), *Charters, vouchers, and public education.* Washington, DC: Brookings Institution Press.

Miron, G., & Applegate, B. (2000). *An evaluation of student achievement in Edison schools opened in 1995 and 1996.* Kalamazoo, MI: The Evaluation Center, Western Michigan University.

Miron, G., & Horn, J. (2002). *Evaluation of Connecticut charter schools and charter school initiative: Final report.* Kalamazoo, MI: The Evaluation Center, Western Michigan University.

Miron, G., & Nelson, C. (2000). *Autonomy in exchange for accountability: An initial study of Pennsylvania charter schools.* Kalamazoo, MI: The Evaluation Center, Western Michigan University.

Miron, G., & Nelson, C. (2002). *What's public about charter schools: Lessons learned about school choice and accountability.* Thousand Oaks, CA: Corwin.

Miron, G., Nelson, C., & Risley, J. (2002). *Strengthening Pennsylvania's charter school reform: Findings from the statewide evaluation and discussion of relevant policy issues.* Kalamazoo, MI: The Evaluation Center, Western Michigan University.

Molnar, A. (2001). Calculating the benefits and costs of for-profit public education. [Retrieved April 30, 2001 from http://olam.ed.usu.edu/epaa/v9n15.html]

Molnar, A., Morales, J., & Wyst, A. V. (2000). *Profiles of for-profit education management companies, 2000–2001.* Milwaukee: Center for Education Research, Analysis, and Innovation, University of Wisconsin–Milwaukee.

Monk, D. H. (1994). Subject matter preparation of secondary mathematics and science teachers and student achievement. *Economics of Education Review*, *13*(2), 125–145.

Mueller, D. C. (1979). *Public choice.* Cambridge, UK: Cambridge University Press.

Mulholland, L. (1999). *Arizona charter school progress evaluation.* Phoenix: Morrison Institute for Public Policy, Arizona State University.

Murnane, R. J., & Phillips, B. R. (1981). Learning by doing, vintage, and selection: Three pieces of the puzzle relating teaching experience and teaching performance. *Economics of Education Review 1*(4), 691–693.

Murphy, J., & Shiffman, C. D. (2002). *Understanding and assessing the charter school movement.* New York: Teachers College Press.

Nathan, J. (1996). *Charter schools: Creating hope and opportunity for American education.* San Francisco: Jossey-Bass.

National Center for Education Statistics. (2000). *SASS and PSS Questionnaires, 1999–2000* (NCES No. 2000-310). Washington, DC: U.S. Government Printing Office.

National Center to Improve the Tools of Educators. (1996). *Learning to read: Reading to learn.* Washington, DC: Distributed by the National Center to Improve the Tools of Educators and the United States Department of Education.

National Education Association. (2002). *New roles, new rules? The professional work lives of charter school teachers.* Washington, DC: Center for the Advancement of Public Education.

National Reading Panel. (2000). *Teaching children to read: An evidence-based assessment of the scientific research on reading and its implications for reading instruction.* Washington, DC: Author.

Nelson, B., Berman, P., Ericson, J., Kamprath, N., Perry, R., Silverman, D., & Solomon, D. (2000). *The state of charter schools: Fourth year report.* Washington, DC: U.S. Department of Education, Office of Education Research and Improvement.

Nelson, C., & Applegate, B. (2002). *Developing a cross-state comparable method of measuring student achievement in charter schools*. Kalamazoo, MI: The Evaluation Center, Western Michigan University.

Nelson, C., & Hollenbeck, K. (2001). *Does charter school attendance improve test scores? Comments and reactions on the Arizona achievement study* (Staff Working Paper No. 01-70). Kalamazoo, MI: W.E. Upjohn Institute for Employment Research.

Nelson, C., & Miron, G. (2002, April). *Professional opportunities for teachers: A view from inside charter schools*. Paper presented at the annual meeting of the American Educational Research Association, New Orleans.

Newmann, F., Marks, H. M., & Gamoran, A. (1996). Authentic pedagogy and student performance. *American Journal of Education, 104*(4), 280–312.

Newmann, F., Smith, B., Allensworth, E., & Bryk, A. (2001). Instructional program coherence: What it is and why it should guide school improvement policy. *Educational Evaluation and Policy Analysis, 23*, 297–322.

Niskanen, W. (1971). *Bureaucracy and representative government*. Chicago: Aldine.

Noblit, G., & Corbett, D. (2001). *North Carolina charter school evaluation report*. Raleigh, NC: Department of Public Instruction.

Odden, A., & Busch, C. (1998). *Financing schools for high performance*. San Francisco: Jossey-Bass.

Odden, A. R., & Picus, L. O. (2000). *School finance: A policy perspective* (2nd ed.). Boston: McGraw-Hill.

O'Neill, P. T., Wenning, R. J., & Giovannetti, B. (2002). Serving students with disabilities in charter schools: Legal obligations and policy options. Retrieved December 10, 2003, from http://www.Special%20Ed%20Charters%20Article%20Reformatted.pdf.

Osborne, D., & Gaebler, T. (1992). *Reinventing government: How the entrepreneurial spirit is transforming the public sector*. New York: Plume.

Ostroff, C. (1992). The relationship between satisfaction, attitudes, and performance: An organizational level analysis. *Journal of Applied Psychology, 77*(6), 963–974.

Pack, J. R. (1987). Privatization of public-sector services in theory and practice. *Journal of Policy Analysis and Management, 6*(4), 523–540.

Patton, M. Q. (1990). *Qualitative evaluation and research methods* (2nd ed.). Newbury Park: Sage.

Perrow, C. (1986). *Complex organizations: A critical essay*. Glenview, IL: Scott, Foresman.

Peterson, P. E. (1990). Monopoly and competition in American education. In W. H. Clune & J. F. Witte (Eds.), *Choice and control in American education* (pp. 47–78). London: Falmer.

Plank, D. N., & Sykes, G. (1999). How choice changes the education system: A Michigan case study. *International Review of Education, 45*(5/6), 385–416.

Podgursky, M., & Ballou, D. (2001). *Personnel policy in charter schools*. Washington, DC: Thomas B. Fordham Foundation.

Powell, J., Blackorby, J., Marsh, J., Finnegan, K., & Anderson, L. (1997). *Evaluation of charter school effectiveness.* Menlo Park, CA: SRI International.

Price, J. H. (1998). America's quiet revolution. *Insight on the News, 14,* 40–42.

Public Sector Consultants, Inc., & Maximus, Inc. (1999). *Michigan's charter school initiative: From theory to practice.* Lansing, MI: Author.

Ravitch, D. (2000). *Left back: A century of failed school reforms.* New York: Simon & Schuster.

Rebarber, T. (1997). *Charter school innovations: Keys to effective charter reform* (Policy Study No. 228). Los Angeles: Reason Public Policy Institute.

Reinking, D., & Bridwell-Bowles, L. (1991). Computers in reading and writing. In R. Barr, M. L. Kamil, P. B. Mosenthal, & P. D. Pearson (Eds.), *Handbook of reading research* (Vol. 2; pp. 310–340). New York: Longman.

Reynolds, K. (2000). *Innovations in charter schools: A summary of innovative or unique aspects of Michigan charter schools.* Kalamazoo, MI: Western Michigan University.

Rhim, L. (1998, April). *Franchising public education: A study of the linkage of charter schools and private education management companies in Massachusetts.* Paper presented at the Annual Meeting of the American Educational Research Association, San Diego.

Rhim, L. M., & McLaughlin, M. J. (2000). *Balancing disparate visions: Charter schools and special education.* Alexandria, VA: National Association of State Directors of Special Education.

Rhim, L. M., & McLaughlin, M. J. (2001). Special education in American charter schools: State level policy, practices and tensions. *Cambridge Journal of Education, 31*(3), 373–383.

Richards, C., Sawicky, M., & Shore, R. (1996). *Risky business: Private management of public schools.* Washington, DC: Economic Policy Institute.

Robertson, P. J., Wohlstetter, P., & Mohrman, S. A. (1995). Generating curriculum and instructional innovations through school-based management. *Educational Administration Quarterly, 31*(3), 375–404.

Rofes, E. (1998). *How are school districts responding to charter laws and charter schools?* Berkeley: Policy Analysis for California Education.

Rogosa, D. (2002). *A further examination of student progress in charter schools using California API.* Stanford, CA: Stanford University, Department of Statistics. Retrieved October 7, 2002, from http://www-stat.stanford.edu/~rag/api/charter.pdf.

Romer, T., & Rosenthal, H. (1979). Bureaucrats versus voters. *Quarterly Journal of Economics, 93*(4), 563–587.

Routman, R. (1996). *Literacy at the crossroads: Crucial talk about reading, writing, and other teaching dilemmas.* Portsmouth, NH: Heinemann.

Rowan, B. (1990). Commitment and control: Alternative strategies for the organizational design of schools. In C. B. Cazden (Ed.), *Review of research in education* (Vol. 16; pp. 353–389). Washington, DC: American Educational Research Association.

Rowan, B., Raudenbush, S., & Cheong, Y. (1993). Teaching as a nonroutine task: Implications for the management of schools. *Educational Administration Quarterly, 29,* 479–500.

Rowley, C. K., Tollison, R. D., & Tullock, G. (1988). *The political economy of rent-seeking*. Boston: Kluwer.

RPP International. (1998). *A national study of charter schools: Second-year report*. Washington, DC: Office of Educational Research and Improvement.

RPP International. (1999). *The state of charter schools: Third-year report*. Washington, DC: Office of Educational Research and Improvement.

RPP International. (2000). *The state of charter schools: 2000*. Washington, DC: U.S. Department of Education, Office of Educational Research and Improvement.

RPP International. (2001). *Challenge and opportunity: The impact of charter schools on school districts*. Washington, DC: Office of Educational Research and Improvement.

RPP International & University of Minnesota. (1997). *A study of charter schools: First-year report*. Washington, DC: Office of Educational Research and Improvement.

Rutter, M. (1979). *Fifteen thousand hours: Secondary schools and their effects on children*. Cambridge, MA: Harvard University Press.

Sanders, S. L., Skonie-Hardin, S. D., Phelps, W. H., & Minnis, T. L. (1994, November). *The effects of teacher educational attainment on student educational attainment in four regions of Virginia: Implications for administrators*. Paper presented as the annual meeting of the Mid-South Educational Research Association, New Orleans, LA.

Sanders, W. L., & Horn, S. P. (1998). Research findings from the Tennessee Value-Added Assessment System (TVAAS) database: Implications for educational evaluation and research. *Journal of Personnel Evaluation in Education, 12*(3), 13.

Sanders, W. L., & Rivers, J. C. (1996). *Cumulative and residual effects of teachers on future student academic achievement*. Knoxville: University of Tennessee Value-Added Research and Assessment Center.

Schnaiberg, L. (1999, December 1). Entrepreneurs hoping to do good, make money. *Education Week*, 1.

Scott, J. (2001). *Reinventing urban school governance: Privatization, decentralization and charter school reform* (unpublished doctoral dissertation), University of California at Los Angeles.

Seastrom, M. M., Gruber, K. J., Henke, R., McGrath, D. J., & Cohen, B. A. (2002). *Qualifications of the public teacher workforce: Prevalence of out-of-field teaching 1987–88 to 1999–2000* (NCES No. 2002-603). Washington, DC: U.S. Government Printing Office.

Slovacek, S. P., Kunnan, A. J., & Kim, H. (2002). *California charter schools serving low SES students: An analysis of the Academic Performance Index*. Los Angeles: Charter College of Education, California State University, Los Angeles.

Smylie, M. A. (1994). Redesigning teachers' work: Connections to the classroom. In L. Darling-Hammond (Ed.), *Review of research in education* (Vol. 20; pp. 129–177). Washington, DC: American Educational Research Association.

Smylie, M. A., Lazarus, V., & Brownlee-Conyers, J. (1996). Instructional outcomes of school-based participative decision making. *Educational Evaluation and Policy Analysis, 18*(3), 181–198.

Snow, C. E., Barnes, W. S., Chandler, J., Goodman, I. F., & Hemphill, L. (1991).

Unfulfilled expectations: Home and school influences on literacy. Cambridge, MA: Harvard University Press.

Snow, C. E., Burns, M. S., & Griffin, P. (Eds.). (1998). *Preventing reading difficulties in young children.* Washington, DC: National Academy Press.

Solmon, L., Paark, K., & Garcia, D. (2001). *Does charter school attendance improve test scores? The Arizona results (Arizona education analysis).* Phoenix: The Center for Market Based Education, Goldwater Institute.

Southern Regional Education Board. (2001). *Reduce your losses: Help new teachers become veteran teachers.* Atlanta, GA: Author.

Spuhler, L., & Zetler, A. (1994). Montana teacher support program: Research report for year two 1993–94. East Lansing, MI: National Center for Research on Teacher Learning. (ERIC Document Reproduction Service No. ED 390 802)

SRI International. (1997). *Evaluation of charter school effectiveness.* Washington, DC: Author. Retrieved January 4, 2002, from: http://www.lao.ca.gov/sri_charter_schools_1297-part2.html.

Starr, P. (1989). The meaning of privatization. In S. Kamerman & A. Kahn (Eds.), *Privatization and the welfare state* (pp. 15–48). Princeton, NJ: Princeton University Press.

Stigler, G. J. (1998). The theory of economic regulation. In R. B. Ekelund (Ed.), *The foundations of regulatory economics* (Vol. II; pp. 81–99). Cheltenham, UK: Elgar.

Stout, R. T., & Garn, G. A. (1999). Nothing new: Curricula in Arizona charter schools. In R. Maranto, S. Milliman, F. Hess, & A. Gresham (Eds.), *School choice in the real world: Lessons from Arizona charter schools.* (pp. 159–172). Boulder, CO: Westview.

Strauss, R. P., & Sawyer, E. A. (1986). Some new evidence on teacher and student competencies. *Economics of Education Review, 5*(1), 41–48.

Stringfield, S. (1994). Outlier studies of school effectiveness. In D. Reynolds, B. Creemers, P. Nesselrodt, E. Schaffer, S. Stringfield, & C. Teddlie (Eds.), *Advances in school effectiveness research and practice* (pp. 74–89). New York: Pergamon.

Summers, A., & Wolfe, B. (1977). Do schools make a difference? *American Economic Review, 67,* 639–652.

Symonds, W., Palmer, A., Lindorff, D., & McCann, J. (2000, February 7). For-profit schools: They're spreading fast. Can private companies do a better job of educating America's kids? *Business Week,* 69–71.

Taylor, B. M., Pearson, P. D., Clark, K. F., & Walpole, S. (1999). Effective schools/accomplished teachers. *The Reading Teacher, 53*(2), 156–159.

Taylor, D., & Bogotch, I. (1994). School-level effects of teachers' participation in decision making. *Educational Evaluation and Policy Analysis, 16,* 302–319.

Teddlie, C., & Stringfield, S. (1993). *Schools make a difference: Lessons learned from a 10-year study of school effects.* New York: Teachers College Press.

Texas Education Agency. (2001). *Texas open-enrollment charter schools: Fourth-year evaluation.* Austin: Texas Center for Educational Research.

Texas Education Agency. (2002). *Texas open-enrollment charter schools: Fifth-year evaluation.* Austin: Author.

Theobald, N. D. (1990). An examination of the influence of personal, professional, and school district characteristics on public school teacher retention. *Economics of Education Review, 9*(3), 241–250.

Thomsen, S. R., & Gustafson, R. L. (1997). Turning practitioners into professors: Exploring effective mentoring. *Journalism and Mass Communication Educator, 52*(2), 24–32.

Tiebout, C. (1956). A pure theory of local expenditure. *Journal of Political Economy, 64*, 416–424.

Tirozzi, G. (1997, April 9). Statement made before the Subcommittee of Early Childhood, Youth and Families, United States House of Representatives. Retrieved spring 2002: http://www.ed.gov/Speeches/04-1997/970409.html.

Triant, B. (2001). *Autonomy and innovation: How do Massachusetts charter school principals use their freedom?* Washington, DC: Thomas B. Fordham Foundation.

Twain, Mark. (2001). *The adventures of Huckleberry Finn.* New York: Modern Library.

Tyack, D. B. (1974). *The one best system.* Cambridge, MA: Harvard University Press.

U.S. Department of Education. (2002). *Meeting the highly qualified teachers challenge: The Secretary's annual report on teacher quality.* Washington, DC: U.S. Department of Education, Office of Postsecondary Education, Office of Policy, Planning, and Innovation.

U.S. General Accounting Office (USGAO). (1995). *Charter schools: A new model for public schools provides opportunities and challenges* (HEHS-95-42). Washington, DC: Author.

Vanourek, G., Manno, B. V., Finn, C. E., & Bierlein, L. A. (1997). *Charter schools in action.* Indianapolis, IN: Hudson Institute.

Vanourek, G., Manno, B. V., Finn, C. E., & Bierlein, L. A. (1998). Charter schools as seen by students, teachers, and parents. In P. E. Peterson & B. C. Hassel (Eds.), *Learning from school choice* (pp. 187–211). Washington, DC: Brookings Institution Press.

Vergari, S. (2000). The regulatory styles of statewide charter school authorizers: Arizona, Massachusetts, and Michigan. *Educational Administration Quarterly, 36*(5), 730–757.

Viteritti, J. P. (1999). *Choosing equality: School choice, the constitution and civil society.* Washington, DC: Brookings Institution Press.

Walberg, H. J., & Bast, J. L. (2001). Understanding market-based school reform. In M. C. Wang & H. J. Walberg (Eds.), *School choice or best systems: What improves education?* (pp. 3–38). Mahwah, NJ: Erlbaum.

Walsh, M. (1999, November 24). Ka-ching! Businesses cashing in on learning. *Education Week.*

Weglinsky, H. (2000). *How teaching matters: Bringing the classroom back into discussion of teacher quality.* Report prepared for the Milken Family Foundation and Educational Testing Service. Princeton, NJ: Educational Testing Service.

Weglinsky, H. (2002). How schools matter: The link between teacher classroom practices and student academic performance. *Education Policy Analysis Archives, 10*(12). Retrieved February 24, 2002, from http://epaa.asu.edu/epaa/v10n12/.

Weick, K. (1976). Educational organizations as loosely coupled systems. *Administrative Science Quarterly, 21*, 1–19.

Weiss, C., & Cambone, J. (1994). Principals, shared decision making, and school reform. *Educational Evaluation and Policy Analysis, 16*, 287–301.

Wells, A., Jellison Holme, J., & Vasudeva, A. (2000). Diversity and inequality: Montera charter high school. In B. Fuller (Ed.), *Inside charter schools: The paradox of radical decentralization* (pp. 144–176). Cambridge: Harvard University Press.

Wells, A. S. (1993). *Time to choose: America at the crossroads of school choice policy.* New York: Hill and Wang.

Wells, A. S. and Research Associates. (1998). *Beyond the rhetoric of charter school reform: A study of ten California school districts.* Los Angeles: UCLA Charter School Study.

Wells, A., Lopez, A., Scott, J., & Holme, J. (1999). Charter schools as postmodern paradox: Rethinking social stratification in an age of deregulated school choice. *Harvard Educational Review, 69*(2), 172–204.

WestEd. (1998). *The findings and implications of increased flexibility and accountability: An evaluation of charter schools in Los Angeles Unified School District.* Los Angeles: Author and University of Southern California.

Wexler, E., & Huerta, L. (2000). An empowering spirit is not enough: A Latino charter school struggles over leadership. In B. Fuller (Ed.), *Inside charter schools: The paradox of radical decentralization* (pp. 98–123). Cambridge, MA: Harvard University Press.

White, P. A. (1992). Teacher empowerment under "ideal" school-site autonomy. *Educational Evaluation and Policy Analysis, 14*(1), 69–82.

Whitty, G., Power, S., & Halpin, D. (1998). *Devolution and choice in education: The school, the state, and the market.* Bristol, PA: Open University Press.

Wilson, J. Q. (1989). *Bureaucracy: What government agencies do and why they do it.* New York: Basic Books.

Wilson, W. (1887). The study of administration. *Political Science Quarterly, 2*, 197–122.

Wise, A., Darling-Hammond, L., & Berry, B. (1987). *Effective teacher selection: From recruitment to retention.* Santa Monica, CA: RAND.

Wohlstetter, P., & Griffin, N. C. (1997). *First lessons: Charter schools as learning communities.* Philadelphia, PA: Consortium for Policy Research in Education.

Wohlstetter, P., & Griffin, N. (1998). *Creating and sustaining learning communities: Early lessons from charter schools.* Philadelphia, PA: Consortium for Policy Research in Education, University of Pennsylvania.

Wohlstetter, P., Griffin, N. C., & Chau, D. (2002). Charter schools in California: A bruising campaign for public school choice. In S. Vergari (Ed.), *The charter school landscape: Politics, policies, and prospects* (pp. 32–53). Pittsburgh, PA: University of Pittsburgh Press.

Wohlstetter, P., Mohrman, S., & Robertson, P. (1997). Successful school-based management: A lesson for restructuring urban schools. In D. Ravitch & J. Viteritti (Eds.), *New schools for a new century* (pp. 201–225). New Haven, CT: Yale University Press.

Wohlstetter, P., Smyer, R., & Mohrman, S. (1994). New boundaries for school-based management: The high involvement model. *Educational Evaluation and Policy Analysis, 16,* 268–286.

Wohlstetter, P., Wenning, R., & Briggs, K. L. (1995). Charter schools in the United States: The question of autonomy. *Educational Policy, 9*(4), 331–358.

Woods, P. A., Bagley, C., & Glatter, R. (1998). *School choice and competition: Markets in the public interest?* London: Routledge.

Wright, S. P., Horn, S. P., & Sanders, W. L. (1997). Teacher and classroom context effects on student achievement: Implication for teacher evaluation. *Journal of Personnel Evaluation in Education, 12*(3), 57–67.

Yancey, P. (2000). We hold on to our kids, we hold on tight: Tandem charters in Michigan. In B. Fuller (Ed.), *Inside charter schools: The paradox of radical decentralization* (pp. 66–97). Cambridge, MA: Harvard University Press.

Yin, R. (1994). *Case study research: Design and methods* (2nd ed.). Beverly Hills: Sage.

Youngs, P., & King, M. B. (2002). Principal leadership for professional development to build school capacity. *Educational Administration Quarterly, 38*(5), 643–670.

About the Contributors

Eileen M. Ahearn, Ph.D., is a project director and senior policy analyst at the National Association of State Directors of Special Education in Alexandria, Virginia, where she conducts research and policy analyses of special education issues. Most recently, she has directed research on special education in charter schools, and she currently directs a national technical assistance project in that area. She has extensive experience in policy work at the state and federal level as well as in teaching and administration in public school systems.

Katrina E. Bulkley is an assistant professor of educational policy at Rutgers University. Her work focuses on issues of school reform, particularly in the area of charter schools and school choice. She has published articles on charter schools in *Educational Policy* and the *Educational Policy Analysis Archives*. She is currently conducting studies of educational management organizations that operate charter schools and traditional public schools both nationally and in Philadelphia.

Marisa Burian-Fitzgerald is a doctoral student in education policy at Michigan State University. She is a former research associate for the Education Statistics Services Institute of the American Institutes for Research and received a B.A. from Stanford University.

Derrick Chau is a RAND/Spencer Foundation postdoctoral fellow in education policy at RAND Education in Santa Monica, California. His research interests include charter schools and systemic education reforms.

Bruce Fuller is professor of education and public policy at the University of California, Berkeley. His work focuses on the decentralization of public aims and organizations, including preschooling, school choice, and family policy. A sociologist by training, Fuller worked for a state legislator and governor, then at the World Bank, before seeking refuge in the university.

Marytza Gawlik is a Ph.D. candidate in education policy at the University of California, Berkeley. Her work examines various forms of political decentralization and their consequential impact on organization and school re-

form. Currently, her thesis focus is on how deregulation, choice, and accountability work as a reform model toward attaining both deinstitutionalization
and increased levels of autonomy across equity, governance, teacher profes-
sionalization, parental involvement, and pedagogy.

Emlei Kuboyama Gonzales, J.D., M.A., is associate director for Policy Analysis for California Education (PACE), an independent policy research center
jointly operated out of the University of California at Berkeley and Stanford
University schools of education. Ms. Kuboyama Gonzales works primarily
on K–12 issues and the linkages between secondary and postsecondary education. Previously, Ms. Kuboyama Gonzales served as an attorney for the
San Francisco regional office of the U.S. Department of Education, Office
for Civil Rights, and the U.S. Department of Justice, Civil Rights Division,
in Washington, D.C.

Paul T. Hill is director of the Center on Reinventing Public Education and
acting dean of the Daniel J. Evans School of Public Affairs at the University
of Washington. He is co-author, with Robin J. Lake, of *Charter Schools and
Accountability in Public Education* (2002).

Cheryl M. Lange, Ph.D., is a founding partner of Lange Consultants, an
evaluation, research, and program-planning firm. She has more than 25 years
of experience as a researcher, consultant, and educator. In addition to consulting in the areas of evaluation and program planning, she has conducted
research for more than 10 years on school-choice options, including studies
of charter schools, alternative schools, and open enrollment.

Christopher Lubienski examines education policy and politics and has particular interests in economic theory and organizational behavior in school
reform. As a fellow in Brown University's Advanced Studies Program, he is
studying schools' internal and external responses to increased competition.
Lubienski is an assistant professor of historical and comparative studies in
education at Iowa State University.

Michael T. Luekens works in Washington, D.C., for the Education Statistics Services Institute of the American Institutes for Research. He is currently
studying education policy at the George Washington University Graduate
School of Education and Human Development. He received a B.A. from Wake
Forest University.

Margaret J. McLaughlin, Ph.D., is a professor of special education at the
University of Maryland, College Park. Her specialty is special education

policy, and she currently directs several national projects investigating educational reforms and special education. She teaches graduate courses in disability policy and has published extensively in areas related to school reform and students with disabilities.

Gary Miron is principal research associate at Western Michigan University's Evaluation Center. Along with conducting evaluations of charter schools in five states, he studied national voucher reform in Sweden and school restructuring in Europe. He has authored or edited eight books/monographs, including (with Christopher Nelson) *What's Public About Charter Schools? Lessons Learned About Choice and Accountability* (2002).

Christopher Nelson is senior research associate at Western Michigan University's Evaluation Center, where he has conducted evaluations of charter school laws in four states. He is co-author of *What's Public About Charter Schools? Lessons Learned About Choice and Accountability* (2002).

Sandra Park is a doctoral student in education policy at the University of California at Berkeley and a research assistant at Policy Analysis for California Education (PACE). Her research interests include charter schools and accountability.

David N. Plank is co-director of the Education Policy Center at Michigan State University and a professor in the College of Education. He is a specialist in the areas of educational policy and education finance. He received his Ph.D. in the economics of education from the University of Chicago in 1983. He has worked as a consultant in education policy development for the World Bank, USAID, the United Nations Development Program, the Ford Foundation, and ministries of education in several countries in Africa and Latin America. He has published four books and numerous articles and chapters in a variety of fields, including the history of education and the economics of education. His current research focuses on issues related to charter schools and school choice and on the development of effective accountability systems in education.

Lauren Morando Rhim, Ph.D., is a faculty research associate at the University of Maryland, College Park. Her primary areas of research are market-based reforms, school choice, and the inclusion of children with disabilities in these reform initiatives. She is currently directing a study of special education in charter schools: Project Intersect: How Special Education and Charter Schools Coexist.

Gregory A. Strizek is a senior research analyst at the Education Statistics Services Institute of the American Institutes for Research. Dr. Strizek received his Ph.D. in political science from The Ohio State University in 1998. His current research interests include charter school policies and practices, school indicators, and survey measurement issues in education research.

Gary Sykes is a professor in the departments of educational administration and teacher education at Michigan State University, where he specializes in policy related to teaching, teacher education, and educational choice. He co-edited (with Linda Darling-Hammond) *Teaching as the Learning Profession: Handbook of Policy and Practice* (1999) and has published on a variety of educational policy issues.

Priscilla Wohlstetter is the Diane and MacDonald Becket Professor in Educational Governance at the University of Southern California's Rossier School of Education, where she also directs the Center on Educational Governance. Her research on charter schools has appeared in such publications as *Kappan*, *Educational Policy*, *Education and Urban Society*, and *Teachers College Record*. She is currently principal investigator for a U.S. Department of Education study of strategic alliances in charter schools.

Index